SEEKING URBAN SHALOM
Integral urban mission in a new urban world

international society for urban mission

Copyright © 2014 by International Society for Urban Mission

Published 2014 by International Society for Urban Mission

All rights reserved. No part of this publication may be reproduced, stored in a retrieval system, or transmitted in any form or by any means – electronic, mechanical, photocopy, recording, or any other – except for brief quotations in printed reviews, without prior permission of the publisher.

National Library of Australia Cataloguing-in-Publication entry

Title: Seeking urban shalom : integral urban mission in a new urban world / Darren Cronshaw, editor.

ISBN: 9780992394103 (paperback)

Subjects: Church work with the poor.
City missions.
City churches.
Urban poor.

Other Authors/Contributors: Cronshaw, Darren, editor.
International Society for Urban Mission, issuing body

Dewey Number: 261.8325

Editor: Darren Cronshaw
Design: Les Colston

Contents

Foreword
Tony Campolo   5

Introduction: From Shantaram to Shalom
Darren Cronshaw   9

The Word on the Street: Biblical Reflections on God's Reign in the City
C. Rosalee Velloso Ewell   17

Sowing Seeds of Shalom in the Neighborhood
Geoff and Sherry Maddock   27

Urban Economic Shalom: Possible Place of Peace and Economic Growth
John H. Quinley, Jr. with John H. Quinley, III   51

Release the Oppressed and Others Suffering from Injustice
Cori Wittman and Aimee Brammer   71

Empowering Children and Young People: Imagining a Better Future in the Global City
Amy Brock-Devine, Elizabeth Barnett, Kimberly Quinley and Matthew Wilson   99

A Movement of the Spirit: Fuelling Church Movements among the Urban Poor
Paul Cameron and Doug Priest   131

Joining God in the Challenges and Opportunities of Multi-faith Cities
John Baxter-Brown, Sharmila Blair and Rosalee Velloso Ewell   163

Recruit, Equip and Sustain Christian Leaders in a New Urban World
Lynette Leach, Scott Bessenecker and Andrew Menzies   179

Interviews with Urban Missionaries
Mari Muthu, Natagamon Roongtim (Earth) and Mary Kamau   207

Lessons from the Good Samaritan
Shane Claiborne   217

Foreword
Tony Campolo

Modern urban life is qualitatively different from what anyone experienced during previous stages of human history. The religious certitudes that marked the homogeneity of those who lived in the small towns and villages of the pre-industrial revolution are no more.

Confronted by those with other religious beliefs and the secular value system of the dominant society, those who live in huge metropolitan areas are prone to make relative their religious convictions. What once were assumed to be religiously legitimated moral absolutes gradually have come to be viewed as socially generated mores. The constraints that once confined behavior within close-knit communities have slowly come to be replaced by a freedom that too often is more of a burden than a blessing. The anonymity that comes from being surrounded by millions of people, none of whom have any knowledge of the identity or personhood of anyone else, can give to the individual a sense of living in a lonely crowd.

The urban citizen soon realizes that he or she is autonomous and, as such, must create his or her own identity and meaning. For many, this responsibility is too much of a burden to bear. Endeavoring to create meaning out of what seems to be the absurdity of modern secular urban life is a formidable task. Furthermore, the ways in which that task is approached can lead toward lifestyles of nobility and heroism on the one hand, or to horrendous and self-destructive forms of behavior on the other. There is also a third possibility: there are those who will sink into the dull conformist lifestyle prescribed by the media and simply tip-toe through the urban jungle, hoping only to arrive at death safely.

This book will introduce you to some of the authors and activists who fit into the first of these three categories. You will become acquainted with Christians who have not conformed to the ways of this urbane world, but, instead, are marching to the beat of a distant drummer. These are they who have heard the call of the ancient Nazarene and, like long ago fishermen in a place far away, have heeded His call to, "Come follow me!" Turning their backs on the allurements of a consumeristic way of life and the sensate pleasures of Babylon, these women and men have opted to find the meaning of their own lives in doing good for the social misfits, to whom I have already alluded. They are willing to do whatever can be done to rescue these people from the anomie and estrangement that leaves them dangerously trapped in this modern form of Babylonian captivity.

The second group of urbanites to be considered are those men and women who have not been able to cope with the disorientation they have encountered in city living. This group often finds temporary escape from their feelings of lostness in a variety of self-destructive pleasures. Sexual promiscuity is one very common form of escape, wherein the ecstasy of orgasms offers temporary and brief excursions into feelings of aliveness and joy. I say "temporary and brief" because, after these sensual feelings have ended, and the momentary relief from the emotional emptiness is over, they are likely to flee desperately to new partners in an effort to satisfy their renewed longing for ecstatic relief. These needy people, having satisfied their sensate desires, usually leave behind an array of persons who have lost some of their humanity because they become aware that they have been "used," but not loved.

Many of us find it difficult to understand the sex trade which is one of the urban world's diseases, or to comprehend why so many men seek out prostitutes and thus support the sex trade and the trafficking of women. We must recognize that prostitutes are more likely to be victims than perpetrators of the sex trade. Some of these women are virtual slaves who are forced to do what they do. Others were abused when they were very young, sometimes by family members, and as a consequence of such abuse, have had their self-worth denigrated. Usually, it is downhill from there on as these women live out the definitions of self that follow such degradation. As you read this book, you will learn how some brave and dedicated foot soldiers of God's Kingdom minister, both to the victims and victimizers who are caught in this evil reality.

Drug addiction and alcoholism provide other means of temporary escape from the emptiness that marks those who become lost in the matrix of urban evil forces. Because these escapes also are only temporary and almost always destructive, I need not spell out for you what drug addiction and alcoholism do to careers, families, and emotional wellbeing. Evidence of this vast and evil economic system that supports the sale of drugs and alcohol abuse can be found on street corners in every city.

We must be thankful for Spirit-led agents of God's Kingdom who are committed to rescuing the perishing and caring for the dying. The kind of work they do can be debilitating and, as you will learn by reading the essays that follow, only those who "wait on the Lord" by practicing spiritual disciplines can experience the restoration that enables them to keep at it day-in and day-out. Without regularly nurturing spiritual renewal, a man or woman who reaches out to needy urbanites will too soon experience burnout. The number of social workers who give up after just a few years of trying to rehabilitate the casualties of alcoholism and drug addiction is legion. Many former social workers tell story after story of how disillusioned they became as case after case in which there had been reason to hope for progress ended with the relapses of their clients. Under such circumstances, to "keep on keepin' on"—as they say in African-American churches—requires spiritual strength from a transcendental power.

In addition to the social pathologies that mar urban life, there are the vast number of city dwellers of whom it can be said, "They measure out their lives in teaspoons and live in quiet desperation." So often the fate of these people is to endure mundane lifestyles, routinized by dreary repetitious work schedules with little or nothing to challenge them to invest their lives in something that might prove to be meaningful. These are the hollow people of the city who are tossed about by the winds of secular society. The opiate of these brothers and sisters that keeps them from paying attention to the absurdities in their lives is sometimes reality television shows that seem to them to offer what they fantasize is real life, because their own reality is so lacking in vitality. According to one survey, 80 percent of urban dwellers hate their jobs and long for retirement. They, nevertheless, find fulfillment in all kinds of distracting activities ranging from preoccupation with sports teams to intense engagement with the arts. But as they rush back and forth between museums, theaters, and ball games, so many are running far too fast so that it is easy to conclude that they must be running *from* something – perhaps themselves.

Such misled people can be dangerous because the emptiness of their lives may make them easy prey for those dictatorial manipulators who seek to create those totalitarian movements that almost always start in cities. It has been said that "when the children tire of their games, it is then that they turn to torturing the cat." Thus, the sadomasochism that usually accompanies mass movements generally emerges from those who are looking for something they believe will alleviate the angst that has made them restless.

Don't get me wrong. I am not suggesting that all urbanites are pathological or emotionally dead. There are huge numbers of city dwellers who have found the joyful emancipation that can come from fleeing the constraints of small intimate communities. In the freedom that can come from urban anonymity, there are many people who are able to express themselves in creative activities. Maybe I, like the French sociologist Jacque Ellul, paint too dismal a picture of urban life.

I must continually come back to the good news that there are still the heroic men and women you will meet in this book who radiate an astounding aliveness. In the midst of struggle and hardship, these are they who have found life's meaning in doing God's work in the urban world. Led by the Spirit, they are reaching out to the homeless and the poor. When they see Jesus in the faces of the poor, these urban missionaries are connecting with an energy source that transcends time and space. They are responding to a divine imperative. In the midst of the suffering and disillusionment that too often surrounds them, their sacrificing of self for the sake of God's needy people gives their lives an ultimate meaning. These laborers for the Kingdom do not toil for material rewards, yet we who read their stories have a sense that every one of them will one day hear a voice saying, "Well done, thou good and faithful servant." It is the hope of these heroes that some of you will join them in their efforts with your prayers and your gifts. Perhaps among the readers of this book there even will be some who will accept the challenge to go to the city and work alongside them.

These urban heroes work not only to rescue individual city dwellers who seem lost, but also seek to change those social structures and institutions that so often are responsible for the aimlessness and injustice that are often a part of urban life. The Apostle Paul calls these societal systems "principalities and powers." In this book you will meet some of those who long for the actualization of the vision for the city that was articulated a long time ago by the prophet Zechariah:

> "Old men and old women shall again sit in the streets of Jerusalem, each with staff in hand because of their great age. And the streets of the city shall be full of boys and girls playing in its streets … In those days ten men from nations of every language shall take hold of a Jew, grasping his garment and saying, "Let us go with you, for we have heard that God is with you." (Zechariah 8:4-5, 23)

They live with the expectation that the good work begun in them and through them will be completed on the day of His coming (Philippians 1:6) and that God's Kingdom will be actualized in their cities.

Introduction
From Shantaram to Shalom
Darren Cronshaw

When I read Shantaram, the 2003 novel by Gregory David Roberts, my eyes were opened to the precarious life of people in slums in Asia. It is a classic story of a tragic character who is running away from his past and finds meaning and purpose through new relationships and serving his adopted community. "Lindsay Ford", as the main character calls himself on his fake passport, was a convicted bank robber and heroin addict who escaped Melbourne Australia's Pentridge Maximum Security Prison in broad daylight in 1980. He was escaping through Mumbai (Bombay), India, en route to Europe, but stayed and grew to love the city. Lindsay meets the taxi driver Prubaker whom he hires as a guide. As their friendship evolves, Prubaker takes Lin home to his village and introduces him to his mother, who sees something of peace in Lin and gives him a new name Shantaram, "Man of God's Peace." On their trip back they are robbed, forcing Lin to live in Navy Nagar slum. An added benefit is the shelter the slum provides him from the authorities, and it opens up a whole new world of engaging his adopted city.

On the day of his arrival in the slum, a fire sweeps the neighborhood — yet another blow to poor and struggling inhabitants. In response, Lin sets up a free health clinic. As he grows to love and serve his adopted community, he learns their customs and culture, becomes fluent in *Marathi*, trades with a leper community, and experiences the joys and betrayals of life in Mumbai. The story takes exciting twists and turns with the promise and loss of love, a stint in abusive Arthur Road Prison, employment with the Mafia, and weapon smuggling to Afghanistan. It is the first but middle book of a planned trilogy, so more exciting adventures are coming that will continue to explore the theme of alienation and its conflict, exile, and search for meaning that Roberts says is characteristic of the twentieth-century. But what most fascinated me was Shantaram's love for the Asian city of Mumbai and its food, transport, music, dance, movies, Sufi poetry, and people.[1]

The author, Gregory Roberts, did literally escape from Pentridge in 1980. After being captured and finishing this book based loosely on his experience in India, he is an activist

---

1   Gregory David Roberts *Shantaram* (London: Abacus, 2003). See also his essay which is instructive concerning the novel's background and literary layers: Gregory David Roberts, "The Architecture of the Novel, *Shantaram*" (2010), accessible at http://www.shantaram.com/

and helps with the World Health Organization, Doctors without Borders, and other charities and NGOs. When asked how eager volunteers might help alleviate poverty, he points to organizations who are overcoming discrimination, helping abandoned orphans and elderly people, and expressing compassion to people with HIV/AIDS. His hands-on-work and his international advocacy are admirable. But the bottom line of his advice is: "if you open your heart to India, you'll always get back a lot more than you give."[2] Roberts' novel and life story challenge me to be a "Person of God's Peace" committed to practically engaging tangible needs of urban poverty and seeking urban shalom, and remind me to expect to grow and learn so much from those I seek to serve.

A second book that has significantly opened my eyes to the needs in slums and squatter neighborhoods, and particularly the need for integral mission that addresses spiritual, emotional, and physical poverty — is Ash Barker's *Slum Life Rising*. Drawing on experience in another Asian city and its slums — Bangkok, Thailand — Barker grapples with the humanitarian, demographic, theological, personal, relational, and team-building challenges of responding to the huge and expanding humanitarian crisis in urban slum and squatter settlements. Without avoiding the complex financial, power, and health dilemmas, he pronounces an imagination-grabbing call to incarnational mission as "enfleshing hope" in situations that are often very desperate and under-resourced. He describes this context of mission as a "perfect storm" of poverty with its overwhelming enmeshed and complex challenges:

> "The various 'fronts' of poverty kept thundering together, causing misery to multitudes: evictions, fires, floods, urbanisation, vulnerable employment conditions, dangerous housing conditions, sewerage inadequacies, superstitions, corrupt officials, language barriers, sanitation problems, AIDS and other preventable infectious diseases, premature deaths of children, the disabled and the elderly, and often no meaningful connection with Christians."[3]

What is an appropriate Christian response to this new urban world? Ministry in this context is challenging from many angles. There is a desperate need for bold and compassionate incarnational mission — workers who are prepared to suffer exile from

---

2 http://www.shantaram.com/, CaringSharing tab.

3 Ash Barker, *Slum Life Rising: How to Enflesh Hope within a New Urban World* (Melbourne: UNOH Publications 2012), 15; reviewed by Darren Cronshaw in *Transformation: An International Journal of Holistic Mission Studies*, 30:1 (January 2013), 77-78.

their own consumerist world and relocate, adopt a simpler lifestyle, learn local culture and language, advocate for justice, and minister compassionately (Shantaram style, but without the vice!). Where is incarnational mission happening at its best, and what can we learn from its best practice?

The International Society for Urban Mission was formed in 2012 to encourage urban Christians to seek God's Shalom in cities, especially in the Majority World, and to come together to seriously grapple with issues of urban poverty. ISUM facilitates solidarity, reflection, and leadership development through sharing resources and training, Urban Learning Exchanges, the *New Urban World* journal, and the ISUM Summit for Urban Mission. The first ISUM Summit met in Bangkok 26-29 January 2013, hosted by the Evangelical Church of Bangkok. It was a significant gathering of 200 diverse activists, leaders, and thinkers collaborating and seeking to discern together how to foster God's reign in our increasingly urbanized world. The gathering was not isolated to conference talks, but invited participants to experience Thai culture and go as small groups to 30 immersion experiences to learn from Bangkok activists and diverse mission contexts. Participants then gathered the lessons from these local experiences and brought their own stories and insights from the Summit into seven ISUM working groups whose task was to draft the seven briefing papers now forming most of this book. We wanted reflection that was grounded in grassroots engagement and serious conversation with one another, and seeking God together, around the relevant biblical, strategic, demographic, and global justice issues.

The overall theme of the Summit and this book is Integral Urban Mission. In cooperating with the mission of God, we want to engage with compassionate service, advocacy for justice, faith-sharing, church planting, and care for creation. ISUM assumes these different expressions of the mission heart of God are all valid and integrally related. They represent what really is good news about Christian hope — that God cares for people and their circumstances and world. As Michael Frost pleads: "We feed the hungry because in the world to come there will be no such thing as starvation. We share Christ because in the world to come there will be no such thing as unbelief".[4] To foster shalom, it is imperative that we cooperate with God in the breadth of his concern for the world and its cities.

Rosalee Velloso Ewell, in "The Word on the Street: Biblical reflections on God's Reign in the City," reminds us that cities are not new in God's plan and have always been places of the best virtues and the worst vices. She draws on Genesis, Isaiah, and Philippians to

---

4   Michael Frost, *The Road to Missional: Journey to the Center of the Church* (Grand Rapids: Baker, 2011), 28.

examine how we can hear the gospel invitation to dwell in cities, not just reside; share life, not just have the same postcode; and live the good news on the street for others, not just live for our own sake.

The first working group briefing paper is "Sowing Seeds of Shalom in the Neighborhood," compiled by Geoff and Sherry Maddock. These urban missionaries and micro-farmers from Lexington, Kentucky are passionate about neighborhood transformation. They encourage Christians to embrace mission wherever they are "placed" locally not just in global generalizations; as neighbors not just church members; and taking an interest in justice and ecology not just individuals and their salvation. I love their encouragement to walk, plant, bake, and shop locally as expressions of neighborliness.

John H Quinley Jr, with John H Quinley III, discuss a variety of economic responses to urban poverty in "Urban Economic Shalom: Possible Place of Peace and Economic Growth." International macroeconomic theory and microfinance, business as mission, and social entrepreneurship all have a place if they can help foster a new economic way of being for the world's poorest. God is concerned with unjust economics which affect the poor, and the Quinleys want to invite people to pray and to work to make a difference with alternative economic frameworks.

Cori Wittman and Aimee Brammer investigate the imperative and dilemmas of working for liberation in their chapter "Release the Oppressed and others Suffering from Injustice." They examine the complex and multifarious world of human trafficking, the biblical inspiration to set such people free, where interventions are needed (not just raids and rescues but viable restoration), case studies of structural breakthroughs, and a wealth of practical implications.

Amy Brock-Devine, Beth Barnett, Kimberly Quinley and Matthew Wilson, in "Empowering Children and Young People: Imagining a Better Future in the Global City," urge us to recognize the vulnerability of children in cities. Through a practice of "reverse-dreaming," their working group imagined a city without exploitation of children and then discussed what the church would need to do to help the city get to that positive future. This paper is honest about the challenges but also optimistic about protecting and healing children and young people.

Paul Cameron and Doug Priest have collated and edited "A Movement of the Spirit: Fueling Church Movements among the Urban Poor." They celebrate stories of urban missionaries building relationships and trust, learning from voices inside slums, integrating evangelism with social action, and empowering local leaders. For example, Second Chance Bangkok is a recycling shop where UNOH is serving the needy and inviting other neighbors to come alongside and help, and along the way generating employment and hosting a Bible study. This chapter urges joining with God's integral mission and God's fueling of church movements.

John Baxter-Brown, Sharmila Blair and Rosalee Velloso Ewell, in "Joining God in the Challenges and Opportunities of Multi-faith Cities," explore the dynamics of living and dialoguing with people from diverse religious backgrounds and implications for witness and collaboration. The writers reflect on their visits to a Buddhist temple, Bangkok Breast Cancer Support Group and Bangkok Refugee Centre, and discuss the document "Christian Witness in a Multi-religious World". They underline how important it is for Christians to deepen their understanding of their own faith, to broaden their understanding of what others believe, and to engage in evangelism with boldness and respect.

Lynette Leach, Scott Bessenecker and Andrew Menzies address key personnel matters in "Recruit, Equip and Sustain Christian Leaders in a New Urban World." They discuss the huge needs and opportunities for recruiting people for tough urban contexts, equipping them for ministry with accessible training, and sustaining them with intentional support networks and spiritual practices. Among other things, urban missionaries need to be resilient, especially through inevitable disappointments and potential crises of faith. Young people from the affluent West and leaders from the Majority world are taking an interest in urban mission, but better recruitment, mentoring, and support are key needs if we are ever going to redress the imbalance and lack of workers in slums.

Mari Muthu, Natagamon Roongtim (Earth), and Mary Kamau share in interview format the challenges and opportunities of their urban mission contexts in India, Thailand, and Kenya.

Shane Claiborne in "Lessons from the Good Samaritan," teaches profound implications from this familiar story. His challenge includes not being so busy not to be interrupted by people's pain and injustice, and not to be too comfortable avoiding places where people get beat up. As well as reading the story with the Good Samaritan's compassion as an example, he also urges working to make the streets safe in the first place, and to find grace even when you find yourself in a ditch, beaten up by life, and abandoned by religious folks. Finally, it is a story that shows the Samaritan using his own resources as well as collaborating with the innkeeper to restore the injured traveller. We need one another, which is the basis of the Summit and ISUM's role in helping us seek urban shalom.

There are some important recurring themes through the chapters. Foundationally, for example, we are invited, like the exiles Jeremiah addressed, to plant ourselves and seek the shalom of the city in the place where God sends us (Jeremiah 29:4-7). There is an imperative to develop appropriate servant leaders and incarnational missionaries. And we need to encourage and learn from the best practices of indigenous missionaries as well as help Western mission workers bridge the gap of power and finance.

Missional strategist Alan Roxburgh maintains the resources for discovering God's vision and dream are found within the people of God in that place. A key discernment practice is *listening, conversation, and dialogue*. Says Roxburgh: "The great reality of the church is that by the Spirit, God's imagination for the future is already among God's people, and so the work of leadership is in the cultivation of the environment that will allow this imagination to gather energy".[5] Be encouraged to open yourself to new directions and insights through the experiences and conversations this book echoes.

My confession is that I don't live in a slum or squatter settlement. Our church is in the inner-eastern suburbs of Melbourne, Australia. Our home is rare in our street not to have a swimming pool and multiple cars. But ISUM members help open my eyes to see the poverty that does exist in my neighborhood, and help open my heart to be involved locally and globally in seeking urban shalom.

I say deep thanks to those who have helped with editorial comment and proofreading and to the ISUM Summit organizers, hosts, presenters, working group facilitators, and briefing papers compilers. Other associated articles, interviews, and videos from the Summit are accessible at www.newurbanworld.org. We look forward to your response to this book, and hope to see many of you at the second Summit hosted in Kuala Lumpur, June 28-July 1, 2014. It is ISUM's hope that the conversations, reflection, prayer, and activism generated from ISUM resources and gatherings will help us as we seek Shalom and cooperate with God's mission in this new urban world.

One in two humans are urbanites, one in three are living in urban poverty with one in six living in urban slums. So one billion people are "living in shit," to borrow from Mike Davis' description of the reality and struggle of slums around the globe. This is a stark and growing reality that the church, worldwide, is barely beginning to grapple with. Christian responses to the rise of slums have been inadequate with only 1 in 500 international missionaries and around 1 in 10,000 national Christian workers, pastors, and evangelists focusing on slums." But this largely unreached and forgotten group of

---

5   Alan J Roxburgh, *Missional Map-Making: Skills for Leading in Times of Transition* (San Francisco: Wiley, 2010), 179.

people will likely grow to 2 billion by 2030 and 3 billion by 2050.[6] This is one of the most urgent and missiologicaly significant issues of this century. With slums on the rise (or sinking away), we might ask where would Jesus be found today? Jesus would be, and Jesus is, working alongside urban mission workers to stand in the gap for some of the most marginalized and vulnerable people on the planet. This first volume of the International Society for Urban Mission, *Seeking Urban Shalom: Integral Urban Mission in a New Urban World* is a conversation to learn from committed practitioners working at the grassroots of neighborhood community development, advocacy, liberation, church planting, inter-faith dialogue, and leadership development.

Darren Cronshaw
Editor

---

6 Barker, *Slum Life Rising*, 21-23, 102.

The Word on the Street: Biblical Reflections on God's Reign in the City

C. Rosalee Velloso Ewell [1]

What does God have to say about cities? What does God have to say about mission and evangelism? What do we already know about cities and what can we learn from the Bible? What is new for our age? What might be the signs of the reign of God in the city today? What is the word on the street? Where is the Word on the street?

Cities are not new or novel to our times. They have always played a role in God's mission. Many times they have been very central to that mission and often God has asked very demanding things of his servants in relation to a particular city. Think of Jonah and Nahum—which prophet would you rather be? The prophet from the marginalized and oppressed people who is sent to the center of the empire, to the seat of power to tell them "repent!" and then to see God save that horrible city—the city of your enemies? Or the prophet who gets to say, "Finally, justice will be done and Nineveh will be destroyed!" In general, when we think of our cities, of the corruption, the violence, the abuse, the poverty, we much prefer to be Nahum and to think of God's mission as doing away with all this horrible stuff. It is easier to be Nahum than to be Jonah.

Similar stories follow for cities like Babylon or Jerusalem or Rome. Babylon is at once both the object of prayer in Jeremiah and the trope for all that is evil and against God in the book of Revelation (cf. Jeremiah 29:7; Revelation 18:2-24). Jerusalem is at once the city of David, the city of the beautiful temple for Israel's God, and the city for which Jesus cries, the city that turns away its prophets, condemns and kills the messiah. Thus, even a cursory sketch of the Bible suggests at the very least that the Scriptures are ambivalent when it comes to cities.

However you read the first chapters of Genesis, it seems we did not start off as city people: there was the garden and then a more pastoral society. But as the numbers increased and people started living together in larger groups, we begin to see how close living conditions bring out both the good and the bad—the virtues and the vices are

---

[1] This chapter was originally published as an article in *New Urban World Journal* (May 2013), 33-43

exaggerated and made more evident in cities. It is in cities where we witness God's care and the goodness of his people towards the vulnerable, the sick, the oppressed; but it is also the place where we see the increase in violence, in the practice of oppression, and forcing some to the margins. Close living conditions promote the exaggeration of both virtues and vices—the sociological impact of condensed living has both a sinful and a salvific impact.

While the biblical texts have much to say about life and living, this study will focus on "dwelling"—what it means to live the Good News in the city and the Word on the street. Mission thinkers (and the field of missiology in general) can sometimes get caught up in methods, in analyses and strategies for mission and thus fail to imagine what it means to live and to dwell, we fail to reflect on the Word that dwells on the street. Yet dwelling is an extremely important concept in the Bible and it is a concept that relates directly to God's mission for his people.

Ivan Illich, a Catholic theologian who died in 2002, argued in a speech to the Royal Institute of British Architects that modern cities have reduced dwelling to housing.[2] To dwell is human, Illich wrote. Wild beasts have nests, cattle have stables, cars have garages. Only humans dwell—"To dwell is an art... Spiders are hard-wired by their genes to weave a web of its own kind... but the human is the only animal who is an artist, and the art of dwelling is part of the art of living—it is the art of loving and dreaming, of suffering and dying. A house is neither a nest nor a garage."[3]

What if we thought of Christian mission as a recovery of a sense of dwelling? What sort of impact might this have on our cities? How might this help us find the Word on the street?

When I ask the question: Where do you live? I am not asking for an address. It is a question that asks for the place where your daily existence gives shape to the world. "Just tell me how you dwell and I will tell you who you are."[4] The problem is that in today's cities people cannot ask this question anymore—at least not fully. Cities are made for consumers and commuters, whether they commute from fancy skyscrapers to the office, or from the slum to the street. We have reduced dwelling to residence. Again following Illich, for the resident, the art of living is fortified—he needs an apartment and security more than he needs a neighbor. He has no need for dwelling, just as he has no need for the art of suffering because he counts on medical assistance, and, he has probably

---

2 Ivan Illich. "Dwelling," in *In the Mirror of the Past* (London: Marion Boyars Publishers, 1984).
3 Illich, "Dwelling", 55-56.
4 Illich, "Dwelling", 55.

never thought about the art of dying. Residents—those who live in settlements, look the same from Shanghai to New York, from Lima to London. Everywhere you find the same garage for humans—shelves to store the workforce overnight. There seems to be little difference between many apartment complexes and large scale chicken coops—neither is dwelling, certainly neither are at all close to the biblical image of God dwelling among us, of God becoming flesh, and pitching his tent with us.

Cities are a concentrated place of corrupt power and the church in the city must be very careful in its witness to this power lest she also become corrupted by it. Cities alienate— you can be completely alone with 15 million people around you. This also is not the biblical vision for the city or for the ways in which God calls us to dwell and to witness.

Part of the challenge for us is to recognize that cities make *koinonia* (biblical fellowship) seem invisible, unreal, or impossible because those who can flourish in the city are the ones with resources. It is harder and harder to find yourself depending on others, to share life with others—not just an apartment block, not just sharing square footage, but genuinely sharing life. Dwelling is about sharing life.

So much of urban mission seems to presume that mission is about servicing what we already have—providing more services within the system—more food for the hungry, more shelter for the homeless, more Bible studies for the middleclass. I am not arguing against shelters or food or Bible studies. But I am challenging the idea that cities are neutral and that we just need to make the best of it, do the best we can to patch things up and make up for the inequalities. What if cities are like the Titanic? Moving around the deck furniture will not do us much good! What if we see the city more like the tower of Babel? It is not neutral, but is a sign of a proud and self-sufficient people that says, "We will make a name for ourselves" rather than "Come Holy Spirit, dwell with us." It is important to remember that God judges certain forms of life.

> "Come, let us build ourselves a city, and a tower with its top in the heavens, and let us make a name for ourselves, otherwise we shall be scattered abroad upon the face of the whole earth" (Gen 11:4).

> "Out of Haran, God called Abram... so Abram went" (Gen 12:1-5).

The people who tried to build the tower were afraid of being scattered so God confuses them and they are scattered indeed. But, already at the end of Genesis 11 and beginning of chapter 12, we read about God's calling of one particular man. Amongst the scattering of peoples, God builds a relationship with Abram and his family. It is tumultuous, filled with ups and downs, betrayals and faithfulness. God dwells among his people as a visitor near the oak tree at Mamre, as a tower of fire by night, as bread and water and life. Ultimately, God dwells with us in Jesus. And here we have dwelling in its full sense—in Jesus we are taught the art of living and of dying, of being in relationship, whether in Jerusalem or in provincial Nazareth, or London or Bangkok.

God's renewal does not necessarily mean, "Let us patch up this mess." Rather, let us build an ark and start anew. Perhaps the hope is not in redeeming the city as it is, but in finding alternative ways of dwelling, offering new spaces where God's dwelling is seen and heard and touched and tasted. This might very well look like homeless shelters or Bible studies, but it is more than that as well. It is seeing mission as finding ways to share life with others and to build relationships because this is how God chose to do things with us.

In the first verses of the gospel of John we read about God dwelling among us—coming literally in the flesh to share life with us in all its fullness, in all its messiness, in all the joys and challenges, unto death. It is this type of dwelling to which Christians are called—to live the good news so that the world might know of this God that came to dwell with us, so that the world might know the Word on the street.

> For I am about to create new heavens and a new earth...
>
> Be glad and rejoice forever in what I am creating; for I am about to create Jerusalem as a joy and its people as a delight.
>
> I will rejoice in Jerusalem and delight in my people;
>
> No more shall the sounds of weeping be heard in it, or the cry of distress.
>
> No more shall there be an infant that lives but a few days, or an old person who does not live out a lifetime...
>
> They shall build houses and inhabit them;
>
> They shall plant vineyards and eat their fruit...
>
> Like the days of the tree shall the days of my people be...
> (Isaiah 65:17- 22).

This is God's vision for the shalom of the city and it reminds us of the famous text in Jeremiah 29: seek the peace of the city. It is indeed a revolutionary vision even— or perhaps because of—its simplicity. It is the small things like building houses and planting gardens that shape this vision for the city. Though our contexts and ministries are varied, these verses give us a glimpse into the ways God calls us to participate in shaping his vision for the city—a place where child mortality is no more and where old people actually have a role, or are really cared for, no matter what disability or illness they might have (v. 20), a place where the hard work put into building a house is shared work and work that is enjoyed by the very ones who have put brick upon brick (v. 21). Building houses and planting gardens require care and the help of others—they are by nature community-building activities. You have to learn how to be a neighbor. The fruit of a garden is meant for sharing. God's vision for building houses and planting gardens is a community vision—a community whose days will be like the days of the tree—the tree of life. Embodying the Word on the street is learning to be this tree. Are we reading the Bible and shaping our lives to be this tree?

Let us look at another text in Isaiah and one that might be a bit more challenging. It is doubtful that anyone disagrees with the vision of the city of Isaiah 65, but in this other text, Isaiah 58, the prophet strikes closer to home partly because he gives us a vision for what the tree looks like and how it grows.

In some translations the subheading for Isaiah 58 reads "False and True Worship." In other versions it reads "The True Fast." It fits within the general section in Isaiah that begins in chapter 56, where the prophet turns his full attention to the characteristics of the new era—the time of the Lord, salvation for all the nations and the glory of Jerusalem—this glory that was described in Isaiah 65 and many other texts. But here Isaiah looks at the characteristics of this new era by contrasting the blessings promised by God with the distressing attitude of the people of God. Here, he argues, humbling yourself is useless if it is merely a matter of appearing humble.

True worship is lived; it is embodying the Word of God. The faith that is lived is not simply about fasting or false humility—it is an active, holistic faith. It is faith that loosens the bonds of injustice, lightens the weight of those with heavy burdens, and sets the prisoner free.

It is a glorious picture, a revolutionary picture, a picture of peace and justice that has often been picked up by Christians in Latin America and around the world to describe what the church needs to do—to denounce the injustice of dictatorships or colonialism. Yes, the text can be used this way. But the prophet warns us—are we criticizing the other while doing nothing ourselves for justice in our own house? We cannot pretend to be humble with fasting and prayers when we are not even a people who strive for justice in our own homes and in our church or our own institutions and mission agencies.

Using Isaiah's texts for public protests is not wrong. In fact, it is a very good reflection of one important sign of God's kingdom: the justice, freedom, and peace that Jesus brings. And yet, there is more to this chapter in Isaiah that we in the church can easily forget because it is perhaps harder to deal with. It is more challenging because it is closer to home. It is sometimes easier to pray for a violent enemy across the border than it is for a next-door neighbor with whom we do not get along. Or we pray and work for world peace, but not for reconciliation with someone in the church or in the community that we do not like. Maybe one reason this Isaiah text is so revolutionary is because it reminds us to incarnate the good news for those that are.

> Is not this the fast that I choose:
>
> to loose the bonds of injustice, to undo the thongs of the yoke, to let the oppressed go free, and to break every yoke?
>
> Is it not to share your bread with the hungry, and bring the homeless poor into your house; when you see the naked, to cover them, and not to hide yourself from your own kin?
>
> Then your light shall break forth like the dawn...
>
> Then you shall call and the Lord shall answer...
>
> If you remove the yoke from among you, the pointing of the finger, the speaking of evil,
>
> if you offer your food to the hungry and satisfy the needs of the afflicted, then your light shall rise in the darkness and your gloom be like the noonday sun (Isaiah 58:6-10).

In verse 7 and again in verse 10, Isaiah says, share your bread. He also reminds us to share shelter, clothing, and healing—the poor should not just get what is left over, but we are called to give of our very selves on behalf of the needy (v.10). Isaiah makes no distinction between the ethnicity or faith of the person that is to be served. Service and peacemaking, that is, being the hands and feet of Jesus on the street, knows no discrimination.

Sandwiched between verses 7 and 10, he says, "in these things your light will shine very brightly and God will answer your cry for help." Then, at the end of verse 9, he hits closer to home again:

> Remove the yoke from among you, the pointing of the finger, the speaking of evil (Isaiah 58:9).

The revolutionary character of God's people has everything to do with the daily matters of how we treat one another and how we use our tongue. This is about sharing the burdens in-house, within the community, within the family, within the church. It is about saying things that build others up rather than put them down, it is about not gossiping, not blaming others or coming up with excuses for ourselves. Here, in a chapter about revolutions and the promises of God, the prophet says, "Watch how you speak!" This is harder to do, but this is also the Word on the street.

Let us look at one more passage. Paul's letter to the Philippians is an extraordinary book. Some commentators say it is the apostle's swan song; but really, it is a call to subversion. For Paul another world is possible.[5] This letter, one of the so-called "prison epistles," was dictated by Paul during the years he was imprisoned in Rome. Some think he wrote while in Caesarea, still others say Ephesus. Wherever the place of writing, his message continues to be the same. What we must keep in mind is that Paul was in jail. He had endured beatings and threats, disappointments, and near-death experiences. He was persecuted, oppressed, and the victim of all sorts of violence. Now in prison his future was nebulous at best. The authorities, both civil and religious, did not sympathize with him or with his teachings. Despite all this, Philippians inspires faith, hope, love, joy, and a fighting and victorious spirit. Paul is grateful for the Christians in Philippi for their "communion in the gospel" (1:5) and for their "sharing in grace" (1:7). Paul responds in the only way a human being can and should respond: with a deep and joyful sense of gratitude.

After citing the glorious hymn of Christ's humiliation and service—a hymn that calls to memory what true humility is, in contrast to the false humility noted in Isaiah—this hymn is about God's faithfulness in exalting Jesus above all. After the hymn, Paul again reminds the Christians of what it looks like to embody God's Word on the street.

> Work out your salvation with fear and trembling, for it is God who is at work in you, enabling you both to will and to work for his good

---

5 Pedro Arana, *Latin American Bible Commentary*, forthcoming.

> pleasure. Do all things without murmuring and arguing, so that you may be blameless... in a crooked and perverse generation, in which you shine like stars in the world (Phil 2:12-15).

The Philippians are not perfect and Paul knows fully well the challenges of living out the faith, especially under difficult circumstances, as was the case for this small group that gathered by the riverbank to worship. Even for them, as the oppressed and persecuted minority in their place, there was the challenge of treating one another well. As was the case in the Isaiah text, here too we are warned of how we speak. The prophet said, "Do not speak evil." Paul says, "Do not murmur or argue" (v. 14).

It is so tempting and so easy to complain, especially in Christian circles. Just as children need to learn how to work out their differences, to be kind to one another, and not jealous, so also we need to learn to do the same—to know when to speak and what the right manner of speaking might be when there are disagreements or when we feel an injustice has happened. Too quickly we think we are always right. Yet, we must open ourselves to the humility Paul speaks of, open ourselves to the possibility that we might be wrong and that God wants to transform us and to make us instruments of his justice, but that God does it God's way, not our way.

How do we embody the humility of Christ? How do we live out the good news in the way we treat one another and the way we treat our neighbor?

What is extraordinary and wonderful in this Philippians text is that like the Isaiah passage, here also is the promise that if we are careful in these seemingly small things like not murmuring or arguing, we will shine like stars! In Isaiah it says our gloom will be brighter than noonday (Isaiah 58:10); you will shine like stars in the darkness (Philippians 2:15). This is the good news on the street. It is not lived for its own sake, but is lived so that others might also have this hope that is within us. It is evangelistic shining—the good news that is lived is the good news that shines as brightly as the tropical sun, such that others will want to join in with this very strange people and will join their stories to the one great story of Jesus.

God is at work in you, says Paul (Philippians 2:13). It is truly extraordinary to recall that God himself dwells among us so that we are enabled to work for God's pleasure. This is a call and a promise to all of God's people. We are all supposed to shine like stars in the darkest night. Whatever urban ministry we are in, whatever work God has for you, you are challenged to remind yourself about not whining, not complaining, not pointing the finger, but to live and exemplify in word and service the peace of Christ, even among those people with whom we do not get along. In these small acts of faithful speech and true worship, in doing justice, and sharing bread, God's promise is that God's people will shine like stars.

Dwelling in the city (or anywhere else) has to be personal. It is sharing the love of Jesus one person at a time, even in a city of millions. It is about building new forms of sharing life together that are lifeboats, not chicken coops, that make the living Word possible.

Mission is about building friendships in the loneliest of places, of visiting the prisoner and finding ways to share in his life even behind bars.

There is a small group of believers who gather weekly in New Delhi, India, to read sacred texts and to share a meal. The people that gather have been told by the city and by their culture that they are in competition with one another; they are taught to oppress others and to accept their position as oppressed. Yet in the upper room at this house, leaders of the backwards castes are offered food and shelter under one condition—to share the table with those you do not get along with and with people with whom you are in competition. It is a new form of sharing space and of learning what reconciliation really means. It is a form of dwelling that challenges the powers that be in that city and that culture.

The prophet Amos said that the day would come when there would be famine in the land—not the famine of food or drink, but famine of the Word of God (Amos 8:11-12). People will search high and low, from north to south and east to west, but they will not find the Word of the Lord. The city can numb our senses so that we become lukewarm. Yet God dwelling among us is anything but lukewarm. The Word has come and God has called each of us to be voices and hands and feet, together for that Word on the street. Not just the word of service, but the living and revolutionary Word that is the Bible. Is the Bible the word on the street?

We are called to a vibrant, living faith that shows the world, urban or rural, that another world is not only possible, but already dwells among us. What are the signs of the fullness of life? Where are these found in the city? Christian mission must be about such signs— learning from them, strengthening them, and sharing them in other cities so that if and when judgment comes, the church will be seen not as servants shuffling furniture on the deck of a sinking Titanic, but as those building the lifeboats, proclaiming the Word on the street, and shining like stars.

Sowing Seeds of Shalom in the Neighborhood

Geoff and Sherry Maddock[1]

Our world is urbanizing at an unprecedented pace and scale. The future of Christian mission depends on God's people taking this growing urban context seriously and asking questions about the scope of biblical reconciliation. This chapter argues that central to God's redemptive work in the world is the transformation of neighborhoods. This task of urban mission must go beyond old categories of anthropology and individual human need to embrace an ecological agenda in order to meet the biblical vision of all things being made new. Through disciplined observation (action and reflection) Christian neighbors can be equipped to develop a theology of place that will form, guide, and inspire faithful service. This chapter offers a theological framework alongside a set of principles, disciplines, and practical suggestions for the urban dweller who wants to be involved in the work of neighborhood transformation.

Introduction

> "I do not think that the geographical parish can ever become irrelevant or marginal. There is a sense in which the primary sense of neighbourhood must remain primary, because it is here that men and women relate to each other simply as human beings and not in respect of their functions in society." (Lesslie Newbigin)[2]

> "When Jesus bids us, 'Come, follow me!' he doesn't call us into the ether, or even into the whole world for that matter. He calls us into particular places, places that we can see, walk, smell and inhabit. God's call is not a call to be everywhere; it's a call to be somewhere." (Simon Holt)[3]

---

1   This chapter was originally published as an ISUM Summit Briefing Paper (#1).
2   Lesslie Newbigin, *Sign of the Kingdom* (Grand Rapids: Eerdmans, 1980), 64.
3   Simon Carey Holt, *God Next Door: Spirituality and Mission in the Neighbourhood* (Brunswick East: Acorn Press, 2007), 77.

It is the purpose of this paper to explore the inspiration, practices, and hopes for transforming neighborhoods. Integral urban mission calls us to partner with God's work of making our neighborhoods into places where God's Kingdom is coming "on earth as it is in heaven." We begin by affirming some foundational assumptions about mission:

- God longs to renew the world in every dimension.

- Jesus represents God's self-disclosure as a way to express love for the Created world. This is most clearly represented through what we call the incarnation.

- Human persons are universally called to join with God in the work of reconciliation and redemption.

- By their very nature, human persons are placed creatures – each one is bound by the limits of life-span (time) and particular location (place).

- Being limited creatures is good news. We are at home in this world and each one of us can join in the work of re-creation in particular, placed, and tangible ways.

- Human persons increasingly live in urban areas and invariably form neighborhoods in which to live.

- Therefore, every resident of a given urban setting has a place and a way to live-out the human vocation of joining with God's mission.

In the work of neighborhood transformation, a paradigm shift in theology is required. It is essential that we redefine our thinking about conventional, culturally sanctioned places where God is believed to be present and at work. In order to work in apostolic ways, our identity must be anchored in our vocation as neighbors, outside the walls of church buildings. Our core understanding of ourselves as followers of Jesus, as sent and placed people, must guide us in the pioneering work of place-making and integral mission.

There are many ways to join with God's renewing work. Missionaries organize in all kinds of ways to love and serve the world. Often it is by managing efforts through affinity groups to address the needs of particular populations and subcultures (e.g. refugee resettlement, housing and food programs, drug and alcohol recovery programs, counseling and support groups, reading groups, sports clubs, church communities, etc.) These are all legitimate ways to join with God in mission. In this paper, however, we want to focus on the grounded and geographically defined realm of mission best described as "neighborhood transformation".

Neighborhoods and the New Urban World

By way of introduction we think it is important to address the relevance of neighborhood transformation for this time in mission history. It is no surprise to anyone that our world is going through unprecedented changes. This is a time of great upheaval. Concerns about climate change, energy costs, food production, and political instability are front-page news in today's world. This is not to mention the global re-shaping of the Christian church.[4] We live in a new urban world.

The recent work by Ash Barker gives us a snapshot of a rapidly urbanizing world. Barker points out that in spite of the myriad difficulties to be faced by people in urban settings, each week an average of 1.3 million people will leave their rural home-place and move into cities – "That is around seventy million people annually. Since World War II the urban population has grown by 2.5 billion, a more than six-fold increase, making it one of the largest migrations in human history."[5] Humans around the globe are experiencing unprecedented density in already crowded cities. This is the "new normal" and it issues an urgent call to God's people for a new commitment to make their homes and serve out their vocations in urban, and therefore neighborhood, settings.

Again, we are all neighbors and for most of us, we live closer than ever to one another. This doesn't have to be bad news. The redemption of the forces of urbanization, dwindling resources and tumultuous circumstances comes in so many ways as the people of God commit to a place, inhabit a neighborhood with love, and manifest kingdom commitments side-by-side with the least of these. The economy of this world is one of scarcity, but God's people are empowered to manifest an economy of abundance.

---

4 See especially Philip Jenkins, *The Next Christendom: The Coming of Global Christianity* (New York: Oxford University Press, 2002); Phyllis Tickle, *The Great Emergence: How Christianity is Changing and Why* (Grand Rapids: Baker Books, 2008); Ann Morisy, *Bothered and Bewildered: Enacting Hope in Troubled Times* (London: Continuum, 2009).

5 Ashley Barker, *Slum Life Rising: How to Enflesh Hope within a New Urban World* (Melbourne: UNOH, 2012), 68-69.

What do we mean when we talk about neighborhood?

Much can be said about how humans dwell and gather in urban settings. A neighborhood can be limited to just a couple of blocks or span a whole section of a city. Whatever size and regardless of experience, neighborhoods are made up of the interactions between people and the immediate environment, built and natural, in which they reside.

As mentioned above, the term "neighborhood" implies geographical limits. These limits invoke a descriptor used to help us interpret our experience of the world, namely "place." While theologians and church leaders have made great efforts to explore and parse God's relationship with humans (e.g. worship, liturgy, prayer) and the way humans relate to each other (e.g. Christian ethics, reconciliation, forgiveness, discipleship, evangelism, etc.), relatively little attention has been given to this concept of place and what the bible might say about how humans should relate to the rest of God's created world.[6] This is especially true when it comes to how humans relate to the environment (variously called ecology, the natural world, nature, creation) from within urban settings. The work that has been done on this human-creation relationship has more often been focused on wilderness or rural settings. While this is extremely valuable, our rapidly urbanizing world demands a renewed effort to understand place-based mission for the built environment. We believe that salvation is indeed reconciliation between God and humankind. We also believe that all creation is caught up in this salvation work so that God intends to, "save people *with* their environment, not *out* of their environment."[7] This is the good news of missional theology predicated on the seminal event – the incarnation.[8]

Belonging to a Place

Our urban neighborhood places are made up of all kinds of interactions, activities, and people. As urban neighbors we develop relationships in our given context in order to belong, and by belonging we find more and more opportunities to join in with and to initiate transformation. To belong to a place is to know our neighborhood and also to

---

[6] Several notable exceptions: Walter Brueggemann, The Land: Place as Gift, Promise, and Challenge in Biblical Faith, Second Edition (Minneapolis: Fortress Press, 2002); Norman Habel, The Land is Mine: Six Biblical Land Ideologies (Minneapolis: Fortress Press, 1995); Howard Snyder, Salvation Means Creation Healed: The Ecology of Sin and Grace (Eugene: Cascade Books, 2011); Craig G. Bartholomew, Where Mortals Dwell: A Christian View of Place for Today (Grand Rapids: Baker Academic, 2011); Fred Bahnson and Norman Wirzba, Making Peace with the Land: God's Call to Reconcile with Creation (Downers Grove: InterVarsity Press, 2012).

[7] Howard Snyder, *Salvation Means Creation Healed: The Ecology of Sin and Grace* (Eugene: Cascade Books, 2011), 121.

[8] Ashley Barker, *Slum Life Rising: How to Enflesh Hope within a New Urban World* (Melbourne: UNOH, 2012), Part C.

be known. As people come to know us and we discover what God is already up to in the households and byways of our neighborhood we are increasingly empowered to offer a credible witness to the good news of Jesus. This is a complex and long-term endeavor.

Urban neighborhoods are places of intersection where we find figurative and literal crossroads. We can think about this using the metaphor of a four-way-stop or a roundabout. If people don't learn to yield (give-way) to one another, there will be collisions and conflict. Navigating intersections in urban neighborhoods with acute sensitivity and undergirding hope requires us to learn the rules and to get into the flow and rhythm of a place. Genuine belonging will come from these dedicated efforts of adaptation and familiarization.

We will come to "belong" in our urban habitats as a result of locating our vocation, rest, work, and friendships there. Regardless of context, it is clear that each person belongs to several groups and sub-cultures at the same time. We may belong in various ways to a place of employment, recreation (e.g. sports team), entertainment (a coffee shop or movie theatre we frequent), and a place for buying and selling (market, grocery store, or corner store). While we visit these places and may even develop relationships with the proprietors and regulars therein, we always go out from these places and return to our place of residence. We may be fortunate enough to find these places overlap in the same neighborhood forming multiplex relationships. This enriched form of relationship, "housed" in a matrix of multiple networks, provides the best opportunity for Christian service and influence. In turn, we discover the importance of status, roles, and, more specifically, personal identity. These complex ways of relating to the world around us are expertly described by Michael Rynkiewich in his book, *Soul, Self, and Society*.[9] Suffice it to say, belonging to a place is not as simple as just sleeping there when the sun sets. It is a textured, layered, and always-underway process that changes your identity over time and makes that particular place different by virtue of your presence there.

So, when we talk about neighborhood we are describing our "place of residence" as being made up of people, structures, animals, plants, and the various relationships that bind them all together. And since we consider neighborhood to be primary and universal across contexts and cultures, that is to say we are all neighbors to someone, we emphasize the centrality of the role of "neighbor" to our Christian identity. Neighbor – this fundamental dimension of identity that is developed through the process of belonging or being a part of a neighborhood – involves every part of us.

---

9 Michael Rynkiewich, *Soul, Self, and Society: A Postmodern Anthropology for Mission in a Postcolonial World* (Eugene: Cascade Books, 2011) see especially chapter 4.

What do we mean by transform?

To be involved in neighborhood transformation is to be concerned with the personal, spiritual, physical, social, economic, political, and ecological dimensions of a given place. By listing these various aspects of life we mean to invoke words like holistic and integral. We are not simply suggesting we should do evangelism and social action but rather to reframe these as interpenetrating parts of the whole gospel. It is, as they say in our beloved Kentucky, "all-of-a-piece".

This explanation from the Micah Network is helpful to define the dynamics of integral mission:

"Integral mission or holistic transformation is the proclamation and demonstration of the gospel. It is not simply that evangelism and social involvement are to be done alongside each other. Rather, in integral mission our proclamation has social consequences as we call people to love and repentance in all areas of life. And our social involvement has evangelistic consequences as we bear witness to the transforming grace of Jesus Christ."[10]

We claim the good news of Jesus is for all areas of life and that God's best hopes and plans for the world will include every dimension of what it means to be human. In addition, we recognize that if the gospel is good news it is, at least in some significant way, good news now. Gospel transformation will be for this place and for now and not just for another place (usually thought of as a place we call heaven) sometime in the eternal future.

The cosmic-in-scale and always-unfolding drama of God's work can be thought of in terms of three dimensions – creation, reconciliation, and redemption. It helps to locate neighborhood transformation in this larger frame of the mission of God. We call this larger frame the *missio Dei*. While we believe that God's creation (including but not limited to humans) is foundationally very good, we also know there has been a severe corruption to this original goodness. We believe God's new-creation has already been inaugurated through Jesus and continues by the power of the Spirit. While we anticipate the full redemption of all things, our work as Christian people is to be caught up in and enact reconciliation in all dimensions of life. This is what we mean when we talk about transformation. It is transformation with a particular hope, rooted in the bigger story of God's work in the world that God so loves. It is not simply an effort to make things vaguely better; it is the Creator God being reconciled to humans and all creation. We plan for, invest in, and work toward a reconciliation that prepares us for full redemption.

---

10 http://www.micahnetwork.org/integral-mission

We dare to believe that we can experience and offer a foretaste of this great hope in the present, in our various places.

The healing of wounds caused by sin is another helpful way to think of transformation. Our efforts at transformation will only take root and flourish as we acknowledge and confront (confess and repent) the sin we find in and around us. In his recent book, Howard Snyder calls the problem we face in our world "The Ecology of Sin." Salvation represents more than just individuals "being saved," because God longs to make "all things new". Snyder goes on to describe the task of transformation in this way:

> "The Gospel is about healing the disease of sin – and the healing of all creation through Jesus Christ by the Holy Spirit. Sin is the disease; salvation is the cure. New creation is the final fruit – something greater and more glorious than healing sin's disease. But we, and all history, cannot reach that new creation without first facing squarely the disease of sin and God's way of healing it. Healing sin is the necessary step toward a larger goal."[11]

Transformation will welcome and name salvation along with the fruit of new-creation. At the same time this transformation work will undermine and confront those things dividing, oppressing, and poisoning our neighborhoods. In gardening terms we are to cultivate the seeds of life-giving, soil-replenishing plants while weeding out the plants that choke and degrade. Transformation is slow work requiring disciplined attentiveness. A transformed neighborhood will become a place where human persons can flourish in health alongside the health of all other elements of that place (plants, soil, air, animals)

As a way to illustrate neighborhood transformation we want to share a story of place-making on a city corner. This account conveys the small, but meaningful ways of reconciliation – between people, between God and humans, and between humans and the world.

In Bangkok, missionaries living in the heart of the city and working among the homeless tell a story of a rabbit:

> "Just like many urban neighborhoods, our landscape is made up primarily of concrete, and beauty can sometimes be a bit hard to find. About six months ago a lady who is a regular on our streets purchased a baby rabbit, and brought it to the corner where she works. Her

---

11 Howard Snyder, *Salvation Means Creation Healed: The Ecology of Sin and Grace* (Eugene: Cascade Books, 2011), 65.

friend, who lives nearby and also works that corner, shares in the care of the little white rabbit, whom they have named "Nom Sote" (which means "fresh milk" in Thai). Nom Sote lives in a decent sized cage, perched on a push-cart on the side of the road where these women spend their days waiting for customers. It didn't take long for my two small children to discover the long-eared newcomer living just a block from our house. My one year old son quickly took to pointing and squawking emphatically whenever it seemed to him that our path might cross into the rabbit's territory. It was beautiful, in the simplest sort of way, to have a little white rabbit sharing the corner with these women, just across the street from where several other neighbors spend their nights sleeping outside. A bit of life, just for the sake of having life. A few months after the rabbit first appeared in our neighborhood, a little triangle-shaped garden sprang up on that same corner. We learned from the women that the garden was actually intended to be the "rabbit's garden", and that a man they knew who worked in a nearby building had decided to plant Thai spinach on that corner so Nom Sote would have plenty of fresh greens to indulge in."[12]

Three points to take-away from this story:

- *We are hardwired to connect to each other and to nature.* It has long been common belief among Christians that we must cultivate community if we are to see the flourishing of human life. What is often missed is the equal and inherent longing to be connected with God's good earth and other creatures. Urban neighbors will do well to anticipate this divine reality in their efforts to seek the welfare of their place.[13]

- *Everything is connected* – Golden Rule of Gardening #30.[14] Plucked from a sustainable gardening manual, this wisdom holds that everything we do affects everything else. Actions always have implications, seen or unseen, anticipated or unexpected. We believe this provides a foundational insight to neighborliness

---

12   Iven and Kashmira, Bangkok. www.ivenandkashmira.info.

13   See Richard Louv, *Last Child in the Woods: saving our children from nature-deficit disorder* (Chapel Hill: Algonquin, 2008). This is an excellent book about the deep need for humans to connect with "nature" in order to be healthy and flourish.

14   Carol Deppe, *The Resilient Gardener: food production and self-reliance in uncertain times* (Vermont: Chelsea Green Publishing, 2010), 25.

in an urban space – one act, such as a rabbit or a garden, can set off a cascade of grace and connection for the people of that place.

- *Life begets life.* This story bares witness to the God-given rule of creation – you will reproduce what you are ("by their fruit you shall know them"). When we labor with love, even in the smallest ways, goodness will come. Hope-filled, generative micro-actions in a neighborhood contribute mightily to the broader unfolding movement of shalom in that place.

Biblical Basis for Neighborhood Transformation

As followers of Jesus we are given new lives. These new lives carry the full grace of forgiveness and membership in the family of God. They also carry a calling – to pair our beliefs with a rigorous ethical imperative. We might call this the missional mandate of the gospel message – to enact the love of God as exampled by Jesus. Because all human persons are limited and placed, this missional mandate is rooted in particular places. From Old Testament theologian Walter Brueggemann we understand that all covenants in Scripture include a triangle of main actors – God, people, and land.[15]

Through this lens of God, people, and land we come to see that the scriptures are always pointing us toward place-based healing and renewal. We see this from the Garden of Eden, to the vineyards of the Judges, to the courtyards of Kings and Prophets on to the highways, byways, and hillsides of the New Testament. God's ultimate hope is revealed when grace (undeserved merit) and peace (shalom) are experienced by placed people under the loving rule of the Creator God. With this perspective, we turn to a story in the book of Jeremiah about how an experience of dis-placed people is redeemed.

Jeremiah 29:4-7 (NRSV):

> "This is the Message from GOD-of-the-Angel-Armies, Israel's God, to all the exiles I've taken from Jerusalem to Babylon:
>
> 'Build houses and make yourselves at home. Put in gardens and eat what grows in that country. Marry and have children. Encourage your children to marry and have children so that you'll thrive in that country and not waste away. Make yourselves at home there and work

---

[15] Walter Brueggemann, *The Land: Place as Gift, Promise, and Challenge in Biblical Faith, Second Edition* (Minneapolis: Fortress Press, 2002).

> for the country's welfare. Pray for Babylon's well-being. If things go well for Babylon, things will go well for you.'"

This part of the story of exile demonstrates an unequivocal command for shalom and the common good. During this time in history the people of God are prisoners of Babylon, stranded in a completely foreign land among their enemies. As captives, they are longing to be set free, to be rescued from the tyranny of their evil, oppressing neighbors. But here is the twist so often present in our Judeo-Christian story – God, through Jeremiah, calls out to these oppressed people and gives clear instructions. Instead of sending in the "angel-armies" to evacuate the exiles, God does something entirely different.

> "Make yourselves at home there and work for the country's welfare."

In this passage, the instruction to be home-makers is issued twice. The call to make yourself at home includes building houses, planting gardens, and raising families. It is through the efforts and processes of settling-in that relationships are established and given sustainable life. These are the generative, fruit-producing actions that create belonging. Hospitality is implied and central to this home-making mandate. The homes of Christians are not meant to be fortresses where we retreat from the world, but instead places of welcome and of sending-out.

The Hebrew word translated here as "welfare" is actually shalom - work for the country's shalom. Shalom, when translated from the Hebrew simply as peace, is rather anemic. In actuality shalom encompasses so much more including right order, justice, and wholeness. There is no stronger biblical word to describe God's hope for humanity. Shalom is the fullness of restoration and right-living.

Can you imagine what a bitter pill this was for the people of God to swallow? It is still bitter to us as we look around at a hostile world. We might personally experience this bitterness in the face of neighborhood conflict and dis-ease. Yet the words of Jesus ring in our ears, "love your enemy." This love of enemy is manifest through the committed act of making a home, settling into a place and binding yourself to it through food and family.

All too often we respond to hostility by shrinking the message of shalom to our personal lives and the confines of church buildings. This call to cultivate the common good is expansive and must not be limited in this way. It is a call to shalom that has at its heart a people and a place (salvation is always place-based). It radiates out from our city, to our county and region, to our state, to our nation, and to the whole world. It is curious that one of the most common verses Christians used to affirm personal blessing comes just a few lines after this incredibly challenging passage in Jeremiah 29:11 (NRSV):

> "For I know the plans I have for you, 'declares the Lord', plans to prosper you and not to harm you, plans to give you hope and a future".

Many of us have read this verse out of context and without acknowledging the enemy-loving and place-embracing exhortation that precedes it. It is as if we have watched only the last part of a movie with a happy ending. It seems to end well but we have no way of knowing what was sacrificed, endured, and achieved to reach that good outcome. Australians have several ways of describing someone who has come to a difficult place in their lives. One of our favorites is to say of such a person that he or she has "lost the plot." When we lose the plot we have missed or forgotten the plotline, the narrative, or the thread of events that bring us to the present moment.[16] In the same way, we get the gospel wrong when we fail to recognize the expansive love of God and when we read scripture outside of the "God, People, Land" lens. The plans God has for this world (a prosperous, safe, and hopeful future) can only come about through a serious commitment to "seek shalom" and "make a home" in our respective cities.

We can see that during a painful time of exile for the people of Israel, God speaks through Jeremiah with a clear call:

- Make a life in a place that is not your own, a foreign, hostile, and unfamiliar context.

- Stay put, work to belong, be fruitful, and flourish.

- Practice an economy of abundance in exile – building, gardening, raising families.

- Immerse your life in the lives of those around you – be a good neighbor!

In the same way that "The Word became flesh and blood, and moved into the neighborhood" (John 1:14, The Message), we move into neighborhoods as an act of hopeful engagement with a world God so loves. Just as Jesus moved in and around real neighborhoods, we move into neighborhoods with real street names, rich histories, empty lots, ramshackle housing, and cracked footpaths. Simon Carey Holt says it beautifully,

---

16 To this end we must learn to read scripture as a whole narrative and avoid the dangerous habit of just picking out our favorite parts. Sean Gladding has written an excellent book that helps us understand the grand plot of the bible. *The Story of God, the Story of Us* (Downers Grove: InterVarsity Press, 2010).

> "The story of the incarnation is the story of God en-fleshed in a particular place at a particular time and within a very specific community. So too for us, the call of God is to be in a particular place and there to embody the presence and grace of God. It's a call to locality. Quite simply, it's a call to the neighbourhood."[17]

The mission of God is particularized in the person of Jesus and we find that we are grafted into his ministry by discovering particular, placed, and neighborly ways to love and serve the world. We are, as Jesus reminds us, being sent into the world in the same way that he was sent by God – announcing the reign of God and living out the implications.

"Just as the Father sent me, I send you" (John 20:21 NRSV).

Paul restates Jesus' example and call for practical, placed faithfulness. In order for us to live out the breathtaking scope and scale of God's reign we must find time and affection for the people who live in our neighborhood. What a curious truth. To throw our arms around the many laws, commands, traditions, ideas, and insights of our faith, we need only throw our arms around our neighbor with compassion and concern.

> For the entire law is fulfilled in keeping this one command: 'Love your neighbor as yourself (Galatians 5:14 NRSV).

Just as the incarnation is God's affirmation of God's plans to reconcile and redeem the whole world, these words from Jesus, echoed by Paul, speak to a remarkable, and for many of us, inexplicable, confidence in the ability of Christians to carry forward the work Jesus started. God invites, empowers, and compels us to continue the work started in Christ.

Although we can be confident that we are guided by the will of God, the power of the Spirit, and the example of Jesus, it would be naïve of us to simply start performing random acts of kindness on our street and expect something meaningful and sustainable to emerge (although, many have done a lot worse!). Instead, we should feel compelled to do the hard work of paying attention to what God is already up to in our context and nuance our actions in light of what we observe.

With Jesus as our example we must learn to *exegete* our neighborhoods to properly understand the implications of our presence in that place. To exegete a neighborhood

---

17 Simon Carey Holt, *God Next Door: Spirituality and Mission in the Neighbourhood* (Brunswick East: Acorn Press, 2007), 77.

is to interpret what is going on, thereby gaining knowledge about that place. The pioneering British neuroscientist, Wilfred Trotter, said of knowledge, "(it) comes from noticing resemblances and recurrences in the events that happen around us".[18] With the written word we exegete by looking for patterns in language, syntax, and grammar. We ask questions of the text – who is the main character in this story? what is the main point of the story? to what other stories does this text implicitly and explicitly refer? In a similar way we can exegete our neighborhoods. This includes learning the history, culture, and politics of a place. As Walter Brueggemann writes, "Place is space that has historical meanings, where some things have happened that are now remembered and that provide continuity and identity across generations."[19]

It also means taking time to learn what trees, plants, birds and other creatures make their home there, not to mention finding out what kind of soil is under your neighbors feet, air above their heads, and if they have access to healthy food and clean water.

We do an enormous disservice to scripture when we skim across the top of accounts about Jesus' ministry, failing to consider the importance of place names, geographical features, and historical references. We show the same disrespect to our neighborhoods when we fail to go deep with our observation and understanding. It is true that the good news of Jesus is for all places, but it must still be communicated and received in particular places.

Theology of Place – from anthropology to ecology

To continue forward in this exploration of the biblical mandate for neighborhood transformation, it is important to first pause and reflect on the very nature of God. Both in our academic work and experience in urban ministry, we find ourselves reassured by a vision of the world that reflects the divine economy. Although the world in which we dwell is racked with scarcity, greed, scapegoating, and death-dealing, we are convinced there is an alternative economy. This alternative system moves to the rhythm of God's abundance and generosity.

By using the word "economy" here, we are intentionally pointing back to its Greek origin in the word, *oikos*. *Oikos* is where we derive the words economy and ecology.

---

18   Cited in Maria Popova, "The Art of Observation and how to Master the Crucial Difference Between Observation and Intuition", Brain Pickings, http://www.brainpickings.org/index.php/2013/03/29/the-art-of-observation/, accessed 2 April 2013.

19   Walter Brueggemann, *The Land: Place as Gift, Promise, and Challenge in Biblical Faith, Second Edition* (Minneapolis: Fortress Press, 2002), 4.

It means to imply an extended household where the culture and practices of that household are generated by the master of the household – the *kyrios*. So, the *kyrios* of the *oikos* decides if the household will be a place of hospitality and generosity or a place of harsh rules and miserly conduct. To translate this into our discussion of an economy (household and set of relationships) built on the lordship (*kyrios*) of Jesus is to say that our world (ecology) is created in love and ruled to be a place of welcome and abundance. All of it is under the loving headship of a self-giving, outwardly-oriented God – Father, Son, and Spirit[20]. This divine economy is interdependent and generative.

As image-bearers, these same characteristics should also be evident in the shape and inclinations of our humanity. Self-giving and outwardly-oriented love should be cultivated and celebrated in our lives. If we are made in the image of this relational, interdependent God then we are at our best and most human when we give ourselves to others and when we nurture communities of interdependent relationships.

In the work of neighborhood transformation, our theology must be first and foremost relational:

- Relationship with a Triune God.
- Relationship with one another - in the world and in the church.
- Relationship to the place (the natural and built environments) around us.
- Relationship to other creatures.

As we have stated above, this set of relationships - with God, with our neighbors, with the place around us - is echoed throughout the Biblical narrative. Our relational, other-oriented God is working out shalom in this unfolding story and in our time. Based on this understanding of God's order and design of creation one of the most compelling definitions of shalom we have heard is the act of God mending the universe.[21] What does this Christian vocation of mending look like? How do we take up the role of co-creators with our Creator God and help mend what is broken in the world?

How do we sow seeds of Shalom?

So, what does this alternative economy of shalom look like in the gritty reality of neighborhood life? In the words of Walter Brueggemann, "There is an alternative to the

---

20   We are indebted to Mary Fisher for this insight into the character of the Trinity.

21   Daniel Erlander, *Manna and Mercy: A Brief History of God's Unfolding Promise to Mend the Entire Universe* (Mercer Island: The Order of Saints Martin and Teresa, 1992).

kingdom of paucity – the practice of neighborhood. It is a covenantal commitment to the common good."[22]

An image or road map for transformation can arise out of the tangible and necessary discipline of neighborliness. Here are some guiding, but by no means exhaustive, disciplines that can serve integral urban mission:

1) Identify influences (good and bad), opinion leaders, and stakeholders.

2) Look for and understand microclimates in the neighborhood. The idea for this discipline comes from permaculture. A microclimate is the climate of a small area that is different from the area around it. It may be warmer or colder, wetter or drier, or more or less prone to frosts.[23] It acknowledges that differences within a place can be very localized with pockets of distinct characteristics. It is critical to intimately know the particulars of your place like a gardener knows her garden.

3) Ask questions:
   - What does the Kingdom of God look like for my neighborhood?
   - Where is God already at work?
   - If God is mending the universe, how is that happening for my neighbors? (e.g. healing broken relationships, reconciling people with each other and the place around them, restoring goodness, beauty, peace, making all things new)

4) Map out civic structures, political entities, social and economic barriers, access points and gateways of connection – geographically and socially.

5) Learn from the unintended consequences or side effects of transformation such as physical or social disruptions to a stable pattern of life, gentrification, and changes in the housing market that displace residents, etc.

Alongside these disciplines we would also suggest four core principles of covenantal living necessary for neighborhood transformation.

---

22 Walter Brueggemann, *Journey to the Common Good* (Louisville: Westminster John Knox Press, 2010), 30.

23 "Cornell Gardening Resources: Microclimates", http://www.gardening.cornell.edu/weather/microcli.html, accessed on 4 April 2013.

1) Commitment

Throughout history the people of God have resolved, by way of covenant, to stay put in a certain place. The resulting stability becomes a gift to both the neighbor and the neighborhood in which he or she resides.[24] This is especially true in neighborhoods where there is great transition and discontinuity. It is also true that relationships take time to form, especially among those who have suffered hardship and injustice. In such communities, where trust is difficult to establish, people are often legitimately skeptical about the possibility of genuine love and concern. From gardening and soil science we learn that it takes around seven years for dirt to become healthy, living soil. A gardener must be patient. It should not surprise us that good things take time. Finally, commitment to a place should not always feel like a hardship. Norman Wirzba describes the process whereby affection comes in the wake of our resolve to be committed to a place.[25] Over time we come to experience a mature love for our context and we derive great joy from practicing fidelity to a place.

2) Awareness

To pay attention is an art and discipline. We never know everything about our neighborhood, so observation will be important as a starting point and an ongoing practice. Following on from our commitment and our growing affection we will, like a loving spouse, learn to be intimately attuned to our place. To be aware requires being students of the neighborhood and the wider culture by engaging in ongoing conversations with neighbors and following the local news (TV, newspapers, radio, etc.)

3) Work

To stay put and pay attention is to create the possibility for wise and loving action. This "joining in" will involve forming partnerships, serving the needy, and collaborating with individuals and groups already at work loving the neighborhood. It will also mean taking risks and experiencing failure. As we live with courage in the face of injustice, and as we fail at our attempts to make things better, we will need to develop the discipline of perseverance. We must take Galatians 6:9 to heart and, "never tire of doing good."

---

24   Jonathan Wilson-Hartgrove, *The Wisdom of Stability: Rooting Faith in a Mobile Culture* (Brewster: Paraclete Press, 2010).

25   Norman Wirzba, "An Economy of Gratitude," in Wendell Berry: *Life and Work*, ed. Jason Peters (Lexington: The University Press of Kentucky, 2007).

4) Radical Hospitality & Generosity

The relationships that form around our staying put, paying attention, and loving action will be precious treasures. They will often be fragile and can only be sustained while we continue to freely give of ourselves. Ash Barker explains what it means to be non-transactional in our neighborhood relationships:

> "For Christians in slum neighbourhoods relationships as shared life between neighbours can be complex, however, there are often power, trust and credibility dynamics to overcome. Without relational integrity Christians can simply use the 'bait of friendship' to hook vulnerable people for their own agendas. These agendas can include making churches bigger, organisations stronger or donors happier. In UNOH we often need to reassure neighbours that, 'the price of our friendship is not your soul.' This says we care about our neighbours as neighbours and not just as a means for us to gain a 'decision for Christ' or whatever else our friendship currency can gain."[26]

Committing to love our neighbors unconditionally is to confront the old economy that always wants something in return. The dynamics involved in this tension between the two economies and the possibility of transformation are beautifully described here by Brueggemann:

> "It is our propensity, in society and in church, to trust the narrative of scarcity. That is what makes us greedy and exclusive, and selfish, and coercive. Even the Eucharist can be made into an occasion of scarcity, as though there were not enough for all. Such scarcity leads to exclusion at the table, even as scarcity leads to exclusion from economic life.
>
> But the narrative of abundance persists among us. Those who sign on and depart the system of anxious scarcity become the history makers in the neighbourhood. These are the ones not exhausted by Sabbath-less production who have enough energy to dream and hope. From dreams and hopes come such neighbourly miracles as good health care, good schools, good housing, good care for the earth, and

---

26 Ashley Barker, *Slum Life Rising: How to Enflesh Hope within a New Urban World* (Melbourne: UNOH, 2012), 234.

> disarmament. The dream subverts Pharaoh's nightmare. Jesus laid it out, having read the exodus narrative:
>
> 'Do not be anxious' – do not trust Pharaoh;
>
> 'Your heavenly father knows what you need' – then provides abundantly;
>
> 'Seek the kingdom' – care for the neighbourhood, and all will be well.
>
> -Matt 6:25-33
>
> The ones who receive the gift have energy beyond themselves for the sake of the world. And we, if we receive well, may be among those who push beyond ourselves."[27]

In summary, we share this story from Bangkok. Pay attention to the way stability builds a foundation for a neighborhood to flourish. Also notice how this transformation is quite fragile in a society where government structures still oppress people and communities.

Here's the story of JetSipRai

> Klong Toey is the biggest slum in Bangkok. It houses approximately 100,000 residents in about 1 square kilometer. Originally workers at the local port were invited to use land nearby for accommodation. After decades the community became the largest slum in Bangkok stretching behind the container yards of the port. The Port Authority wanted to develop part of the land that the slum was on for a container handling facility. The National Housing Authority started to develop the slum by relocating residents off the land to be moved into flats that were then built. A plan was also offered to relocate residents to a remote area outside Bangkok with few facilities nearby but residents refused. Some residents were also relocated to an area of the slum of about 27 acres (70 rai in Thai measurement). The National Housing Authority organized an agreement for the residents to rent this land from the Port Authority for 20 years. This area then became known as JetSipRai (70 rai).

---

27 Walter Brueggemann, *Journey to the Common Good* (Louisville: Westminster John Knox Press, 2010), 34-35.

As the residents knew they could anticipate living in JetSipRai, this area of the slum was rebuilt in a grid system with spaces for the community between alleyways. The slum committee overseeing this area developed a fire response strategy and night watchmen for safety. A Football ground was also allocated for tournaments, markets and fairs. The rent was also collected and given to the port authority. Compared to other areas of the slum close by this area is highly developed and people have a greater sense of stability. However as it became a more desirable part of the slum to live in members of the Thai mafia also tended to prefer to live there. Many residents used money trickled down from dealing in drugs to develop and maintain their houses. Often they used plants to decorate the house. After the "war on drugs" this excess money disappeared and houses returned to their previous appearance.

The agreement has now finished but has been extended with three year terms. The Prime Minister is currently reviewing plans to relocate the slum and turn it into a park and government office buildings. The slum previously survived a plan by the Prime Minister's brother (Prime Minister Thaksin) to turn it into a casino.[28]

Practices of Neighborhood Transformation

While each neighborhood deserves its own careful and contextualized consideration, our working group found common ground in sharing about the following twelve practices. It is fair to say these ordinary examples are widely accessible across cultures and urban settings.

1) Walk – when possible, choose to walk as your mode of transport. Walk daily as a spiritual discipline to participate in the life of the neighborhood – as a time to socialize, observe and pray.

2) Communicate – get to know local government representatives, city officials, religious leaders, and decision-makers that impact the neighborhood. Stay in touch with them and hold them accountable.

---

28 Rod Sheard, UNOH. Bangkok.

Build partnerships and demonstrate grass-root support of civic initiatives within the neighborhood and serve as an advocate on behalf of the neighborhood.

3) Share – tools, supplies, skills such as home repair, knitting, or sewing.

4) Care – initiate and invite others to join in with caring for the most vulnerable in your midst (elderly, sick or infirmed, children, orphans, single-parent families). Relationships and bonds will be strengthened immensely when neighbors serve together for a common cause.

5) Plant trees – a spiritual, environmental, quality-of-life practice of beautification.

6) Bake or cook – loaves of bread, preserves, divide meals you are already preparing to take to neighbors in need, share recipes.

7) Garden – the generosity and fecundity of the garden will always provide produce to share. Garden together with neighbors in community gardens. Urban farming and agriculture serves both community and economic development.

8) Eat together – practice an open kitchen table by inviting neighbors to share meals in your home. Plan community meals like potlucks and picnics. Participate with special events, festivals, and seasonal celebrations.

9) Beautify – participate with or create public art projects, involve youth, adopt a corner of a street or an intersection and plant flowers, build and maintain raised bed gardens on top of car parks and footpaths. Cement and asphalt shouldn't prohibit cultivating beautiful spaces.

10) Start mini-projects in the neighborhood. These can be micro-actions of hope.[29] Ideas include civic improvements, neighborhood clean up, painting a fence or a mural, installing a historic marker, or celebrating something.

11) Join or participate in neighborhood associations or local civic organizations. Attend the neighborhood church instead of commuting across the city.

---

29 Ann Morisy, *Bothered and Bewildered: Enacting Hope in Troubled Times* (London: Continuum, 2009).

12) Dwell in neighborhood "third spaces" – spend time in area parks, plazas, markets, or public libraries in the neighborhood where people encounter each other and socialize. Patronize local businesses and shop as locally as possible as an effort to build up multiplex relationships. Waste time wandering and lingering in your neighborhood.[30]

These two stories shared in our working group by Jon Owen (UNOH, Sydney, Australia), illustrate the potential for how some practices described above can promote neighborhood transformation.

> One of the things I love about focusing on transforming urban neighborhoods is that it forces me out of the abstract and into the concrete realities of the everyday concerns of my direct neighbors. It drags me out of my thoughts which have the capacity to never cease and into the only place I can truly be, which is present to the moment.
>
> The pursuit of shalom is the search for the abundance that exists in our neighborhoods. We need to bring our whole selves to the task of being attentive to her gifts. This comes through walking away from a mindset of scarcity which communicates that as the minister in this area I have all the resources and its my job to give them to you as I see fit. Apart from being a fast track to messianic complexes, anxiety and burnout, it is a fundamental misunderstanding of the good gifts that God bestows upon all.
>
> The pathway to abundance is sharing what we have with one another. So my wife, Lisa, started sharing what she knows about cooking with some local mums, in turn they began to teach each other what they knew and pretty soon some dads joined in too. From here they decided that each week they should prepare an extra meal which could be delivered to another family who was having a tough week, pretty soon this happened every week.
>
> The slow movement from scarcity to abundance - the mad scramble for limited food parcels has been transformed into a place of abundant

---

30   Simon Holt calls this "the spiritual discipline of dawdling", in *God Next Door: Spirituality and Mission in the Neighbourhood* (Brunswick East: Acorn Press, 2007), 101.

sharing of meals. Let us never forget that even the teaching of Jesus himself was not enough to reveal who he was, but the sharing of food was! (Luke 24:13-31).

Sharing sparks imagination, which leads to unprecedented creativity within urban neighborhoods.

We have a neighbor who is a virtual shut in and lives in squalor. There is seemingly no way to engage him, yet we both have a shared passion - we can't stand mowing our lawns. I own the only lawn mower and it is a cheap one that he borrows when the lawn is too much or he gets an eviction notice from the local authorities. My poor lawn mower shudders every time he approaches.

The mower is finite and will break down - proving costly. As someone committed to simplicity is there anything that would thrive on grass? Then one day in conversation we struck upon the idea - what if we bought a sheep together and shared it between our yards? It worked! We soon realized that our lawns are not enough - so we now share the sheep around the neighborhood, mainly with single mums who are busy enough without having to attend to their gardens.

All of a sudden a few have approached us who know a little about sheep care and are willing to share their knowledge, including the most despised family in our street who accidentally smothered their baby one night while they were passed out stoned. There is a beautiful knock on effect as we together care for this sheep we are learning to care for each other. Kids are being brought into the conversation around animal care. We even have plans to buy more together.

All of a sudden the scramble for lawnmowers has been transformed into abundance. (There is hope for Aussie suburbia yet!)

Conclusion – coming home to the promised land

> "Transformation begins at the neighborhood level when people decide that the neighborhood is the promised land."[31]

Christian mission has always advanced through the faithful witness of humans willing to be sent and willing to be placed. These two motions of being sent and placed are not opposite or competing forces but instead interpenetrating parts of being human creatures. However we experience our being sent and being placed, invariably we return at the end of each day to a neighborhood and to a home. This is our most essential identity – to be a neighbor. Our identity, therefore, is contingent on others. To be a neighbor is to be in relationship with God and with those who live around us. The fact that the entirety of the laws and ethics of our faith can be distilled down to practicing love for God and love for neighbor should stop us in our well-worn tracks and direct our attention to the place in which we live.

It is, however, easy to assume that true mission happens elsewhere. Many of us feel underwhelmed by the prospect of going across the street instead of across the oceans to serve in mission. While we fetishize "elsewhere" we miss opportunities to partner with God in the ordinary and everyday of our lives right where we live. We need to remember that the current place of our dwelling is just as significant as any other place we might want to be. We need not be geographically promiscuous.[32] There is a promised land. It's your neighborhood.

We hope this brief exploration into neighborhood transformation inspires the reader to join in with the mission of God. There is no need for an anointed calling, advanced training, or specialized education. One simply needs to go home.

---

31 Stanley J. Hallett, "To Build a City", in *Signs of the Kingdom in the Secular City*, eds. David J. Frenchak and Clinton E. Stockwell (Chicago: Covenant, 1984), 7.

32 Fiona Allon, "'Geographic Promiscuity': Mobility, Postmodernity, and the Problem of Home", in *Imagined Places: The Politics of Making Space*, eds. Christopher Honston, Fuyuki Kurasawa and Amanda Watson (Bundoora: School of Psychology, Politics and Anthropology, Latrobe University, 1998), 213; quoted in Holt, *God Next Door*, 47.

Urban Economic Shalom: Possible Place of Peace and Economic Growth

John H. Quinley, Jr. with John H. Quinley, III

The concept of Urban Economic Shalom is God's idea. Repeatedly scripturally mandated, we've tended to continue to hit and miss the goal now as much as in ancient Israel. Urban poverty has been tackled by modern macroeconomic theory and International Development with a rasher of tools devised to address the plight of the poor, some unwieldy and equivalent to sweeping vacuously over nations with international development billions. Other ways include, no more or less, than simply being with the poor – one on one – the hands and heart of Jesus. In between the extremes, comes myriad methods as varied as major microfinance organizations to coffee shops, and multi-million dollar consulting firms to antenna manufacturing concerns and small leather or jewelry workshops. In the midst of the fray, groups of "new friars" seek to take a place to bring peace to the city, and deliver God's hope among the least of these. How this all fits together is anyone's guess. I suspect we will need the guidance of God's spirit to help us work uniquely yet collaboratively to see Urban Economic Shalom become reality.

1. Its Not God's Fault: The Biblical Basis of Economic Urban Shalom

Throughout the whole of scripture, God shows without question care for the plight of the poor and calls for justice delivered to them by the people of God. Economic Shalom is clearly God's idea with an expectation of action put to His people through the ages. It is certainly no new concept. Some of the earliest biblical challenges concerning poverty are shown by Robert D. Spender in his *Theology of Poor and Poverty*:

> Beyond direct legislation a number of institutions contained special provisions for the poor. Gleaning laws focused on the widow, fatherless, stranger, and poor (Lev 19:9-10 ; 23:22 ; Deut 24:19-22). During the Sabbatical year debts were to be canceled (Deut 15:1-9) and Jubilee provided release for Hebrews who had become servants through poverty (Lev 25:39-41, 54). During these festivals the poor

could eat freely of the produce of all of the fields (Exod 23:11 ; Lev 25:6-7, 12).[1]

Gleanings laws, debt limitations, as well as, special provisions for the poor, widow, and orphans essentially show that we must make certain specific provision for the poor in our society. Otherwise, we find ourselves actually at odds with God himself as he identifies closely with those who society is often very happy to ignore, dismiss, or exploit.

So, while God makes special place and provision for the poor, many – who claim His name and care – make a mockery of the poorest of God's creation.

The book of Amos dramatically frames Israel's lack of care for the poor, and delivers strong rebuke. Here Spender describes the poor's lot:

> The poor are bought and sold, trampled, crushed, oppressed, forced, and denied justice by those who are in a position to do otherwise. Their treatment is a striking example of the waywardness of God's people from the covenant obligations and their unique relationship with the Lord. Amos underscores this situation [2]

Amos is quite graphic in his portrayal of the poor's oppressors: "They sell the righteous for silver, and the needy for a pair of sandals. They trample on the heads of the poor as upon the dust of the ground and deny justice to the oppressed" (Amos 2:6-7).

Yet, God never relents in His calls for intervention among the oppressed: "But let justice roll on like a river, righteousness like a never-failing stream!" (Amos 5:24)

Not only biblical literature, but the whole of world literature is actually full of chronicling the perils and protagonists of poverty and oppression.

2. The World's Greatest Writers Tried to Move Us

World literary history confirms this well with the writings of Dickens in England, Hugo in France, and a veritable parade of pain in Russian writings from Tolstoy, Dostoyevsky, and Chekhov often themed amidst squalor, and fully interlaced with physical and spiritual poverty.

So, whether "Let them eat cake." was actually uttered by Marie Antoinette, or as Jean Jacques Rousseau referenced to a "great princess,"[3] either would display utter

---

[1] Robert D., Spender. Baker's Evangelical Dictionary of Biblical Theology Online, "Poor and Poverty, Theology of.", accessed May 27, 2013. http://www.biblestudytools.com/dictionaries/bakers-

[2] Spender, "Poor and Poverty".

[3] "Bartleby.com", accessed April 12, 2013. http://www.bartleby.com/73/1347.html.

disconnectedness and disregard to the common peoples' plight and affirm Victor Hugo's take in *Les Miserables*, "There is always more misery among the lower classes than there is humanity in the higher."

David Herman clearly asserts in his, *Poverty of the Imagination: Nineteenth-Century Russian Literature about the Poor*, that essentially urban poverty is the primary lens for viewing most of the western world in the nineteenth century:

> The primal scene of all nineteenth-century western thought might involve an observer gazing at someone poor, most commonly on the streets of a great metropolis, and wondering what the spectacle meant in human, moral, political, and metaphysical terms. For Russia, most of whose people hovered near the poverty line throughout history.[4]

So, if these postulates are true for the historical developing western civilizations, the projection of the utter pain in the development of Asian, African, and all the majority world stories must be many multiples and are all but yet untold to the world at large. For example, obviously the highly awarded 2008 film, *Slum Dog Millionaire,* is certainly as close as most of the Western world may ever come to a Mumbai slum, and became something of a modern wakeup call for the world at large in reference to majority world urban slums.

3. But, How Can We Help?

This question has loomed continually over the centuries and, until the beginning of the 19th century, there was no sense that there could ever be any significant help for the poorest of the world. Bryant Myers points to this in his Walking with the Poor:

> With a radical change in the trajectory of economic history around 1800, a wide range of new ideas emerged – creating wealth, markets as systems, ordinary people as creative contributors, and the idea that God's world could be improved by human creativity. Science and technology emerged as ways to create wealth and increase human well-being. In the West, material improvements in the human condition were rapid. More recently, China, India, Brazil, and Indonesia have assumed this same trajectory. Sadly, this is less the case for Africa and Central Asia. While this process was wildly uneven and some

---

4 David Herman, *Poverty of the Imagination: Nineteenth-Century Russian Literature about the Poor Studies in Russian Literature and Theory*, (Evanston, Illinois: Northwestern University Press, 2001), x.

benefited a great deal more than others, the fundamental historical shift that took place at the beginning of the nineteenth century is a historical fact that resulted in the creation of the idea that we now call development or poverty eradication.[5]

Working within the larger world of International Development and poverty eradication, for better or worse, is the playing field we all come to today in the wake of the first global ISUM Summit. So, how will we move forward now? Let's look at Shane Claiborne's ISUM challenge.

4. Just Do It?

In the first ISUM Summit keynote address, moments after explaining that his "dreds" had had to go for a recent trip back to Afghanistan (he had also been in Iraq on a peace team during the Shock and Awe campaign on Baghdad) this prophetic activist, "Ordinary Radical", Shane Claiborne put us on the edge of our seats, and on his inside committed view concerning the possibilities for peace in the urban slums of the world. Throwing out his punchline-like, tongue-in-cheek, slam you in the gut challenge – but all the while smiling: "We throw up our hands, asking God why won't God do something. And God responds, "I did do something – I made you. Now get out and do something!"

The International Society for Urban Mission (ISUM) Summit held in Bangkok the last week of January 2013, did not happen in a vacuum or without a long history leading together the some 200 participants who gathered. They came from around the globe, for various reasons, but one overriding agreement seemed to rule the hearts of all those hearing Shane's clarion call: God cares greatly for the urban poor and their plight, and expects us to act accordingly, indeed, on His behalf.

In some ways, these are very clear marching orders. Just do it! Sounds like we just got dropped in the middle of shooting a NIKE commercial. Too bad solving urban poverty isn't as straightforward as producing an award winning NIKE commercial: for that, you simply take the requisite budget to secure the best creative and technical talent the ad world can muster and there it is—ready to garner more creative accolades. Ready to "Take It to the Next Level", "Write the Future"- and "Just Do It"- bolstering market share and global sales figures.

"Do something!" That is not very specific is it? It reminds me a bit of my father, who I remember used to posit regularly enough: "Do something, even if it's wrong." He didn't

---

5 Bryant Myers, *Walking with the Poor* (Maryknoll, NY: Orbis Books, 1999), 12.

really expect that we should make some foolish or inappropriate move, rather he was cheering for my sister and I to consider the options, make a good decision, and act with significant commitment.

So, coming off the ISUM Summit, it is pretty clear to all, it is incumbent on us all: to act. Perhaps, even to launch forward in new endeavors, or maybe carry on as we have started with more certainty and redoubled resolve than ever before. Yet, far less certain, however, would be the manner and methods that seem most appropriate to all. To each of us, however, as we consider the "What to do?" question, Micah 6:8 seems to ring out in our hearts.

> To act justly, and
>
> to love mercy,
>
> and to walk humbly
>
> with
>
> your God.

But, one might say, that is not so much instruction on, "What to do?" as it is "How do we do?" Micah outlines a framework for Urban Economic Shalom rather than specifies practices of how to implement it. That might be a fair summary, but the popular passage certainly moves us all forward in a clear direction.

Seeking the peace of the city, indeed, seeking economic development that empowers the urban poor is not an easy task. Delivering Economic Urban Shalom is now a major remaining task for the church today. Today's problems include a single mom ordering the dollar specials for her children in an urban food desert. Yet, fixing problems like this will require more than ranting against massive multinational corporations, indeed it could take challenging corporate leadership to turn around to help serve up solutions and build the communities they serve. It will take planting "urban gardens" by the thousands, and mentoring youth by the hundreds of thousands to work in them. Meanwhile, add to that teaching them English and computer literacy, keys for global youth discovering new opportunities and growing up in a way that is not bounded by their birthplace.

Seeking "Urban Economic Shalom" is going to take work and require painful persistence. But no matter what we do – it will need to be a labor of love. We will foster shalom as we display God's love working in and through us. In the ISUM working group presentation for Urban Economic Shalom, a short paragraph erupted full of desires that we hoped could lead us all forward, and which led us to this paper. More than anything, however, it did clarify just how we all desired to serve.

5. Serving Like Jesus

> WE DESIRE: to see Economic Urban Shalom: Christ centered mustard seed initiatives and groups serving alongside the poor, learning and loving together, making priorities to be people and families, always over money. So we commit to serving one's neighbors, like Jesus, but also ready to challenge vile systems of injustice at the macro level and bring about growing impact in communities – no matter what, no matter where – serving like Jesus.

We felt this was not just some cliche, rather a helpful focusing strategy. In the ISUM Summit second keynote address, Ruth Callanta, spoke on "Serving Like Jesus." Some would have to be forgiven for thinking she was just sharing on how she launched, built, and now continues to run CCT – Center for Community Transformation – a massive microfinance ministry in Manila and across the Philippines, and for thinking further: "What has this got to do with my own work in the slum I awake in every morning?" It actually has everything to do with it, for certainly more than anything, Ruth told us no matter what we do – we must "Serve Like Jesus." This priority can remain equally true whether we lead organizations with thousands of staff, and multi-million dollar budgets, or if we lead a "kids club" in a slum community.

The how to "serve like Jesus" for Step Ahead Integrated Community Development, includes finding microfinance economic solutions for great-grandmothers and grandchildren in Klong Toey slum community, the largest of its kind in Bangkok with over 100,000 inhabitants. Indeed, having CCT as a mother program and Ruth Callanta and David Bussau as mentors, since 2002, Step Ahead has sought to serve among the urban poor with economic development, mentoring, and training among mostly women and children. Sometimes the work can span a family of four generations like in this example of a very committed Great Grandmother.

This is an incredibly arduous story that began over twenty years ago. "Feung" had a daughter who left home, leaving her own baby daughter, "Naen", in the care of her Grandmother Feung. The father, for better or worse, never figured prominently in this story. He was, as the term is used, as though missing days from school, "absent". The mother, facing the increasing pressures of her life, followed suit. Grandmother Feung over the next two decades heard very little, and received no help from her daughter. Feung fought hard for her granddaughter doing the best she could. Sadly, before Naen turned ten, misfortune multiplied and Feung's husband died. So, all the care of her granddaughter fell to her alone. Selling her food to order in the markets of Klong Toey slum community was the most certain opportunity she could find. This was all complicated by the local money lender, who would threaten her if she could not pay on time the onerous interest payments (usually over 20% month) for her small working capital loans (less than $50).

After a few more years, Feung's situation came full circle: her grand-daughter gave birth to her own baby girl – "Sofa". Feung had become a great-grandmother. Clearly, Naen, not yet twenty years old, needed help to raise her daughter, as the help of the father was not to be found. Today, a great-grandmother, and mother look after baby "Sofa" together. Feung, now nearly 70, today continues to sell delicious curries, standing in the gap for the futures of her granddaughter and great granddaughter. Step Ahead's place was to help with microfinance, prayer, mentoring, and encouragement in the love of God.

Across the community, Urban Neighbors of Hope (UNOH) staff began to grow close to a woman working in Klong Toey selling her delicious fresh food to order. UNOH worker Anji Barker was impressed enough to start cheering for her to start a cooking school, and not just any cooking school: a cooking school for expats and tourist to Thailand. Initially, Poo demurred saying, "I can cook, OK, but I could never teach cooking for tourist and foreigners." Against all odds, and perhaps against best consultation practice, Anji pressed her that she believed she could do it. She believed in her. The story of Poo's Helping Hand's Cooking School that finally became just the brand "Cooking with Poo" is a runaway success story. In Thailand's tourist industry at one point recently "Cooking with Poo" pulled more interest online for bookings than the Grand Palace tour.

After the success of the cooking school, Poo published the cookbook *Cooking with Poo* through UNOH Publications which now drives the demand for the school and creates a potentially much greater income stream than is possible in the cooking classes.[6] "Cooking with Poo" is now a Business as Mission (BAM) that is changing more than her family's life but also employing a handful of helpers who are learning how to do the business as well.

With the success of Cooking with Poo behind them, and with Poo's consultancy, UNOH also last year launched a Cafe/Catering business on the edge of Klong Toey

---

6 Urban Neighbors of Hope, "Cooking with Poo" Accessed April 15, 2013. http://www.cookingwithpoo.com/.

community with a view of training young, inexperienced youth from Klong Toey to run a Thai/Aussie Cafe called: Munjai Cafe. Munjai means confidence in Thai language and that is exactly what this BAM is building with Thai youth, along with steady sales, and a dedicated clientele.

Last year because of growing relationship between Step Ahead and UNOH, it was discovered the two organizations had unwittingly collaborated in supporting an amazing micro-entrepreneur. Living in Klong Toey community for 35 years, Mrs. Vimon Romphum joined as a respected community member client since the beginning of Step Ahead nearly ten years ago. Her first loan, for just under $100 was to sell second hand merchandise and noodles in the community. Later, her son had an idea for a niche market as he had studied Japanese food preparation. He convinced her she could do it, and now she makes and sells a delicious kind of Sushi in several weekly market fairs. Her market is mainly local youth coming out from school and home delivery. Japanese Sushi is actually a new strongly developing cuisine in Thailand today, and the savvy recognition of this market opportunity opened bigger economic doors than she had ever seen before. After nearly ten successful loans mostly for working capital, she generally accessed just over $200 to keep her business moving forward until she no longer found the loans necessary.

On one visit, the Step Ahead program assistant noted that there was a lot of nice new Sushi menus and marketing around. After asking about the nice advertizing, it was found that the good folks at UNOH had essentially become her ad agency and translation service. This kind of unintentional collaboration challenges Step Ahead and UNOH to look for more good ways to serve in Klong Toey together.

6. More BAMs and Organizations Seeking to Serve Like Jesus

A major network that strengthens BAM and grassroots business initiatives is **Ten Thousand Villages**. Started by an innovative business woman of faith Edna Ruth Byler in 1946. Then in 1962, her business initiative was fully embraced by the Mennonite Central Committee (MCC). MCC works for peace and development around the world and has helped lead the BAM model because they believe its an integral tool for peace building. Ten Thousand Villages is apart of the fair trade movement where artisans receive a fair income. If people receive a living wage they will be less likely to go to war, if needs are met people are at peace. Ten Thousand Villages has today grown to a global network of social entrepreneurs working to empower and provide economic opportunities to artisans in developing countries around the globe with sales in excess of 20 million dollars.[7]

Sari Bari founded by Sarah Lance, opened in 2006 after four years of steady presence and friendships with women in the red light areas of Kolkata, India. The love, solidarity, and desire for freedom born out of these friendships became the foundation of Sari Bari's work for hope, justice, and freedom.

Sari Bari functions as both a for-profit business a well as a non-profit trust. This kind of hybrid model works very well in social business and is very innovative. The Sari Bari women learn an artisanal trade by recycling old saris into bags, scarves, blankets, and other accessories and profitably selling them. The story of Sari Bari is not just about profit, but about coming into a narrative of how they help build this story of the women who work for them. Therefore, each Sari Bari product is marked with the name of the woman who made it. [8]

Founded by Annie Dieselberg in 2005 in Bangkok, Thailand, NightLight's mission is to do "whatever it takes" to affect change within the global sex industry. The local offices build relationships with victims of commercial sexual exploitation and those who are at-risk and provide hope, intervention, rescue, and assistance by offering alternative vocational opportunities, life-skills training, and physical, emotional, and spiritual development to those seeking freedom. NightLight builds support networks internationally to intervene and assist women, men, and children whose lives are negatively impacted by the sex industry.

In Bangkok, **Nightlight**[9] operates as a business (NightLight Design, Co. Ltd) and a non-profit (NightLight Foundation). In the United States, NightLight operates as a 501c3 with branches in Atlanta, Branson, and Los Angeles.

Hagar was first started in 1994 in Cambodia and in 2009 started branches in Afghanistan and Vietnam. The U.S. state department has named Hagar founder Pierre Tami as "one of the its six international heroes in the struggle against the modern-day slavetrade" .

Hagar Catering & Facilities Management Ltd. (HCFM) is a social enterprise with a partnership between Hagar Social Enterprise Group (HSEG) and private investors from

---

7   Ten Thousand Villages, "Ten Thousand Villages: Our History." Accessed May 28, 2013. http://www.tenthousandvillages.com/.

8   Sari Bari, "2012 Annual Report." Accessed May 28, 2013. http://saribari.com/resources/img/2012_Annual_Report.pdf.

9   www.nightlightinternational.com

international catering businesses. HCFM provides employment opportunities for men and women from Hagar NGO's shelters and social programs.

Hagar's mission is to provide high-quality, professional food catering services to companies and organizations operating in Phnom Penh at affordable prices.

HCFM is Cambodia's largest and most professional food services and facilities management company. They currently produce over 4500 meals daily for the employees of over 13 different companies, hotels and factories. Hagar annual turnover is in excess of $1 million and they currently employ over 135 highly-trained staff.

Hagar currently provide catering services to a number of major international companies and organizations, including Raffles Le Royal, Intercontinental Hotel, and the US Embassy. No other food services company in Cambodia can match their experience, quality, and level of professionalism.[10]

ITSERA PURSES are a community economic development that Step Ahead began after the South East Tsunami and developed further in 2009 with training of an at-risk woman's group making woven leather purses in Pattaya, Thailand. Today, ITSERA (meaning Freedom in Thai language) purses are in development across three provinces in the North East of Thailand, bringing Freedom with Every Bag. (http://stepahead.myshopify.com/products/itsera-hobo)

"Economic Urban Shalom" is not limited to one program, and need not carry any specific branding. It must simply change lives for the better. It does not necessarily mean we are all to take on running microfinance programs, small economic initiatives, or even sizable economic engines of Social Business or Business as Mission. But it will mean that we consider carefully the options available for us, and our teams. Further, it will mean we need to discover who among us is prepared and meant to do serious economic engagement, so that those in our communities have the best opportunities. Or at a minimum, it urges that our teams see how to best network and possibly partner with those around us with a proven track record to serve our networks among the "least of these."

We who seek "Economic Urban Shalom" look with hope and confidence that while none of us will do everything, and many will certainly not do all a Ruth Callanta has done, all of us are able to network, learn, facilitate, and be a part of discovering the economic solutions that God has for our neighbors to experience growing "Economic

---

10 Hagar International, "Hagar Caterig and Facilities Management." Accessed May 28, 2013. http://www.hagarcatering.com/.

Shalom" in their own communities. Before we consider further our own particular place in all this, it is instructive to look back at the last few decades to see what vehicles of service were developed and to consider how they may yet work for us and the urban poor.

7. David, Muhammad, and Goliaths

When speaking of solutions to poverty and urban slums, it is all but impossible to do so without looking back to the passionate, visionary, and breakthrough work in the 1970s of leaders and organizations like Muhammad Yunus and the genesis of The Grameen Bank, David Bussau and the launch of Opportunity International, Accion in Brazil, or John Hatch and his conception of the Village Bank and FINCA.

These unlikely disparate players, while unaware of their similar work, or the cumulative impacts their innovations would bring, had paradigm rocking ideas which surged around the globe: from Bangladesh, to Indonesia, and reaching right across South America to essentially birth the much touted and hoped-in modern microfinance movement. This movement has become a focus of poverty eradication/reduction/alleviation over the last half a century, delivering us to the current shores of "Financial Inclusion". Over those decades, most informed observers until today, continually evaluated that while microfinance was certainly never a panacea for poverty, urban or rural, it has offered monumental opportunities for massive programs with unparalleled reach and impact in opening economic possibilities to the poor.

Even with significant problems or achievements, depending on one's point of view of Initial Public Offerings (IPOs) and mass commercialization, certainly these small loans disbursed by the millions delivered possibilities that no macroeconomic development program with its dams and roads ever hoped to deliver – and without bringing with it inevitable crippling national debt, and the enabling of despots, autocrats, and creation of aid traps. So, even with its most recent problems (some perceived and some real), microfinance can not be dismissed as inconsequential or finally unneeded. The reality is that the only alternative that shows no sign of disappearance is the local money-lender, one whose only motivation from time immemorial is exorbitant profit.

8. The Macro-Movement of Micro-Finance

According to the Microcredit Summit Campaign, as of December 31, 2011, 3,703 microfinance institutions reported reaching 195,014,970 clients, 124,293,727 of whom were among the poorest when they took their first loan. Of these poorest clients, 82.7%, or 102,749,643, are women. That is massive reach and impact, that only the most jaded can easily dismiss. Meanwhile, another very important fact is not reported in the statistics, yet it is a reality that those working and motivated by God himself can never diminish: that all of these microfinance clients are greatly loved by God himself.

Larry Reed, Chairman of the Microcredit Summit Campaign, would quite agree and hope for our global and local, wise and inspired, and humble and love-motivated inputs with all these micro-entrepreneurs. Larry was once the President of Opportunity International the largest Christian microfinance organization in the world. Perhaps standing with millions of micro-finance clients across the globe is actually a huge opportunity to work together with the working poor: making hundreds of millions of non-financial, mentoring and training inputs humbly in the love of God.

9. Not Your Grandfather's Christian Development Movement

Also during the 1970s and 1980s, another important group of leaders and organizations keenly focused on solutions to poverty, but didn't fit into a tight economic development solution matrix. Dr. Ron Sider of Eastern University, quietly shook the church in 1978 with *Rich Christians in an Age of Hunger*. This book was a challenge to responsibility that had never really been articulated so clearly before. For example, he argued that while some urban missionaries, such as Vinay and Colleen Samuel and David and Carol Bussau felt called to live and minister among the poor, almost all of us can afford to fund a $500 microloan. Essentially, Dr. Sider challenged that all Christians should take an important part in fighting global poverty and displaying a witness in the process.[11]

In 1982, John Perkins challenged the church again in his book *With Justice For All* looking at church planting among the poor in the USA.[12] A few years later in 1984, Viv Grigg's *Companion to the Poor* would next look at the crushing needs in the slums around the globe and deliver a radical and strategic call for communities to live among the poor as servants delivering God's love to their neighbors.[13]

These works set the stage for Bryant Myers, now Professor of Transformational Development at Fuller Theological Seminary and bringing over 30 years of senior leadership with World Vision International to write *Walking with the Poor: Principles*

---

11 Ronald Sider, *Rich Christians In An Age Of Hunger* (Nashville: Thomas Nelson, 2005), xvi.
12 John Perkins, *With Justice For All: A Strategy for Community Development* (Venture, CA: Regal Books, 1982).
13 Viv Grigg, *Companion to the Poor* (Tring, Hertfordshire: Lion Publishing, 1984).

and Practice of Transformational Development published in 1999.[14] Today, it remains a seminal work for all those who care deeply about the solutions to poverty, not least of which over 40,000 World Vision staff.

Further, as an important side issue, World Vision and other mega-sized Christian non-profit organizations can simply not be ignored when the question continues to arise: how should we work with such massively large organizations that have annual budgets in excess of a billion dollars? Perhaps, there is no clear answer but we would be amiss not to acknowledge the importance of this new phenomenon. Certainly, engagement within these organizations as holding tanks of vast amounts of goodwill, wisdom, understanding, (not to mention funds) must register as a significant opportunity for collaboration. Again, Bryant Myers as one of the builders and makers of World Vision today, is an example of a good friend in the world of people caring deeply about Urban Shalom. Furthermore Jayakumar Christian, a global leading voice in terms of serving in the urban slums of the world, is National Director at World Vision India.[15] Therefore, we must choose to all stand together, whether we come from the world's largest organizations or some of the smallest.

All these people and organizations have tilled the soil where today's new innovative thinkers, activists, and ministers such as Ash Barker and Urban Neighbors of Hope (UNOH) from Bangkok and Shane Claiborne of The Simple Way in Philadelphia now pave the way. Perhaps hundreds of groups like them and hundreds of thousands of workers will continue to serve in global fields of fruitful ministry, writing, praying, loving and calling forward more radicals to follow Christ's call into the largest and most congested slums the world has ever seen.

10. If We Are One, What's this Wall About?

It seems many of us who are united and committed to being the hands and feet of Jesus are somehow falling on two sides of a dividing wall. On the one side, there are those who hope for God to fill economic development engines with the fuel of promise and thereby open opportunities among the poor that can remain so elusive. Be it by micro-enterprise development or other economic development programs, or Business as Mission (BAM), and Social Business that generally demand significant funding and

---

14   Bryant L Myers, Walking with the Poor: Principles and Practice of Transformational Development (Maryknoll, NY: Orbis Books, 2011).

15   See for example his book Jayakumar Christian, God of the Empty-handed: Poverty, Power and the Kingdom of God (Monrovia, CA: MARC 1999)

management inputs from outside players would make up and fall on one side as they seek to bring significantly large economic impacts with and among the poor.

On the other side, camped deep in urban slums there are neighbors, or pilgrims, whose call brings them into the closest relationship possible with the poor. Some essentially follow St. Francis' call and example today, whether or not they actually take his vows and don his robe under the auspices of the Franciscan order in Roman Catholic church, they are simple friars with various orders and vows of their own. It is this kind of simple life and "with-ness" that defines the work and commitment to Christ and the "least of these" that these servants demonstrate daily. Sometimes, unfortunately, this call and commitment can seemingly bring disdain for the possible economic tools and infrastructure that could actually really help.

The question begged is: can each side be fully performing the commands and work of Christ with the poor, or has one somehow actually got it right, while the other is essentially missing something? Or even, could it be that each one working diligently on their side of the wall is unaware of the strength available if we worked together and tore down the walls. Perhaps, the hearts of Shane Claiborne, founder of The Simple Way in inner city Philadelphia, and Peter Greer, CEO of Hope International who has Ruth Callanta's Center for Community Transformation – CCT (a ISUM Summit keynote speaker) as a partner are, indeed, of one heart. Look at how CNN recently posed them as Capitalist and Communist and queried them as to which of them could properly claim Jesus for it's leader.[16]

Obviously, Shane and Peter do care for each other as brothers in Christ, indeed, knowing that the other shares the highest commitments to serving "the least of these" and Jesus. But, what of the broad gulf that seems clearly to divide them? Can one discover how to get a "strategic screen shot" of all the strengths that the other possesses, while also holding to their own personal priorities, callings and strategies?

Can the players like David Bussau, Peter Greer, and Ruth Callanta, and their organizations mobilize and serve with hoards of "New Friars" or "Neighbors" moving in to live and love like Jesus in the poorest slum communities of the world and even serve as their partners in economic good?

Can the grassroots movements of committed incarnational workers understand and accept the possible role of microfinance friendly advocates who stand for the clients of MF organizations—along with the employed MF loan officers?

Can they cheer for one another, pray for one another, help one another serve with the

---

16   CNN.com, "Was Jesus a Communist or a Capitalist?." Accessed April 11, 2013. http://religion.blogs.cnn.com/2010/11/23/was-jesus-a-communist-or-a-capitalist/.

poor in the special way they have been called? Then, they can conceivably pray together for but working against the local moneylender with their loan interest that "stings like a scorpion."[17]

If they could, then perhaps the troops in each camp can see we are all really on the same side in this war against poverty, and against Satan himself, who desires only to kill and destroy. If they can, then there is opportunity to dramatically display John 13:35: "By this everyone will know that you are my disciples, if you love one another" and pursue "Urban Economic Shalom" together.

11. The Three Ps of Micro-finance Could Help: Provision, Promotion, or Partnership.

This can happen, if those who provide, or promote microfinance, or partner with major Microfinance players (a concept first put forward by Dr. Russ Mask and David Bussau in *Christian Microenterprise Development*[18]) can see each other as members of the same team with roles as different as Strikers and Goalies on the football pitch, or Guards and Centers on a basketball court. Certainly, urban poverty is no game, but God has plans that can use the various strategic gifts of MBAs and the writing of major programs requiring funding proposals, as well as and informed by time spent one on one just being with neighbors in the most daunting of circumstances in their slum communities.

Paul recognized the contributions of different team members: "For just as each of us has one body with many members, and these members do not all have the same function" (Rom 12:4). In a liberal rewrite on this passage, we might say, "Just as not every member is meant to start an inner city MF program in Philly or the Philippines, not all are called to live and work in an urban slum." We might agree to disagree on some of this, but we can certainly stand together as one family. With wildly varying roles, we commit to love one another, and those who are different to us, whether rich or poor. Finally, we might look together to help those who are our poor neighbors in the majority world connect to financial possibilities that they might not have discovered otherwise.

12. International Development Economics: Development or Devastation?

The Christian world has struggled to address the call and priority of over a billion people now living in urban slums. The development sphere has also wrestled with the same

---

17 Kershaw Burbank, Jr., Ph.D., A CHRISTIAN PERSPECTIVE ON MICRO-ENTERPRISE LOANS AND THE PAYMENT OF LOAN INTEREST, Eastern University http://www.wtrc-tmed.org/resources/Christian%20Perspective%20on%20ME%20Loans%20and%20Interest.pdf

18 David Bussau and Russell Mask, *Christian Microenterprise Development: An Introduction* (Oxford: Regnum, 2003).

realities from a wide continuum of views ranging from Jeffrey Sachs to William Easterly. Sachs is a major force in promoting the United Nations Millennium Development Goals and writer of *The End of Poverty*[19] in which he recommends "clinical economics" and "differential diagnosis" with a top down approach to heal the ailing patient. Easterly comes from the other end of the spectrum, in *The White Man's Burden*[20] which focuses on his views of how foreign aid has through the decades often actually brought more problems than solutions.

Dambisa Moyo who penned, *Dead Aid* "describes the state of postwar development policy in Africa today and unflinchingly confronts one of the greatest myths of our time: that billions of dollars in aid sent from wealthy countries to developing African nations has helped to reduce poverty and increase growth."[21] Finally, Paul Collier from Oxford, weighs in rather squarely in the middle between the two extremes with *The Bottom Billion* where he looks at a rasher of "development traps" that tend to cause an ongoing downward spiral for the world's poorest.[22] Who is right, who is wrong, and just how they add or actually confuse the whole discussion is up to your study and decision. In International Development and Politics, we don't get a vote, except for our reasoned commitments and informed actions.

13. Muhammad Yunus – Equation Changer Extraordinaire

During the mid-seventies, entered an academician turned activist, microbanker, and finally turned global tour de force. Muhammad Yunus: founder of the Grameen Bank and winner of the Nobel Peace Prize in 2006, presses on to the cheers and undaunted through the jeers. The Bangladesh government put Yunus out of leadership of Grameen Bank in moves that are mostly understood to be in the machinations of politics, power struggles, and national jealousies.

Meanwhile, Grameen has launched cell phone companies to deliver impact among the working poor of Bangladesh, as well as forging a collaboration with Dannon – the yogurt giant – to bring better nutrition and hugely increased opportunities too. In 1997, Grameen launched Grameenphone as a joint venture with Telenor (55.8%), the largest telecommunications provider in Norway boasting mobile phone operations in 12

---

19 Jeffrey Sachs, *The End of Poverty: How Can We Make it in our Lifetime* (Nww York: Penguin Press, 2005)

20 William Easterly, T*he White Man's Burden: Why the West's Efforts to Aid the Rest Have Done So Much Ill and So Little Good* (Oxford: Oxford University Press, 2006)

21 Moyo, Dambisa. Dead Aid (New York: Douglas & Mcintyre, 2010).

22 Paul Collier, *The Bottom Billion: Why the Poorest Countries are Failing and What Can Be Done About It* (Oxford: Oxford Press, 2007)

other countries, and Grameen Telecom Corporation (34.2%), a non-profit organization of Bangladesh. The remainder of 10% of the shares belong to general retail and institutional investors.[23]

As of March 31, 2012, Grameenphone had a market share in Bangladesh of 42%. Further, more than simply delivery of massive telecom service they have constantly shown innovative prowess that has served markets across Bangladeshi society. Primary among this lineup of social enterprise success is Healthline, a 24 hour medical call center with licensed physicians. Moreover Studyline is a call center-based service that provides education related consultation. Added to the lineup is Mobicash, for electronic purchase of train and lottery tickets, plus Billpay for paying utility bills through mobile phones, and some 500 local centers across Bangladesh that deliver affordable Internet access and other information based services to people in remote rural villages.[24] With such a plethora of social business successes, there is little doubt that now not only is Yunus the most well known social entrepreneur, but the one who more than anyone else is opening up the business world and society at large to the whole concept of "Social Business".

Turning out more books than anyone on the burgeoning subject, *Creating a World Without Poverty: Social Business and the Future of Capitalism* in 2009, and then *Building Social Business: The New Kind of Capitalism that Serves Humanity's Most Pressing Needs* in 2011 Yunus now stands not only as the most well known innovator in the world of microfinance, and author of *Banker to the Poor*, but also as the leading Social Business Guru. No other globally respected figure wields the requisite clout to see the major corporate and non-profit organization collaborations required to bring massive impact, employment, and profits that can hope to recharge and restore severely ailing economies.

Actually, Professor Yunus in *Building Social Business* envisions a whole new economic reality dawning as he posits:

> "The wonderful promise of social business makes it all the more important that we redefine and broaden our present economic framework. We need a new way of thinking that is not prone to creating a series of crises; instead it should be able to end the crises once and for all... The first piece of this new framework must be to accommodate social business as an integral part of the economic structure."[25]

---

23   Grameenphone, "About-us/Corporate-information/Ownership-structure." Accessed April 11, 2013. http://grameenphone.com/about-us/corporate-information/ownership-structure.

24   Telnor, "Investor Relations." Accessed April 11, 2013.

25   Muhammad Yunus, *Building Social Business: The New Kind of Capitalism That Serves Humanity's Most Pressing Needs* (New York: Public Affairs - Perseus Books, 2010), xxv.

These breakthrough developments should encourage the entire Christian development world, including New Friar types, BAM operators, and MF players. The major question really is how can we engage this movement in the most efficient and effective way that will help us in our work in urban slum communities?

14. What Next? Try the Lord's Prayer, and the 23rd Psalm

The Christian development worker is wise to be aware of all these factors and issues, understanding that while all the learnings amassed from research and study are important for us to be able to use and have in our toolkits, and to help inform our actions, yet knowing the bedrock reality that personal relationship with the poor motivated by the love of Christ himself will always remain the core strength to any of our work. But, could it be that working in a urban community serving alongside a BAM company in China, Turkey, or Northern Africa, or in a slum community collaborating with a major microfinance provider network like Opportunity International or Hope International might not be one way to see His kingdom come on earth?

This is not to say the Christian development worker has no place in study, research, writing, and business, but simply that we do all knowing that the answers and ultimately hope do not lie in our excellence of thought, research, analysis, or marketing, but in God's love.

Finally, "God is our peace", as well as the hope for Shalom among the urban poor. God is the only one who can lead us into all truth, as we seek to make personal, organizational, and business decisions in regard to our own work in discovering the "how" for us in doing the Lord's Prayer: in action, in love, and obedience for our part in building not our kingdoms, but His and Urban Economic Shalom.

Shall we pray?

> Lord may your Kingdom come, your will be done, on earth as it is in heaven. Lord, we know there is no poverty or exploitation in heaven. Help us then discover fulfilling, creative work that will bring provision, joy, and increase of daily bread.
>
> Lord, make us ready to serve one another, forgiving one another as you have forgiven us. May we be delivered from the temptation to exploit our sisters and brothers, rather to love one another as you have loved us, displaying the glory of your character and the power of your love. Amen.

And may we walk in the way of Psalms 23 through the alleys of the world's largest slums:

If the Lord is our shepherd, God can lead us into the lush green pastures that will bring rich rewards and blessing to all that are found there. God can establish and show us how to build supply chains that will mean green pastures of provision can be made for multiplied millions with profits that will bestow blessings and restoration to all engaged. We will not fear drug dealers, moneylenders, or gang leaders—for you are with us. May you be with each family, widow, and orphaned child. We commit Lord to walk in your ways, so that your mercy and goodness will follow us into every corner of the poorest urban slums of the world. Making all those places your dwelling place: places of shalom. Amen.

Release the Oppressed and Others Suffering from Injustice

Cori Wittman and Aimee Brammer[1]

The call to fight injustice and release the oppressed rings loud and clear from the pages of Scripture to secular newsstands, but the practical realities of doing so in modern society can be complex and overwhelming. Christian and secular populations alike are wrestling with the best approaches to right modern injustices leading to enslaved child soldiers, war-torn refugees, exploited migrant workers, victims of human trafficking or other egregious realities in today's world. While the world grasps for solutions to these complex, interconnected challenges, the Bible gives clear guidelines on how to fight for justice and release the oppressed globally and in our own neighborhoods. As Christ-followers, we are called to a deeper understanding of the Biblical mandate to release the oppressed by "doing justice," and to use that framework to then evaluate and engage in situations of injustice. This paper highlights the issue of human trafficking as an example of a modern social issue that the Church is both called and equipped to engage, through collaborative, humble responses driven by an understanding of the character of God to bring God's justice to the earth.

Introduction

What do you picture when you read the word *oppressed*?

Perhaps you envision a billboard advocating the fight against human trafficking or recall a network expose on mistreated migrant workers or child laborers. Perhaps you think of refugee or asylum seeking populations fleeing war or famine. Or perhaps you've been introduced to injustices closer to home as you encounter individuals suffering from disability, unemployment, indebtedness, homelessness, isolation, abusive homes or fatherless communities.

As our society becomes more and more driven toward social justice, stories, photographs, and documentaries of modern injustices pepper our news feeds and strike our hearts, calling us to intervene and be part of the solution.

As a Christ-following community, what is the appropriate response? As an individual in the "minority world" of relative safety and prosperity, how can we engage in the

---

1 This chapter was originally published as an ISUM Summit Briefing Paper (#3).

discussion and the solution of bringing justice to these situations?

Rather than leaping to respond to the latest item sweeping the social justice stratosphere, or becoming overwhelmed and avoiding it altogether, Christians are called to first seek to understand God's heart of justice, and His desire to restore the oppressed and redeem situations of injustice by bringing His heart and character of justice to the earth.

Taken in the context of God's character of justice, and His desire to restore justice, we can then begin to un-package the injustices facing us in today's society. We can begin to understand just how widespread and complex they are, and we can begin cultivating compassionate responses for oppressed peoples not only in faraway lands, but also in our own homes and neighborhoods.

After exploring God's heart of justice, this paper will un-package the issue of human trafficking as just one example of a present-day injustice that is widespread and complex, but one in which God is moving powerfully through His followers throughout the world. It will show that this movement is based less on big programs and viral documentaries and more on the carrying of God's presence into difficult situations, often inspired or facilitated by programs or documentaries, but not ending with them.

It will conclude with recommendations to the Christ-following community as to how to best engage in bringing God's justice and loving-kindness to this earth through prayerful, humble and holistic responses toward situations of modern injustice, centering primarily on boldly carrying His presence into difficult, messy situations.

1. The Biblical Call to Justice

God's demonstration of justice from the beginning book of Genesis until Revelation is a central theme to the meaning of salvation and our reconciliation to Him, to others, and to the earth.

Woven throughout the Old Testament are God's commands to the Israelites regarding right responses to the poor and oppressed, and dire consequences of failing to adhere to these commands. Laws requiring the cancellation of debts, allowing the poor to glean from the fields, setting slaves free, and returning land to original owners in the Jubilee year are just a few examples of God's demonstration of His priority to bring justice to the poor and oppressed.

The book of Isaiah then records God's indictments of Israel for seemingly missing the point and failing to follow these commands, followed by a clarification of His desire that the fatherless, the widow, the oppressed, hungry, homeless, and naked be truly cared for.

> Stop bringing me your meaningless gifts; the incense of your offerings disgusts me! As for your celebrations of the new moon and the Sabbath and your special days for fasting – they are all sinful and false. I want no more of your pious meetings... Get your sins out of my sight. Give up your evil ways. Learn to do good. Seek justice. Help the oppressed. Defend the cause of orphans. Fight for the rights of widows (Isaiah 1:13, 16-17).

> Is not this the fast that I choose: to loose the bonds of wickedness, to undo the straps of the yoke, to let the oppressed go free, and to break every yoke? It is not to share your bread with the hungry and bring the homeless poor into your house; when you see the naked, to cover him, and not to hide yourself from your own flesh? Then shall your light break forth like the dawn, and your healing shall spring up speedily; your righteousness shall go before you; the glory of the Lord shall be your rear guard. Then you shall call, and the Lord will answer; you shall cry, and he will say, 'Here I am.' If you take away the yoke from your midst, the pointing of the finger, and speaking wickedness, if you pour yourself out for the hungry and satisfy the desire of the afflicted, then shall your light rise in the darkness and your gloom be as the noonday. (Isaiah 58:6-10, ESV).

In their book *When Helping Hurts*, Steve Corbett and Brian Fikkert describe God's displeasure with the Israelites as it may be applied to a modern day situation.

> Why was God so displeased? ... God was furious over Israel's failure to care for the poor and the oppressed. He wanted His people to "loose the chains of injustice," and not just go to church on Sunday. He wanted His people to "clothe the naked," and not just attend midweek prayer meeting. He wanted His people to "spend themselves on behalf of the hungry," and not just sing praise music. Personal piety and formal worship are essential to the Christian life, but they must lead to lives that "act justly and love mercy."[2]

God has given us specific instructions on how we are called as His people, the global

---

2 Steve Corbett and Brian Fikkert. *When Helping Hurts: How to Alleviate Poverty Without Hurting the Poor* (Chicago: Moody Publishers, 2009).

Church, to act justly. Again and again we are called *to practice* or *to do* justice with faithfulness and steadfastness (Jeremiah 22:3-5, 9:23).

Do Justice

Our requirement to engage with justice is not a calling that stands alone, but is integrated with *loving mercy* and *walking humbly with God*, as famously articulated in Micah 6:8. It is through first seeking to understand and know God and His mercy that we can begin to understand love, justice, and righteousness (Proverbs 28:5). And it is then that we are each able to respond and pursue justice.

The term for "mercy" is the Hebrew word *chesedh*, referring to God's unconditional grace and compassion. The word for "justice" is the Hebrew term *mishpat*. The call of Micah 6:8 to do justice and love mercy, then, emphasizes both the action (*mishpat*) and the motive (*chesedh*), articulating that "what is good" and "what is required" is this action of doing justice from the motive of merciful love.[3]

In his book *Generous Justice*, Timothy Keller points out that this Hebrew term *mishpat* in its various forms occurs more than 200 times in the Hebrew Old Testament, most often meaning to treat people equitably (Leviticus 24:22—"have the same *mishpat* for the foreigner as the native"). He also uses this term to articulate a broader definition to what it means to *do* justice:

> Over and over again, mishpat describes taking up the care and cause of widows, orphans, immigrants, and the poor—those who have been called 'the quartet of the vulnerable.' .... Today this quartet would be expanded to include the refugee, the migrant worker, the homeless, and many single parents and elderly people. The mishpat, or justness, of a society, according to the Bible, is evaluated by how it treats these groups. Any neglect shown to the needs of the members of this quartet is not called merely a lack of mercy or charity, but a violation of justice, of mishpat. God loves and defends those with the least economic and social power, and so should we. That is what it means to "do justice."[4]

In Isaiah 58, God defines justice as the type of fast, or action, that God delights in the most. His examples of practicing justice are "to let the oppressed go free", "to share our

---

[3] Timothy Keller, *Generous Justice: How God's Grace Makes Us Just* (Riverhead Trade, 2012), 2.

[4] Keller, *Generous Justice*, 4.

bread with the hungry", "to bring the homeless poor into our houses", and "to clothe the naked." Therefore we can see that the call to seek justice for the oppressed requires a *personal response*: the sharing of *our* bread, *our* houses, *our* clothes.

Whether Micah or Isaiah or countless other passages, the focus is on personal and corporate responses of *doing* justice. This act of doing justice was exemplified best in the life of Jesus, per His own understanding of His mission on earth (Luke 4:17-21).

Recognizing Modern Injustices

As a society our senses are heightened to a number of modern injustices, thanks in large part to information being spread by social media. It isn't difficult to identify a handful of clear injustices facing today's society, whether modern day slavery, recruitment of child soldiers or other abuses of human dignity. However, it is far too easy to limit our understanding of injustice to only a relative few popular issues rather than the Biblical mandate against all forms of injustice and exploitation.

The verses in the previous sections refer to "vulnerable" people groups that are more susceptible to injustice than others—widows, orphans, immigrants, and the poor to name a few. The injustice they are most often susceptible to is exploitation by those with relatively more economic or social power.

Exploitation is the taking advantage of weak and vulnerable groups in society; a practice that is explicitly prohibited in Scripture and countered with the command that these groups should be treated with care and concern.[5] A specific warning against exploiting the vulnerable, specifically the poor and needy, appears in the book of Proverbs. "Do not exploit the poor because they are poor, and do not crush the needy in court, for the Lord will take up their case and will exact life for life" (Proverbs 22:22-23, NIV).

Similarly, in the book of Job, lending money and demanding clothing as security; refusing water for the thirsty and food for the hungry; viewing land as possessed solely by the powerful and privileged; sending widows away empty-handed and crushing the hopes of orphans are identified as "wickedness" or sins of the people. (Job 22:5-9) God clearly identifies these "sins" as various forms of exploitation.

God's remedy to situations of exploitation was articulated and recorded by the prophet Zechariah. Again warning against oppressing the vulnerable (the widow, fatherless, foreigners or the poor), God lays out His desire that His people instead administer true justice, and show mercy and compassion to one another. (Zechariah 7:10-11)

In light of this mandate *against* exploitation and *for* merciful and compassionate

---

5   http://www.biblegateway.com/resources/dictionary-of-bible-themes/5310-exploitation

action on behalf of those exploited, it leads us to the question: How do we identify and advocate on behalf of the exploited?

The solution may appear simple: rescue the victims of exploitation and bring the perpetrators to justice. But it's rarely that simple. Exploitation and injustice are complex and weighted definitions that carry with them the requirement of prayerful, collaborative, and informed responses.

The following section will look at the issue of human trafficking as one example of a modern injustice that is complex and multifarious, requiring an abandonment of assumptions regarding perpetrator and victim, causes and solutions, and instead allowing God's heart of justice to guide our understanding and response.

2. Un-packaging Trafficking

In the last decade the issue of trafficking of persons has captured the world's attention, and it has been thrust into the spotlight of mainstream social justice movements. Despite varied approaches, perspectives, motivations, and frameworks that have been applied to the dialogue of ending all forms of exploitation, trafficking, and modern-day slavery, scholars, practitioners, and people of all faiths agree that the trafficking or enslavement of persons is a violation of an individual's human rights and their innate human dignity.

In order to craft an appropriate response to this modern injustice it is important to first understand the complexity of what is meant by the terms "human trafficking" and "modern-day slavery".

What is Trafficking (and What It Isn't)

Human trafficking and modern-day slavery are widely used synonymously. Kevin Bales, President of Free the Slaves, defines slavery as "a relationship in which one person is controlled by another through violence, the threat of violence, or psychological coercion, has lost free will and free movement, is exploited economically, and is paid nothing beyond subsistence".[6]

By international standards, human trafficking is *"the recruitment, transportation, transfer, harboring or receipt of persons, by means of the threat or use of force or other forms of coercion, of abduction, of fraud, of deception, of the abuse of power or of a position of vulnerability or the giving or receiving of payments or benefits to achieve the consent of a person having control over another person, for the purpose of exploitation."* (United

---

6   Kevin Bales, Zoe Trodd, and Alex Kent Williamson, *Modern Slavery: A Beginners Guide* (Oxford: Oneworld Publications: 2009), 31.

Nations Palermo Protocol, 2000).[7] The diagram below may help explain the definition of trafficking further (Note: all three elements must be present).

ACT (What is Done)	MEANS (How it is Done)	PURPOSE (Why it is Done)	
Recruitment Transport Transfer Harbouring Receipt of persons	Treat or use of force Coercion Abduction Fraud Deception Abuse of power or vulnerability Giving payments or benefits	Exploitation including: Prostitution of others Sexual exploitation Forced labour Slavery or similar practices Removal of organs Other types of exploitation	= Human Tarfficking

Source: UNODC (2013)[8]

More simply put, human trafficking is the "deception and/or coercion (the method) to move a person (the action) into an exploitative situation (the purpose)".[9]

Human trafficking therefore is part of a larger framework of slavery and exploitation. As Bales says, "Trafficking is simply a mechanism or conduit that brings people into slavery. It is one process of enslavement itself, not a condition or result of that process."[10]

When approaching the issue of trafficking, some may imagine only young, poor women being moved across borders for purposes of sexual exploitation. In reality, trafficking and slavery target women, men, and children alike, from all backgrounds and socioeconomic statuses, for labour, sex, recruitment of child soldiers or other exploitive purposes.

It is globally estimated that around 800,000 men, women, and children are trafficked annually across international borders into slavery; and that the number of slaves in the world today is 27 million people, although it is important to note that both statistics are widely disputed, under-researched, and purely estimates[11].

In their journal article *Human Trafficking is More Than Sex Trafficking and Prostitution:*

---

7   "Protocol to Prevent, Suppress and Punish Trafficking in Persons, Especially Women and Children, supplementing the United Nations Convention against Transnational Organized Crime", (United Nations Office on Drugs and Crime, 2004), 41. http://www.unodc.org/documents/treaties/UNTOC/Publications/TOC%20Convention/TOCebook-e.pdf

8   UNODC "What is Human Trafficking" http://www.unodc.org/unodc/en/human-trafficking/what-is-human-trafficking.html

9   Sverre Molland. "Human Trafficking and Poverty Reduction: Two Sides of the Same Coin?", Juth Pakai 1:4 (2005), 28.

10 Bales, Trodd & Williamson, Modern Slavery, 35.

11 Bales, Trodd & Williamson, Modern Slavery, 18, 36.

Implications for Social Work, Alvarez and Alessi argue that keeping a narrow focus on women and sexual exploitation directly impacts our identification and assistance of victims of other forms of exploitation, as well as our prevention strategies and messaging, and essentially our influence to affect change at a grassroots and government levels.[12] In fact, victims of trafficking are commonly found in a wide variety of industries including "construction, manufacturing (e.g. textile, metal, wood), industrial fishing and fisheries, agriculture, domestic servitude, mining, quarrying, food processing, forestry, leather and tanning, carpet weaving, [and] livestock."[13] It becomes very personal considering that enslaved and exploited people produce commodities that are sold in our global markets, such as grains, coffee, cocoa, sugar, cotton, and gems.[14]

Tangled: Migrant Workers in Penang is a short documentary that outlines the exploitation and injustices faced by migrant workers in Malaysia, some of whom are unidentified victims of trafficking. Southeast Asia is the number one destination for migrant workers. Within the region, Malaysia is an important destination country for an estimated 2-4 million migrant workers (20 percent of the workforce). These workers are employed in various sectors of primarily "3D jobs" – dirty, dangerous, and disgusting – such as the manufacturing, construction, domestic work, and food industries. The documentary explains a "system" of injustice through which people from all across Asia coming with hopes of finding economic solutions for their families in Malaysia go through a process of being cheated by local agents, asked to sign contracts by middlemen that are not in their native language when they arrive in Malaysia, and the unjust power of recruiters, outsourcing agencies, and employers over workers.

By definition alone, and even more so by modern day examples, we understand human trafficking and the broader issue of modern-day slavery to be a grievous injustice demanding our response. On this point there is little disagreement between secular and Christ-following communities. However, the motivation toward response and the methods whereby we engage may differ based on our understanding of the Biblical mandate against exploitation and the coinciding call to administer *true* justice, and show mercy and compassion to one another.

For the remainder of this paper we will use the term "human trafficking" as understood to be an increasingly exploitative process that is part of the larger framework of modern-day slavery.

---

12   Maria Beatriz Alvarez & Edward J. Alessi, "Human Trafficking is More Than Sex Trafficking and Prostitution: Implications for Social Work", Affilia 27:2 (May 2012) 142-152.

13   International Organization for Migration. *Caring for Trafficked Persons: Guidance for Health Care Providers* (2009), 19.

14   Kevin Bales and Rebecca Cornell, *Slavery Today* (Toronto: Groundwood Books, 2008).

Gray Areas

In the case of human trafficking, there are many commonly held assumptions that prevent "doers of justice" from engaging effectively. One of those assumptions relates to an overly simplified, often black and white, view of perpetrators and victims.

It is easy to come to the table with an emotional response against the perpetrators and compassion for the victims with little understanding that each side of the equation requires much education and solidarity with the oppressed and with each other. It also requires a response of mercy and compassion, as lines between exploited and exploiter are often blurry.

For example, perpetrators aren't always foreign managers or pimps, but sometimes are parents, relatives or economic systems. What happens when you get to know them? Traffickers or other "perpetrators" have names, families. Perhaps they have a broken past or were abused as children. Perhaps he was forced into the business to pay off a debt.

Likewise, victims aren't always forced into the trade, but some enter with a degree of consent. What happens when you find out that the trafficked girl didn't fight back? That she actually volunteered for the job? Perhaps not knowing what all would be entailed, but she thought it would be an improvement over her current abusive situation at home. And at least in this abusive situation she would be making some money for her family.

And what about the young boys who are victims of sexual exploitation? Or the man who voluntarily migrates to earn money for his family but finds himself enslaved on a deep-sea fishing vessel for the next two years of his life? He chose to move, so does that mean he is or is not a victim of trafficking?

Effective engagement in this issue requires a departure from black and white thinking to humble yet bold steps into uncomfortable gray areas. It requires abandoning our fascination with sensational stories about raids and rescues, and instead humbly exploring opportunities for restoration of all individuals involved in the framework of exploitation.

In the last chapter in *From Human Trafficking to Human Rights*, a compilation of experts writing about the connectedness between trafficking and the framework of human rights, Kevin Bales points out how the rescue-raid approach not only inappropriately portrays victims as helpless creatures, but more importantly, it overlooks their own resilience and personal strength to overcome slavery.

> "It is easy to think about slavery in a simple way, as evil slaveholders and innocent slaves, a crime that is truly black and white in its moral contrast. Often, from this viewpoint, slaves are victims who need to be

rescued - helpless, dependent, a little pathetic, and, we expect, grateful for a chance of freedom. What this view misses is the resilience and strength of people caught in slavery, their endurance, intelligence, and compassion.... If we are going to help this push to freedom, we need to recognize and respect the power in every person in slavery, especially when slaves join together and make a decision to struggle together for their own freedom."[15]

Researchers and practitioners alike agree that the issue is far from black and white. The issue of human trafficking must be looked at through a broader lens than only sex trafficking or it's root cause being merely poverty. A more holistic approach, including safety, rehabilitation, and empowerment, as well as inclusion of love, care, and rehabilitation for perpetrators can address the injustice with more sustainability and success.

Dynamic and Multifarious

Human trafficking is far from an isolated issue needing an isolated response. It interconnects with multiple forms of injustice and human rights violations - gender inequality, domestic violence, poverty, globalization, labour abuses, and family breakdown to name a few. The complexity of this multi-layered issue can be further understood through looking at the root causes or systemic breakdowns that lead to an individual's vulnerability to exploitation.

In their book *Modern Slavery: A Beginner's Guide,* Kevin Bales, Zoe Trodd, et al. list some root causes and reasons that trafficking is a growing problem, including "insufficient penalties for traffickers, the growing deprivation and marginalization of the poor, restrictive migration laws, and lack of information about the realities and dangers of trafficking."[16]

Generally speaking, similar factors of vulnerability can make men, women, and children prey to being trafficked into various forms of exploitation and slavery. Using the context of Cambodia to outline some common push, pull, and facilitating factors to being human trafficking, the table below outlines some of these contributing causes.

---

15 Allison Brysk and Austin Choi-Fitzpatrick, ed. "The Anti-Slavery Movement: Making Rights into Reality", in From *Human Trafficking to Human Rights: Reframing Contemporary Slavery,* (Philadelphia, Pennsylvania: University of Pennsylvania Press, 2012), 197.

16 Bales, Trodd, & Williamson. *Modern Slavery,* 43.

PUSH FACTORS	FACILITATING FACTORS	PULL FACTORS
Poverty	Globalization	Labor demand
Debt	History of migration in village	Recruitment practices and advertising
Loss of land and natural disasters	Proximity to urban and border areas	Belief that job will be better than reality
Lack of employment opportunities, especially in rurul areas	Presence of social networks in destination	Peer encouragement and stories
Limited or no access to education	Lack of knowledge about journey, destination and working conditions	Lure of perceived easy money
Familiy relationship breakdown (divorce, death or separation of parents) and domestic violence	Improved transportation and communication infrastructure	Aspirations for an improved livelihood, independence, and urban experiences
Number of siblings and obligation of primarily young women to help their family	Values and attitudes toward female inequality	Opportunity to earn income to help family
Distressing childhood expereinces, including virginity selling or sexual abuse		

Source: **Adapted from USAID and The Asia Foundation**[17]

In *The Irresistible Revolution*, Shane Claiborne challenges followers of Jesus to do justice for the individual while also tackling the structural and societal injustices that the individual is suffering under. He urges us to see our brother and sister, and also the broader scope, by asking "who owns the pond" from which they have been fishing. He challenges us to not only follow the example of the Good Samaritan by lifting up the oppressed lying on the road, though that is indeed important, but also to transform "the entire road to Jerusalem." He borrows a quote from Dietrich Bonhoeffer who said: "We are not to simply bandage the wounds of victims beneath the wheels of injustice, but we are to drive a spoke into the wheel itself."[18]

The following graphic shows the complexity of the "wheels" needing intervention with respect to trafficking in persons in Cambodia, which can easily be contextualized into other country settings, as well as the interconnectedness and complexity of such interventions.

---

17 Review of a Decade of Research on Trafficking in Persons, Cambodia. http://pdf.usaid.gov/pdf_docs/PNADS386.pdf, p. 36

18 Shane Claiborne, *The Irresistible Revolution: Living as an Ordinary Radical* (Grand Rapids: Zondervan, 2006), 152.

Dynamics of Trafficking in Persons: A Conceptual Framework

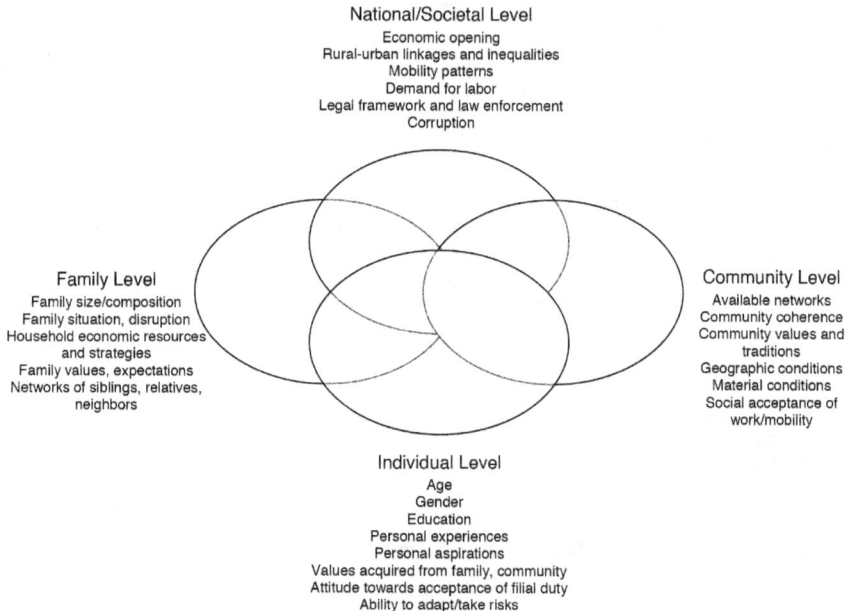

Source: USAID and The Asia Foundation[19]

Understanding the complexity of issues of injustice such as modern-day slavery is important as it forces us to remain humble by being open to learning and dependent on the God of Justice rather than on our worldly responses and programs. It forces us to accept the burden of stepping into a mess that we alone cannot fix, but as a community of Christ followers we are able to join hands and see the Restorer of Justice intervene.

The Call Into Complexity

At this point, it is easy to be overwhelmed by the complexity of the issue, and this paper cannot even begin to unravel the nuances of the issue let alone propose concise solutions. However, by offering a taste, it is the authors' hope that it would create an appetite to dive into the complexity of issues such as this.

Christians are called not to look at human trafficking as a "silo" issue of sexual exploitation with a clear perpetrator and victim, but instead to *understand* and *enter* the complexity of push, pull, and facilitating factors, bringing the character of Christ to the

---

19 Review of a Decade of Research on Trafficking in Persons, Cambodia. http://pdf.usaid.gov/pdf_docs/PNADS386.pdf, p. 36

equation to facilitate deeper, structural root causes that can create sustainable change. This understanding and "entering in" requires a commitment to education.

In the opening chapter of his book *Irresistible Revolution*, Shane Claiborne defines "ordinary radical" as one "who wants to get at the root of what it means to love, and to get at the root of what has made such a mess of our world."[20] This means that the beginning of an effort to release the oppressed must start with an examination of the root, structural causes of injustice, including but not limited to greed, power, and broken relationships. A great place to start for educating yourself about an issue is to look for recommended resource lists of films, books, and articles, normally published on the websites of respected organizations.[21]

There are no easy answers to complex challenges like those referred to in this paper, and there is no single strategy, program or organization that alone can provide a solution. However, through humble collaboration of hearts and minds aimed at carrying God's presence into these situations, leaving authorship and ownership in the hands of God rather than in the hands of men, breakthroughs begin unfolding.

3. Structural Breakthroughs

The interconnected structural issues may become overwhelming in the quest to seek solutions to issues of trafficking or sexual exploitation. In response, the need to determine areas of highest need (or greatest impact) with respect to trafficking, exploitation or other areas of injustice is becoming greater.

Through investments in research, a commitment to collaboration, and a willingness to enter the mess of relationship, organizations around the world are seeing structural breakthroughs.

Research Dividends

An organization focused primarily on intervention with sexually exploited women desired to see more efforts directed toward moving the needle in preventing exploitation. To that end, research was conducted in 2010 to determine factors differentiating Thai women who made the voluntary or semi-voluntary decision to migrate from their homes, largely located in the rural Northeast region, to engage in sex industry employment and those who chose to stay in the rural villages.

---

20 Shane Claiborne, *The Irresistible Revolution: Living as an Ordinary Radical* (Grand Rapids: Zondervan, 2006), 20.

21 For recommended reading lists about human trafficking and modern-day slavery visit the websites of Chab Dai Coalition (www.chabdai.org/downoads) and Polaris Project (www.polarisproject.org).

Though many would simply point to poverty and lack of employment in the rural areas as the main contributing factor to migration, this study showed that family dynamics played a much larger role in differentiating between those who stayed home and those who migrated for sex work. Cultural paradigms regarding marriage, relational fidelity, and imbalanced socio-cultural obligations of daughters played a strong role in determining whether a Thai daughter would find work in the rural area or succumb to family or societal pressure to migrate.[22]

What is the implication of these findings? It was discovered that targeted approaches of providing education or employment to those impacted by the sex industry, without addressing the broader issues of family and relational brokenness, would fail in many ways to "release" individuals suffering from sexual exploitation in bars and brothels. In the same vein, a targeted approach to support stronger family units without addressing broader education and economic systems may also leave an individual with a lack of healthy life options. This understanding led to a shift in approach to prevention, intervention, and re-integration of individuals suffering from sexual exploitation, by broadening the targeted group from the individual to their family and community environment.

Case Study – The Well, Bangkok

> Trafficking isn't the half of it. The family is everything. The engine driving Thailand's huge sex industry is a pandemic of broken families rearing damaged people in an unending cycle. (Jim Larson, Servantworks/The Well Bangkok)

The Well, Bangkok is a Christ-centered ministry established in 2004 with the mission to help transform Thailand through reaching sex industry workers and others at risk, training them as leaders, and sending them to reach others.[23] They do this by developing relationships with individuals "on the margins," including those actively engaged in prostitution, suffering from homelessness or addictions or otherwise in need of relationship, and offering opportunities to receive social services, education, and employment. The Well "reach-teach-send" strategy is based on the story of John 4:39-42

---

22   Cori Wittman. From *Rice Fields to Red Light Districts: An Economic Examination of Factors Motivating Employment in Thailand's Sex Industry*, Kansas State University, 2011

23   The Well is a ministry of Servantworks, a US-based nonprofit committed to finding innovative ways to solve difficult problems to advance the Kingdom.

where an entire community was transformed through a purposeful encounter between Jesus and a woman who had five husbands.[24]

Through the first several years of ministry, the Well was focused on inviting women out of scenes of exploitative employment in Bangkok's red light districts and offering counseling and employment with the goal of seeing these women restored and able to return to their home communities. It became quickly apparent that this road to recovery involved much more than counseling and employment, but required holistic responses to physical, emotional, and spiritual needs not only of the individual but often of their families and communities.

For the last several years, the Well team has been continuing to provide social services, education and employment to hurting individuals while all the time recognizing that an ounce of prevention is worth a pound of cure. In light of the research showing the impact of the health of family units on the likelihood that a woman would resort to bar work or other risky activity, The Well expanded its focus to include husbands/boyfriends and children/teens of affected women. This expansion of focus carried with it a whole slough of complexities, as husbands often carried burdens of physical abuse and drug addictions, and children and teens brought a new onslaught of unique needs.

In light of these complexities, and inspired by the possibility of more breakthroughs, a small team of individuals from The Well decided to locate themselves in the heart of the rural Northeast (Isaan) region from which a 70-80 percent of women exploited in Bangkok's bar districts originate. The goal was to grow a community environment where these cycles of brokenness, originating with vulnerable rural families and communities and ending in Bangkok's bar districts, are broken and redeemed. Through investments in educational opportunities for at-risk teens and young adults, economic development for struggling rural families, and support and trainings for family units, it is believed that vulnerability to exploitation can be decreased and individuals and families can be built up to lead broader social change.

Since early 2012, the small team has operated as a family, collaborating with a number of established ministries and foundations to bring needed services to what is a growing community of individuals on the road to becoming leaders of a changed generation. Through rural residential discipleship, education, and economic development, with an outward focus of serving the broader community, the team is seeing teens and young adults break the cycles of brokenness passed down from their parents and grandparents and grow into leaders.

---

24   http://servantworks.com/the-well/

But this is only one, modest example. Breakthroughs are unfolding all around the world in the midst of situations of injustice. In the world of trafficking and exploitation, these breakthroughs take the form of individuals being rescued from rings of coercion, repatriation for those trapped out of their own country, individuals working to strengthen legal or law enforcement systems, recovery and reintegration of individuals that have suffered exploitation, strengthening economic systems and reducing vulnerability among families and communities. Each of these activities, and many others, are being undertaken by countless heroic ministries and organizations both small and large in highly vulnerable populations throughout the world.

It takes all kinds.

But most importantly, it takes *people*. It takes people willing to "enter the mess" of complex, unjust situations and believe that the God of Justice will both author and orchestrate a renewal of justice.

Collaboration is Key

The first step in seeking structural breakthroughs in any issue of injustice – particularly those weighted in complexity like human trafficking – requires a commitment to being both a collaborator and a learner. No one person, church, or organization can address the world of injustices single-handedly. The Bible says we are called to work together as the Body of Christ, acknowledging each other's unique and significant role in God's story of reversing injustice (Romans 12:4, 1 Corinthians 12:12).

Our commitment to learn and collaborate is two-fold: first, through educating ourselves about the context by studying and talking to practitioners working on the ground and; second, by humbly acknowledging that change is to be expected, and through openly sharing with partners it is possible to proactively adapt our program models to address the shifts we see in injustice, trafficking, and/or exploitation.

Case Study – Chab Dai Coalition

In Cambodia, a coalition of fifty-five faith-based organizations engage with the issue of human trafficking on all levels of its complexity, from prevention to rehabilitation, outreach to police interventions, vocational training to socially responsible businesses, from grassroots awareness-raising to high-level government advocacy. The shelves of their extensive library demonstrate further the reality that the issue is highly complex and intersects with other development and human rights issues. The library has more than sixty categories of resources, all related to the issue of human trafficking: parenting, violence against women, drug abuse and addictions, and demand to name a few.[25]

The Chab Dai Coalition has been working towards ending trafficking and exploitation since it's inception in 2005. The term "Chab Dai" means "joining hands" (in Khmer) and it's vision is to see relationships between partners translate into a continuum of care for survivors of trafficking and exploitation, and open sharing of best practices and lessons learned in order to sustain programs to holistically prevent, rehabilitate, or restore the lives of women, men, and children. Chab Dai also acts as an active bridge-builder between this grassroots network and the Royal Government of Cambodia and larger international and United Nations agencies in Cambodia.[26]

In their report on *Faith Roles in Cambodia's Efforts to Counter Trafficking in Persons*, World Faiths Development Dialogue highlights the individual roles faith based organizations have already had, as well as the important role the coalition plays on strategically looking at longer term, systemic issues through joint-activities like bi-annual member meetings and focus forums. Helen Sworn, Founder & Executive Director of Chab Dai, said:

> Having all of these organizations around the table has created a really beautiful opportunity to be strategic and to ask what impact issues will have on our programs and what we would like to see in five years' time, both programmatically and geographically.[27]

Chab Dai believes that only through collaboration will the world will see an end to human trafficking, exploitation, and all forms of slavery. To that end, Chab Dai helped launch a global project called Freedom Collaborative with the aim to bring together grassroots organizations, government task forces, and researchers on a global platform in order to address the issue from all angles.[28]

Restoration Through Relationship

Running hand-in-hand with the importance of collaboration is the importance of investment in relationships: relationships with other organizations, with governments and systems, with oppressed individuals and their oppressors. In the authors' opinion, the least common denominator in effective efforts is a commitment to both top-down

---

25 Chab Dai Coalition. www.chabdai.org

26 Chab Dai Coalition. www.chabdai.org.

27 World Faiths Development Dialogue. *Faith Roles in Cambodia's Efforts to Counter Trafficking in Cambodia* (2012): 30.

28 Freedom Collaborative. www.freedomcollaborative.org.

and bottom-up, long-term relationships built on foundations of trust and respect. This may sound overly-simplified in contrast to the complex issues outlined above, but there is nothing simple or easy about relationships. Relationships are as messy and complex as the issues themselves.

As a Christ-following community, we must be willing to build long-term relationships with those who are under oppression, between those committed to fighting against oppression, as well as those linked to the oppression itself: pimps, clients or "johns", traffickers, and corrupt government officials. Change will be seen when we engage in personal relationships with people on all levels, and seek to understand their motivations and stories, and together - patiently and faithfully - creating solutions.

Case Study – NightLight Bangkok

Annie Dieselberg is Founder & CEO of NightLight, an international organization committed to addressing the complex issues of commercial sexual exploitation through prevention, intervention, restoration, and education.[29] She explains the complexity of the issue from her perspective and argues that it cannot be defined in black and white terms:

> Trafficking is a complex situation that employs, exploits, profits, and destroys millions of people – humans, with emotions, people with families, people with dreams, and people with bitter disappointments. Some of these people are victims and some are the exploiters. It would be easy to draw the line in the sand to clearly establish the acceptable and the unacceptable; the loveable and the despicable; those worthy of grace and those to condemn. It would be easy – it was easy, until I met Lionel, one of many characters in the drama of human trafficking. Exploitation is wrong – no ifs, ands, or buts about it, but hating an individual simply because of what they do becomes much harder when you know them by name.

She explains how long-term, trust-based relationships with victims and traffickers alike are more sustainable solutions than rescue operations. She also encourages us to engage in the tension of good and evil, and the space between freedom and enslavement:

---

29 NightLight International. www.nightlightbangkok.com.

You might wonder why we don't just call the police to raid the place. We've learned though, that hasty raids do further damage and chase the trafficking ring further underground. We know trusted investigators who are doing their part in this drama. It takes time. I have learned the hard way that when you pick fights with the gatekeeper the door slams shut. Right now we have access to victims and the opportunity to speak into the lives of the traffickers and pimps as well. This is where we live and work – in this tension of hating the sin and the evil but of loving those who are trapped in its grip. Lionel is the gatekeeper and Lionel likes us enough to let us through the gate.[30]

Annie's commitment to building relationships with traffickers and victims alike, as well as engaging in relationships with governmental and intergovernmental organizations, is an example of a Gospel-centered, holistic approach to injustice. She is able to balance the call to befriend the broken-hearted and "administer true justice" by carrying with her the presence of God, and allowing Him to show up and work in the most unlikely places.

This concept of development based on collaboration and incarnational relationship is not new, and with creativity and in relationship may be applied to the oppressed. In 700 B.C. Lao Tsu wrote these words:

> Go to the people, live with them
>
> learn from them, love them.
>
> Start with what they know,
>
> build on what they have.
>
> But with the best leaders when the work is done,
>
> and the task is accomplished,
>
> The people will say,
>
> We have done this ourselves.[31]

---

30   Annie Dieselberg, "My Scandalous Confession," Love Never Fails (blog), April 12, 2013, http://anniedieselberg.wordpress.com/2013/04/12/my-scandalous-confession.

31   Michael Duncan, *Costly Mission: Following Christ into the Slums*, (Monrovia, California: MARC, 1996), 52.

4. Practical Implications for the Church

The social injustices of trafficking, poverty, globalization, and human rights are rooted in deep, multidimensional causes that are not going to be solved overnight. Transformational impact for those who have experienced oppression or suffered from injustice requires long-term investment and commitment. Understanding this is key if we are going to see the oppressed released. However, understanding must lead to action. It must lead to the broader Christ-following community taking steps toward long-term investment and commitment.

In her book *The Invisible*, Arloa Sutter, founder of Breakthrough Urban Ministries in Chicago identifies three kinds of churches: personal piety churches, social justice committee churches, and compassionate to the core churches. Warning against the temptation to settle for the first or second, she reminds that "churches that are compassionate to the core recognize that the gospel is indeed good news, especially for those who have experienced social oppression. Each part of the body of Christ works with the whole, under the direction of Christ, the head, to reach out with compassion to the world Jesus loves and died for."[32]

Sutter then goes on to highlight seven "breakthrough practices" that churches and individuals may adopt to move us away from guilt or confusion and instead into a place of "heartfelt engagement with [the poor]." A few of those practices include adopting the "practice of presence" by intentionally spending time with those less fortunate, being guided by the Spirit rather than driven by need, practicing stewardship and joining a movement with those already investing in solutions.[33] This is the call for the church to release the oppressed: to work as part of the whole, with Christ, to reach out with compassion.

Arloa's breakthrough practices provide strong foundational guidelines for churches to adopt as they relates to releasing the oppressed. The remainder of this section will outline some additional thoughts with respect to ways the Christ-following community can and should effectively engage in "doing justice."

Cause versus Character

How many times have you heard a friend, colleague or celebrity say that they were passionate about? Perhaps even closer to home, how many times have *you* used that phrase?

---

32   Arloa Sutter. *The Invisible*. (Indianapolis, Indiana: Wesleyan Publishing House, 2010), 93

33   Sutter, *The Invisible*, 109.

In light of today's heightened sensitivity to social issues and an increasing interest in engagement, it is important for Christ-followers to stay focused on the character of Christ in bringing restoration to situations of injustice rather than being caught up in "being passionate" for a cause. Many individuals, after being educated about the atrocities of modern day slavery or other forms of exploitation, become passionate about the cause to which they were just exposed. This newfound cause and our passion for it may end up blinding us to the injustices in our own neighborhoods, workplaces or families. Or, it may lead us to jump in and "fight for the cause," only to be quickly disillusioned by its complexity or lack of sensation when you're in the trenches finding solutions. Perhaps the people with whom they are fighting aren't doing it the "right" way. Or, maybe you're told there's another cause that is more worthy of your time, talents or finances, causing you to question your involvement in the first.

The temptation is to allow the cause to become more important than the character of the one that called you in the first place. However, by allowing the character of Christ to season our every action, we decrease the temptation to get overly caught up (and quickly disillusioned) by the sensation of a cause. We can instead maintain a healthy passion for God's commitment to justice, and His call that we be committed to the same.

This does not mean we cannot become passionate about a specific issue or cause. It simply reminds us that we must let the character of Christ heighten our senses to situations of injustice, give wisdom in when and how to respond, and keep us humble and dependent in our responses.

Honor One Another

While we are called to *do* justice, we are also called to *walk humbly* before our God. Following Christ's example of humility and His teaching to consider others better than oneself is a needed foundation for any action toward restoring justice. This humility paves the way for us to honor one another.

Honor the Oppressed

When drawn into the call to release the oppressed or restore justice, we are called to honor those that are oppressed or vulnerable. We may do this by avoiding making the vulnerable objects of pity – either through films or handouts – but instead respecting the dignity of those we are called to love and serve.

Peoples who have been oppressed each have a unique story to share, but that may not mean they want to share it. We are called to be sensitive and understanding of each person's stage of their healing process. Genesis 1:27 boldly states: "God created human beings in God's own image. God created them in the image of God; male and female God created them." Herein the inherent dignity of all women, men, and children lies: each individual was designed with purpose and intention and bears the fingerprints of their creator. We must be mindful of not re-exploiting those who have been released through un-dignifying story telling or "poverty porn".[34]

Another way of respecting the dignity of the oppressed is in collaborating with them to designing programs that empower them as individuals and communities to take steps toward restoring justice rather than offering handouts that may end up doing more harm than good.

After learning some of these lessons the hard way, Michael Duncan, leader of Servants to Asia's Urban Poor in Manila for nine years wrote in his book *Costly Mission: Following Christ into the Slums* that "[d]evelopment was to be a shared process that respected both the dignity of the poor and the missionary." He found that working alongside the poor, rather than on behalf of the poor, creates sustainable, long-term, life-giving change. He writes: "For change to occur and be long-term it must be personal and corporate. People must agree together that they need change. Need-based change is preferable to advice-driven change."[35]

Honor the Oppressors

Slightly more difficult, or counter-intuitive to many, is the call to honor the oppressors, recognizing that they too may be oppressed themselves. As Annie Dieselberg explained their work in building relationships not only with the oppressed, but often with the perpetrators, we find that these relationships cannot be built without an element of honor.

Jesus exemplified this in his decision to dine with Zacchaeus[36]. Though not a trafficker, Zacchaeus was in a position where he was exploiting the poor and vulnerable through excessive tax collection. Jesus didn't condemn Zacchaeus for his exploitive behavior, but instead he showed Him a distinct honor by inviting himself over for dinner.

In the realm of exploitation and trafficking, movement is being made away from condemnation of the oppressors and instead toward a compassionate response. The MST Project is an example of an organization working toward that end by reaching out

---

34 For more information about what dignity and informed consent looks like in media download the "Photography + Protecting Dignity Guide" and "Media & Communication Policy" available on Chab Dai's website: www.chabdai.org/download

35 Michael Duncan, *Costly Mission: Following Christ into the Slums*, (Monrovia, California: MARC, 1996), 54, 93.

36 Luke 19:1-10.

to foreign men that visit red-light districts. They maintain the value that men are part of the solution and describe that, "We see a person, not a perpetrator. We see a man, not a client. We see someone to love, not someone to hate. We love these men because God first loved us."[37]

Honor Fellow "Doers of Justice"

In the call to honor one another, perhaps the least spoken of is the need to honor others working in similar fields or toward similar goals. It is the author's belief that the single greatest impediment to Kingdom advancement and restoration of justice is failure to honor one another, often stemming from a creeping spirit of pride. And those following Christ are just as susceptible – if not even more susceptible – to this crouching tiger of pride as those that do not have the benefit of relationship with Him.

In the midst of heavy, dark, stressful ministry to broken populations, it is easy to unintentionally allow comparisons to be made with others. As we compare best practices, perhaps we think our practices are better than another's. We become protective of those for whom we are caring, rescuing or advocating, and we desire that these precious people deserve the best care possible: ours. We begin to compete for people. For limited fundraising dollars. For name recognition.

We begin to compete rather than collaborate. We begin to let pride in *our way* cloud our focus on *His way*. And often in doing so, we inadvertently fail to honor our fellow laborers.

To avoid this trap of pride, it is important to return to the command of Christ to consider others better than yourself.[38] In this case, we might expand that to also include our ideas, our methods, our organization or our cause. Regardless of the reality of our idea, method, organization or cause being "better" or "worse" than theirs, the important thing is the ability to approach the issue with humility – to above all honor one another in our responses.

One way to maintain this spirit of humility in honoring one another is through prayer. Prayer for fellow laborers, and as importantly, prayer *with* fellow laborers. It is much more difficult to let a spirit of pride cause division when you are willing to sit and pray for one another, and with one another for your common vision that the Kingdom be advanced.

---

37 www.mstproject.com
38 Philippians 2:3

Remember to C.A.R.E.

A focus on the character of Christ and a commitment to honoring one another becomes the foundation for any activity toward releasing the oppressed. In addition, the acronym "C.A.R.E." can help remind us of four important elements in our responses: Collaboration, Accountability, Relationships, and Education.

Collaboration

As mentioned in a previous section of this paper, collaboration is key toward working effectively toward releasing the oppressed. Partnering, forming networks with other organizations, ministries or churches, or otherwise joining forces with other laborers brings synergy, strategy, and all-important humility to efforts toward justice.

Accountability

We must remain mindful of God's corporate and individual call for His people to seek justice for the oppressed. As we form organizations and missions statements, design programs or discuss budgets, let us be transparent with beneficiaries, donors, and our partners. And most importantly, let us remain accountable to the core of Christ's call on our lives and the church with respect to caring for the poor, vulnerable, and oppressed.

Relationship

Those desiring to enter into the work of "releasing the oppressed" must be willing to enter into the mess of relationship. The term "release" implies there must be a physical presence of something moving something from bondage to freedom. As we have explored in this paper, we see that relationships – top down, bottom up, with the oppressed, with oppressors, with each other – these are the foundations whereby justice is restored.

Education

We all must be committed to constant learning and re-learning. Again in the spirit of humility, we must commit to growing in knowledge and understanding of God's heart of justice, the issues of injustice themselves, and in His methods of bringing His justice to Earth. We must be willing to fail and to learn from those failures, and we must also be willing to share what we have learned with others.

Conclusion

> We do justice when we give all human beings their due as creations of God. Doing justice includes not only the righting of wrongs, but generosity and social concern, especially toward the poor and

vulnerable. This kind of life reflects the character of God. It consists of a broad range of activities, from simple fair and honest dealings with people in daily life to regular, radically generous giving of your time and resources, to activism that seeks to end particular forms of injustice, violence, and oppression. (Timothy Keller)[39]

Both Scripture and modern social media give us plenty of examples regarding oppressed peoples requiring just intervention, and given closer examination we may see that they are not generations or worlds away, but very well may be our neighbors. What should be our response?

Our response should be a Spirit sensitive to the calling of God to spend time with the kinds of people Jesus spent time with, to identify with Christ in His sufferings, and *to spend yourselves on behalf of the hungry and satisfy the needs of the oppressed.*

This may mean leaving our comfortable homes to seek out a hurting neighbor or build relationships with teens on the rougher side of town. Or, it may mean stepping out and living out God's heart for justice in a faraway land.

Regardless of our personal call to stay or go, we each must constantly allow God's heart for justice to shape and form our own heart and to train our eyes to recognize injustices around us. We must commit to learning about the context of the injustices in our communities and world from books and those who are oppressed themselves. And finally, we must muster up the guts to faithfully, and in faith, respond in obedience—to "do justice."

A Franciscan Benediction

May God bless us with discomfort

At easy answers, half-truths, and superficial relationships

So that we may live from deep within our hearts.

May God bless us with anger

At injustice, oppression, and exploitation of God's creations

So that we may work for justice, freedom, and peace.

May God bless us with tears

To shed for those who suffer pain, rejection, hunger, and war,

---

[39] Keller, *Generous Justice*, 17.

So that we may reach out our hands to comfort them and
To turn their pain into joy.
And may God bless us with just enough foolishness
To believe that we can make a difference in the world,
So that we can do what others claim cannot be done:
To bring justice and kindness to all our children
and all our neighbors who are poor.
Amen.

References

Alvarez, Maria Beatriz and Edward J. Alessi, "Human Trafficking is More Than Sex Trafficking and Prostitution: Implications for Social Work", *Affilia* 27:2 (May 2012) 142-152.

Bales, Kevin, Zoe Trodd, & Alex Kent Williamson. *Modern Slavery: A Beginner's Guide* (Oxford: Oneworld Publications, 2009).

Brysk, Allison and Austin Choi-Fitzpatrick, ed. *From Human Trafficking to Human Rights: Reframing Contemporary Slavery* (Philadelphia, Pennsylvania: University of Pennsylvania Press, 2012).

Chab Dai Coalition. www.chabdai.org

Claiborne, Shane, *The Irresistible Revolution: Living as an Ordinary Radical* (Grand Rapids: Zondervan, 2006).

Corbett, Steve and Brian Fikkert. *When Helping Hurts: Alleviating Poverty Without Hurting the Poor and Yourself* (Chicago, Illinois: Moody Publishers, 2009).

Duncan, Michael, *Costly Mission: Following Christ into the Slums* (Monrovia, California: MARC, 1996), 52.

Keller, Timothy *Generous Justice: How God's Grace Makes Us Just* (Riverhead Trade, 2012).

Molland, Sverre. "Human Trafficking and Poverty Reduction: Two Sides of the Same Coin?", *Juth Pakai*, 1:4, (2005), 27-37.

Tangled: Migrant Workers in Penang. http://www.youtube.com/watch?v=DNvEbJyozyk

Wittman, Cori. *From Rice Fields to Red Light Districts: An Economic Examination of Factors Motivating Employment in Thailand's Sex Industry*, (Kansas State University, 2011).

World Faiths Development Dialogue. *Faith Roles in Cambodia's Efforts to Counter Trafficking in Cambodia.* (2012).

Empowering Children and Young People: Imagining a Better Future in the Global City

Amy Brock-Devine, Elizabeth Barnett, Kimberly Quinley and Matthew Wilson

Children and young people constitute a considerable proportion of urban slum communities. They occupy an ambiguous place in the missional imagination of many, and are the focus of much benevolent, commercial, and dark intention from within their own countries of origin, neighboring nations, and from remote western sources. Marginalized, exploited, and often bearing an invisible burden, they are also equivocally highly profiled in images and popular narratives. The process of the ISUM Children and Young People stream sought to see, describe, imagine, listen, and dialogue with children in the ways of shalom in the urban slum contexts that are their home.

Introduction

The International Summit of Urban Mission gave attention to a web of dynamics impacting the shape and character of missions in global cities. We recognize that there is a good deal of cross-over between the contexts of the various streams and papers. "Empowering Children and Young People" gathers the perspectives of practitioners focusing their attention on the environments, experiences, and challenges of children and young people in global urban contexts.

The ISUM Working Group for Children and Young People consisted of around 20 Christian practitioners gathered from nine nations: Australia, China, England, Philippines, Singapore, Tonga, United States of America, Vietnam, and Thailand.

The participants undertook a journey together, engaging a three stage interrogative process, principally concerned with discerning challenges to urban shalom as well as identifying a number of positive features of the urban context related to the experience of being young. Resisting binary approaches, participants acknowledged the ambiguities and contradictions present in young lives. Together through Biblical reflection, story-sharing, theoretical inquiry, and creative re-imaging, the group considered three key questions in stages.

"What are the challenges to shalom for urban kids & youth?"

"What are the seeds of hope for shalom of urban kids & youth?"

"What calls to action and invitations to innovation can we commend to the wider church?"

Biblical Interval 1: A Reflection Upon Intervention and Recuperation

In the gospel of Luke, Jesus responds to the question "who is my neighbor" by telling a parable – perhaps drawn from the popular imagination of his time (Luke 10:29-37). A vulnerable traveller has been mugged, beaten, and left to bleed and perhaps die, by the side of the road. Questions are raised in the story about the nature of true piety as religious people pass by this broken human life without intervening. Eventually help comes – from an unlikely place – from across a deep racial and cultural divide. The parable concludes with a picture of hospitality and rehabilitation. The roles of the one who intervenes in the short-term and the one who provides longer-term recuperation are shown as distinct yet working in co-operation with one another.

The parable presents a powerful challenge to travellers through, and dwellers within, today's global cities. Poverty and injustice groans at the edge of the economic superhighway – and this is no mere metaphorical groaning – these are real human voices. Oppression and exploitation in urban sprawl has a face, and very often that face is the face of a child. The vulnerability of the adult traveller in the countryside in Jesus' parable easily mirrors the vulnerability of children and young people resident in cities.

Does the church – the body of Christ in the city – hear these cries? Are we, God's people, attentive or distracted? And what will our role be in the relief of this suffering? Who will engage in the critical work of intervention and who will provide the respite and rehabilitation?

The ISUM working group considering the theme of Empowering Children & Youth spent time visiting, questioning and learning from, two groups in the city of Bangkok who are engaged on a daily basis in the work of both intervention and recuperation; Word Made Flesh and The Hub.[1]

---

1 These groups are representatives of "contextualization" missiologies, as drawn from Wilbert Shenk's typologies: replication, indigenization, and contextualization. Wilbert Shenk, *Changing Frontiers of Mission* (Maryknoll, NY: Orbis, 1999)

Stage One: "What are the challenges to shalom for urban kids & youth?"

"Let us enter equal complaint against stomachs and minds which do not eat. If there is anything more heart-breaking than a body perishing for lack of bread, it is a soul which is dying from hunger for the light" (Victor Hugo, Les Miserables).

The Biblical Context of Children

Children are to be valued both for their presence in the present, and for their prophetic role as signs that point to the future. While often spoken of primarily as "the next generation" or "our future" in political, civic and even faith community speeches and sermons, children must be rightly recognized as fully human, fully present, and to be deeply treasured now. Children have agency now. Through their being and their acting in the world they are "not a state that anticipates full human life, but an enduring reality saturated with meaning and grace."[2] Psalm 8 speaks of God's empowerment of children, prophetically stating *"Through the praise of children and infants you have established a stronghold against your enemies, to silence the foe and the avenger."* The biblical vision reveals childhood as a special and indeed powerful time in the divine ordering of life's journey.

However, Dan Brewster reminds us of the immense scope of biblical material that references children and childhood – over 1700 examples – expanding our vision and awareness of the possibilities of God's action in the lives of children in marginalized communities, both the historical biblical context and our contemporary urban context.[3] Marcia Bunge helpfully collates the plethora of biblical material regarding children into six helpful images as "typologies": lights, signs of the kingdom and bringers of revelation; gifts; bearers of the *imago Dei*; inheritors of sin and moral agents; developing beings in need of instruction; the most vulnerable and marginalized among us.[4] The variety, nuances, and tensions between these biblical images help us not to approach our task of thinking about children and attending to them in a one-dimensional "flat" or "blunt" manner, but with creativity, sensitivity, discernment, and responsiveness to who they are and how God is at work in their orbit, informing our own path of action in their midst.

---

2   David Jensen, *Graced Vulnerability* (Cleveland: Pilgrim Press, 2005), 12

3   Dan Brewtser, *Child Church and Mission* (Compassion International, 2011), 12

4   Marcia Bunge, "The Child, Religion, and the Academy: Developing Robust Theological and Religious Understandings of Children and Childhood" *The Journal of Religion* 86.4 (2006), 549-579.

The biblical patterns demonstrate that God's purposes for children (which also means for each child) are fulfilled in the context of shared responsibility, not only between parents, siblings and extended family but also with the wider community. Many will participate in the growth, development, and empowerment of a child. Amongst them will be some particularly critical individuals who will teach them how to use the gifts that God has placed within them, for their own individual flourishing and also for the good of their city. The ground for the communal contextuality of human life lies in Trinitarian theology, and is not limited only to children, but to all humans.[5] In this we recognize that the flourishing of adults in community is also dependent on the participation of children, who also instruct elders in the use of their particular gifts. Bunge highlights the reciprocal vocations of child and adult in serving one another in prophetic truth-telling and modeling the kingdom.[6] Children are called to honor and obey parents, but also to resist wrong-doing that adults may initiate with a godly vocation to "disobedience". Adults are called to nurture and encourage children, but also to limit the access children have to evil in a godly vocation of restraint. Awareness of the double vocation of children prevents us from looking upon children only as passive objects. Our call to "empower" children is not just because they are young and need elevating, but also because they are rightfully active and inspired participants in the kingdom.

Within the hopeful atmosphere of the Summit there was a mature sense of self-awareness regarding the successes and failures of what we have or haven't accomplished in our efforts to empower urban youth and children. Admitting that we'll never be perfect, nor will we have all the answers, the group possessed a spirit of openness and a resolve to draw from each other's strengths. There was an acknowledgment of the enormity of the challenge and an acceptance that none of us can do this alone. We need each other.

The Community Context of Today's Children

Around the globe two billion people are living in slums, on the sidewalks, under bridges, on riverbanks, and in garbage dumps. Children and young people are integral to all these communities. They live and participate in the midst of urban slums, comprising a significant proportion of the population. They are part of the ecology and economy, living, working, moving, witnessing, knowing, providing friendship, bearing burdens,

---

5 Holly Catterton Allen and Christine Lawton Ross, *Intergenerational Christian Formation* (Downers Grover: IVP Academic, 2012), 111. Allen and Ross draw parallels from social science frameworks of human thriving with biblical Trinitarian theology.

6 Marcia J Bunge, *The Vocation of the Child: Theological Perspectives on the Particular and Paradoxical Roles and Responsibilities of Children* in Patrick McKinley Brennan The Vocation of the Child (Grand Rapids: Eerdmans, 2008), 31-52.

and contributing in all aspects of urban reality and community.

Simply defined, a slum is "a heavily populated urban area characterised by substandard housing and squalor."[7] The United Nations task group, Un-habitat, identify a slum as an area that combines to various extents the following characteristics:

- Inadequate access to safe water;

- Inadequate access to sanitation and other infrastructure;

- Poor structural quality of housing;

- Overcrowding; and,

- Insecure residential status.

These characteristics of slums are often referenced because they are quantifiable and can therefore be used to measure progress toward the Millennium Development Goal to significantly improve the lives of at least 100 million slum dwellers by 2020.

We must be careful, however, not to cast a vision of slums only in negative terms.[8] Those choosing to live incarnationally in slum communities prefer to articulate a tension between the light and the darkness that exists in the slums – a tension between "slums of hope" and "slums of despair."[9]

A Summit participant from Cambodia reflected:

> If we have our identity in God, there is no difference between those who have grown up in the slum, and those who have chosen to live there. Without God, we who live there by choice know that we can get out if we wanted to, but to anyone without a choice, there is hopelessness. But if living in the slum is home, then you also do have a choice - our attitude. Either being thankful or always wanting

---

[7] *Unhabitat Features: Twenty first session of governing Council report*, Nairobi, Kenya, 2006. http://www.unhabitat.org/downloads/docs/4625_51419_GC%2021%20What%20are%20slums.pdf

[8] Un-habitat recognize the pejorative history of the term, but affirm a morally neutral use of the term now. "Today, the catchall term "slum" is loose and deprecatory. It has many connotations and meanings and is seldom used by the more sensitive, politically correct, and academically rigorous. But in developing countries, the word lacks the pejorative and divisive original connotation, and simply refers to lower quality or informal housing."

[9] Cousins, Fry and Olivola, Environmental Health Project, Activity Report 109, Health of Children Living in Urban Slums in Asia and the Near East: Review of Existing Literature and Data. "The urban poor are resourceful survivors who live by the principle of self-help. Many are skilled entrepreneurs. Slums and settlements often turn out to be stable and homogenous communities rather than chaotic agglomerations. The challenge is to tap this strength to create the foundation for health and welfare interventions." (p.16)

something else. So we see kids and adults that love and embrace their slum home, no matter what the situation, they choose to be thankful. And we see drugged-up millionaires, who never really appreciate what they have.

The life of the child in the slum brings this tension of hope and despair into clear focus. The slum can rob a child of some of the most fundamental needs of human development: joy, health, and often quality and sustained education. It is life at its lowest. Children do survive in slums with simplicity and ingenuity on their side, yet survival is precarious, and life still marginal. Preventable diseases are common and claim many young lives. Death in the slums comes earlier: infant mortality rates are very high – and complications in childbirth leave many entering life with disabilities and lifelong health problems. Illnesses go untreated, high-risk behaviors are normative, and everyday environments carry physical and social threats.

Urban children often show great resilience in the face of enormous challenges but there are obvious constraints upon their ability to sustain themselves in life. Most therefore struggle to thrive in the extreme conditions it presents. They are physically, emotionally, and financially vulnerable and economically dependent. The city beyond the slums is unwelcoming, even hostile to them. Whilst in early years the child may be oblivious to these realties they will gradually begin to come to an awareness of the often futile and hopeless trajectory of their future.

John Wesley is frequently quoted as having said *"What one generation tolerates, the next generation will embrace,"* and this tendency has certainly contributed to the shocking situation that urban children around the world now face. What role does the church, as the people of God, have in turning the attention of wider society toward the myriad injustices of the slum? In what ways can we stoke up indignation, and light a creatively channeled anger toward the plight of children born into these circumstances. How can we amplify the voices of the suffering in order to address and reduce the systematic abuses they suffer? Our biblically shaped vision of shalom convinces us that children deserve life, and not just to survive but to thrive.

Therefore, beyond praying and petitioning God *"Why don't You do something about this, Lord"* we are reminded that God did do something. God created us – bearers of God's image. We are God's workmanship (Ephesians 2:10). ISUM participants share a commitment to more than simply describing and documenting the problems, more than canvassing and campaigning. We have a bias to action and involvement – a willingness to *make poverty personal,* believing that, as Viv Grigg said at the Summit, "the way to transform the city begins in the slums."

Amy Brock-Devine, from her perspective working with Lighthouse Slum Neighborhood Community Centre in Bangkok, expresses her response to the call to "make poverty personal":

> I couldn't stand by and watch people talk about "those people that live in the slums, could get out of there if they would just make different choices." I have seen that people in the slums feel judged and unloved. So like most of us, they need love, true unconditional love that helps us think differently and make different (and better) choices.

"Coming to" the slum community, is better recognized as "becoming" one of the slum-dwellers, as Amy says in a call of solidarity with the slum as home:

> I want to be at home in my community, to be there to love, to be readily available, to have those conversations with "my people." Instead of talking about them, I want to talk with them.

But ultimately, the impact of making poverty "personal" is demonstrated in the transformation of truth within Amy:

> And honestly, most the time, "those people in the slums" know how to show that unconditional love way better than those people that are talking about it!

A Child's-Eye View

As concerned adults seeking humbly to understand and compassionately address these issues with integrity, we must acknowledge that our own perspective is altered by the empowerment that is naturally ours through our age and social status. The ISUM working group therefore attempted to imagine ourselves in the position of an urban child or youth, in order to describe the world from their point of view.

Further, we recognize the difficulty of generalization. We take care to describe as thickly as we can what we might see through children's eyes, and resist reducing their experience to familiar and manageable categories. David Jensen writes: "The abundant difference of graced human life under God is invariably smothered once a standard is fixed to mark what humans, or what children are."[10] We want to explore: what is it that children feel? What do they think about?

There are numerous positive features that may be related to being young: the experience of simple pleasures of play and friendship, as well as the sense of being unencumbered

---

10   David Jensen, *Graced Vulnerability*, 43

by the worries and responsibilities of adulthood. Children may carry openness to the spiritual dimension through awe and wonder, instinctive sensing and feeling, and natural searching and questioning.[11] Moreover, as Adams, Hyde and Woolley reiterate,

> A profound lesson learned from implementing the UNCRC (1989) is that at virtually every age from birth onwards children's capacities are greater than previously imagined (UNICEF 2003).[12]

But for many of the children born or trafficked into urban contexts around the world their childhood may be a daily fight for survival and will almost certainly be abbreviated. In the British urban context this phenomenon has become referred to as "kidulthood" – popularized by the 2006 social realist film of the same name by director Menhaj Huda.

A Summit participant recounts the tensions of adult concerns impinging in inevitable ways on the trajectory of children – but also the serendipity of God's Spirit and presence:

> Nella's parents were insisting that she quit school at 15, as they, and almost all of the children in the neighborhood, had done – to begin work at the factory, 10 hours a day, 6 days a week for about $50 per week. But Nella was excelling in our English program, becoming the top student in her 5th grade class, and she had dreams to continue education and become a doctor to help support her family and her community. The extraordinary character of Nella made a great impact on her community, regularly connecting dozens of local children with the center's sports program. We saw her pray for her parents to change their mind and we saw God's Spirit give her strength. A God-encounter between her parents and a university graduate from an even poorer neighboring country, caused her parents begin to consider other options.
>
> When Nella's grandmother had become ill, Nella's mum made plans to remove Nella from school and return to their home country, leaving Nella's father alone, to work. We grieved the loss of this amazing girl, having listened and prayed with her about her dreams but continued to pray for her. You can imagine our delight when we got a phone call from Nella that said her mom had suddenly, but miraculously changed

---

11 Adams, Hyde and Woolley, *The Spiritual Dimension of Childhood* (London: Jessica Kingsley, 2008), 70-71.
12 Adams, Hyde and Woolley, *Spiritual Dimension of Childhood*, 42

her mind and had left for her home nation, leaving Nella to care for her now ailing father, but continuing her studies. Praying with her Father and helping them through the rough emotional moments has been a highlight of our weekly visits to their community. The Father obviously in pain, saying every time, "God is bigger than this." This has been an incredible testimony to God's grace, as we see His children receive and share abundant life in the urban slum neighborhood.

The world of a child like Nella is filled with competing threats and tensions. To be with her mother and return to her homeland? Or to care for her father in the slum and continue the opportunity for education? To continue study or to contribute to her family financially in work? How does a child process and respond to these allegiances and dreams?

Those in the working group engaging with young people in such circumstances suggested the following statements as "windows" into the thoughts of children they know.

- "I see everything. I feel everything."
- "I feel sick, hungry and no one will take care of me."
- "I feel lonely and neglected."
- "I'm a boy, but everyone is treating me like a girl. Maybe I was made wrong?"
- "Somebody is celebrating their birthday, but I don't even know mine."

For the child, the family unit is absolutely vital. Within a healthy family a child finds their identity and their sense of acceptance and personal worth. However, when there is a lack of family, or a dysfunction within family, children are understandably confused and disoriented. If comfort cannot be found in the arms of their parents or siblings then they may turn to other things for comfort. Or they may be exploited by others who sense their vulnerability and abuse it for their own selfish gains.

As they develop from childhood to youth the desire to make a contribution to their family and to their community is a healthy impulse. This is important for building self-esteem, developing a sense of personal fulfillment, and inhabiting their vocation as an active agent and participator in the world.[13]

---

13 Bonnie Miller McLemore, "Children, Chores and Vocation", in Patrick McKinley Brennan, *The Vocation of the Child* (Grand Rapids, Michigan: Eerdmans, 2008), 320

Another Summit participant within Ark International from Bangkok recounts the familiar frustrations of trying to sustain connection with young people:

> "10 year old 'Little Dee' came to our sports program every week with a huge smile on his face and a sense of determination to play this crazy sport of rugby that was so foreign to this Asian son of a single factory working mom. We spoke to Dee's mom about a bridging school program to help him read and write Thai and introduce math concepts. But shortly after that day, Dee became a 'no-show'. Often kids in our communities are very transient, as their parents are not always legal residents. Looking for work where they won't get caught, they take very low paying positions that offer them, at least, a little more financial security than the work force of the poorer nations that they are coming from.
>
> Although the slum is a tight-knit community, rich in relationship and care for one another, even Little Dee's youth leader didn't know where he had gone.
>
> I began to worry and that put us to prayer.
>
> A few weeks later, Dee and his sister walked by our small group, dirty from head to flip-flop covered toe. Dee proudly showed off his bright yellow hard hat. Dee and his sister now worked in the factory, while their mom was home to take care of her new baby. But now so tired after working 10 hour days, Monday to Saturday, with a ½ on Sunday, they didn't want to study anything. I was sad. What solution could we see now?"

When family and community life is disrupted or corrupted, this transitional stage of life becomes fraught with dangers. The need to contribute financially to the family unit may result in the physical labour or indeed the very bodies of children becoming commodified through oppressive, unregulated work, often including physical harm and sexual exploitation. The emotional and spiritual damage of falling prey to these dangers can be immense. For this reason, many turn to drugs and alcohol in order to numb the pain. A predictable cycle of substance addiction often follows.

Stage One Summary

When seeking to see the world from the perspective of a child the group recognized that we ought to resist a binary approach i.e. mindsets that would describe certain features of life and influences upon the young as either entirely bad or entirely good. Rather, the group acknowledged the ambiguities and contradictions present in young lives: parents, employment, education, even urbanity itself all appear as polysemous factors.[14]

The working group concluded this stage by converging on a finite number of issues that appear to reside at the heart of the problem for urban Children and Youth, as follows:

- Broken family relationships – in terms of both the physical separation of the birth parents and also the effects of compromised parenting within dysfunctional families.

- Lack of security – in terms of susceptibility to physical, social, cognitive and spiritual danger and exploitation.

- Limited participation in healthy community – in terms of the child experiencing stigmatization or exclusion.

- Struggle for economic survival – in terms of exclusion from a share of the wealth being generated in the City due to the broken connection between the need and resources.

Finally, it is worth noting that during Stage 1, a majority world participant, from the Philippines, raised an important postcolonial critique of the concept of empowerment. The group agreed that we must be careful to realize that issues of power and powerlessness are often very subjective. What we may perceive as powerlessness from our position of privilege may not be a true interpretation of the situation.

The ISUM delegates participated in two "immersion" experiences to frame, fuel, and form their discussion.

---

14 An immediate and concrete example lies in the case of parents. To have a parent or parents is a good thing, but parents are likely imperfect and inconsistent and may influence the life of their child for both good and ill. Nevertheless, esteem for parents is a core component of a child's psycho-social development and even in corrupted and compromised situations, scaffolding this aspect of a child's self requires care and is not to be dismissed.

Immersion 1: Word Made Flesh (WMF) - Tim and Amy Hupe

Tim and Amy are Americans who have been living and ministering in Bangkok as a family (they have 2 young children of their own) for the last 6 years.

In the city of Bangkok young kids are sent to the streets at night to beg in order to bring in income for their families. On the streets they are very vulnerable, yet WMF have observed that they also show great resilience and a good deal of ingenuity in order to survive.

By way of methodology, WMF begin with a simple approach which is 'to go and sit with', in the most literal sense of that expression. They have oriented their personal schedules around maintaining a consistent late-night presence in the streets and alleys where they know children and young people will be found. In practice they have learned to be aware that their attention towards the vulnerable can actually further expose those they are reaching out to. This means that they have to be very careful – this is particularly the case when dealing with trafficked girls and women who are being 'controlled'.

WMF have recently taken on a new base, a property with a reasonably secure perimeter in close proximity to the specific downtown district of Bangkok most notorious for the illicit nighttime industries. This base now affords WMF the opportunity to have a nighttime drop-in for some of the women in the sex trade. For those who are not Thai but asylum seekers / refugees from other countries they may get an opportunity to advocate for them so that official UNHCR status can be gained which is a big milestone. The nature of Bangkok as a global city was revealed as Amy described the nationalities of women she meets who have been trafficked to the city. Once again the ambiguities of exploitation and complicity were exposed as Amy noted 'I have never met an Uzbek prostitute who didn't know what she was getting into when she came over here – but they bought into a bad deal – they have to service a lot more men than they expected, for a lot less money than they expected'.

The new base has also become home to a little school for the street kids. WMF have implemented a form of play therapy that they learned from the Ragamuffin project in Phomn Phen in Cambodia. The implementation of this play therapy "borrowed" from the neighboring nation of Cambodia is a great example of urban practitioners 'looking sideways' to learn from one-another rather than re-inventing the proverbial wheel.

From a secure Western perspective it is easy to sit in judgment over these parents who appear to be exploiting their own children and literally putting their lives at risk. And yet WMF have resisted becoming calloused by such judgment. Rather they have sought to understand the tragic moral and ethical dilemmas faced by the parents – whose choices are often not choices at all but pressure pushing toward either the dreadful or the terrible. What kind of choice is the choice between hunger and begging? What sort of choice is the choice between homelessness and prostitution? A further layer of complexity upon this issue is that of culture, in particular conflicting notions of shame. WMF had needed to learn that eastern ideas of shame differ from western ideas of shame. What is shameful in the Global West may not be shameful in the Global East, and vice versa. For example incomers from the West have great difficulty understanding why someone would choose to sell their body for sex, and do so regularly for such a small price. It is vital therefore to note that the western approach to social justice can be very black and white and struggles to cope with complexity and ambiguity.

The immersion experience at "Word Made Flesh" identified challenges to urban shalom which are complex and interconnected; in the corrupting power of money in a context of extreme poverty; in desperate choices people are forced to make; as even children are objectified and turned into economic units; where adults ignore problems developing in their children and non-intervention is legitimized as stories circulate on the streets e.g. "don't try to help those street kids; they work for the mafia".

Nevertheless we also observe seeds of hope, sprouting subversive shalom: in the companionship amongst those working the street, summed up in a Filipino phrase "tara me-i" which means "I got your back"; in the sharing of resources amongst the poor and exploited, as kids sometimes pool their begging cash with a kid who is having a bad night; in the quick wit of street kids who catch on when made aware of their basic rights e.g. being taught to say "don't touch me" in English to the Western men who try to molest them.

Immersion 2: The Hub - Illya (Russian project manager)

"The Hub, in a poor inner suburb of Bangkok is not a Christian project but has an excellent holistic approach that is very 'kingdom compatible'. Positioned prominently at a busy street intersection it is a well-proportioned building over 3 floors with a number of special facilities including washing and feeding areas, educational and creative space plus quiet areas for group and individual counseling and therapy. The Hub serves 500 – 1000 kids and youth every year.

The main aim of The Hub is 'harm reduction' by providing a safe place for street kids to rest during the day, to eat a healthy meal, wash, get checked up medically and receive appropriate therapy. The children and youth served by the staff and volunteers of the Hub are mainly Thai by origin, some born in Bangkok, others from out of town. Illya explained that many of those using the center are runaways. The group were told that by far the main cause of kids running away from home is physical / domestic abuse in the home. Illya feels that if this could be stopped the flow of new kids on the street would be almost solved overnight.

The Hub aims to trigger self-awareness in kids. They need to know that the things that are happening to them – such as sexual exploitation – are wrong. They do not know that they are victims. From this recognition pathways out of exploitation can be developed such as referral to a place in an out-of-town boarding school or repatriation to their home town / nation.

The street kids are savvy – they have a strong survival instinct but they make bad choices every day – such as sniffing glue. They are very independent and know lots about making money – mainly from sexual favors through which they can make up to $100 a day – although they can never 'save' money, they always spend it very quickly."

The immersion experience at "The Hub" identified challenges to urban shalom in which human children are marginalized; there are very few places for street kids to hang out, a scarcity of parks, and children are not tolerated in the tourist parks. The voice of children is suppressed – though they have much to say, as keen observers in the world, but there is nobody who will listen. Nevertheless, seeds of hope can be seen to sprout as young people at The Hub are participants not recipients, their increasing awareness unfolds possibilities of alternate and positive choices: e.g. one boy's life was revolutionized when he decided to become a (Buddhist) monk and was accepted as a novice in a monastery community.

Immersion 3: In search of Sanuk, Sunday Program

In Search of Sanuk is a volunteer led initiative, which aims to bring "sanuk," the Thai word for fun, to Bangkok's neediest families. The project uses fun activities to reach out to underprivileged communities, organizing a Saturday School teaching English with the help of local international schools and other exciting activities. Fun is also used (often in combination with food) in many events organized to fundraise and generate interest in finding sponsors for the families we support each month. Fun and food, important aspects of life in every culture, facilitate connections, which reach beyond language barriers and the most heartbreaking circumstances to show we care.

Biblical Interval (2): A Reflection Upon Brokenness and Restoration

In chapter 37 of the book of Ezekiel the prophet is drawn into a vivid vision. The scene is set in a dry and dusty valley full of human skeletons, the aftermath of a cataclysmic defeat. Significantly, the perspective given is not one from afar, but from up-close. Ezekiel recalls being led "back and forth among the bones". He has been led by the Spirit of God into uncomfortable proximity in such a way that he can be left under no illusions as to the scale of the brokenness. The Lord asks him a pointed question, "Son of man, can these bones live?"

At this point it is apparent that Ezekiel attempts to dodge the question by responding "Sovereign Lord, only you know". He is expressing a common human trait, present even in people of faith when they are face to face with overwhelming brokenness – a reluctance to get involved in an issue that bears all the signs of being a hopeless cause.

Is the church – the body of Christ in the city – reluctant to get involved in the lives of the most marginalized and broken children and young people because it sees them as a hopeless cause? Who will have the faith to take hold of the promise of God, to be convinced of his power to "breathe into these slain, that they may live"?

The ISUM working group considering the theme of Empowering Children & Youth chose to adopt a faith-filled stance in the face of the enormous challenges witnessed. Stage 2 thus represented their determination to shift focus from the scale of the brokenness to the creative power gifted by God to the church through his Spirit for the Kingdom work of restoration.

Stage Two: What are the seeds of hope for shalom of urban kids & youth?

Mission is revealing to others their fundamental beauty, value, and importance in the universe, their capacity to love, to grow, and to do beautiful things, and to meet God… Mission is transmitting to people a new inner freedom and hope; it is unlocking the doors of their being so that new energies can flow; it is taking away from their shoulders the terrible yoke of fear and guilt. (Jean Vanier, *Community and Growth*)

> *Stage Two:* **To consider** *"what are the seeds of hope for shalom of urban kids & youth"*

During this stage the working group participants were called to lay aside pragmatic and critical tendencies to consider what kind of future might emerge if the seeds of hope were given opportunity to fully flourish, what would that look like? In order to create an atmosphere of possibilities the group strained to inhabit an imaginary future in which the numerous challenges to shalom had been defeated through the efforts of the church – using "church" in the broadest sense of the word – i.e. as the "Christian community".

It is worth noting that some members of the group found it harder than others to talk hypothetically about such a future – such is the scale of the challenge that even as people of faith we struggle to journey to the future shalom even in our wildest imaginations.

It is of great significance that Jesus himself was born into poverty. He was also born into a strained relational context between un-wed parents. To compound matters he experienced the early stages of his life as a refugee away from his homeland. When he finally returned with his parents to their home village we discover that it was a stigmatized and ridiculed place: *"Nazareth! Can anything good come from there?"* (John 1:46) And yet despite these circumstances we are told that Jesus *"grew in wisdom and stature, and in favor with God and people."* (Luke 2:52).

Given the detailed discussion already undertaken in Stage 1 of the group's journey, the plan for Stage 2 of the investigation was to work through a process of "Informed Imagining" – to ask *"what if these seeds of hope were given opportunity to fully flourish, what would that look like?"*

Imagining a Better Future with Urban Youth and Children

The working group summarized the progress made in the previous stage using a series of "Mess Statements" – brief articulations of the challenges faced, worded in future-oriented problem-solving phraseology, all prefaced by the short phrase "How to...."

- How to protect, heal, and restore children who are facing abuse.

- How to identify and heal the emotional, spiritual, and physical roots of brokenness in children. How to transfer Love.

- How to fix the brokenness of children and young people, help them be accepted, and know that they are valued.

- How to clarify and affirm the value and place of children in family and in society.

- How to reclaim and protect childhood innocence and attribute to it the true intrinsic value that childhood demands.

- How to Be with the community, to Be in the community, to Be the community.

An extensive time of discussion followed revealing both complementary but also divergent viewpoints. Care was taken to allow all the voices from the nine nations represented to be heard. Considerable efforts were also made to uncover connectedness between viewpoints present within the working group and observations made during the immersion visits. The working group drew great encouragement from the fact that around the world followers of Jesus are responding to the brokenness evident in the world around them, seeking to bring healing and shalom.

With regard to children and young people these responses most commonly fall into one of four categories:

- Child-focused initiatives. Relating specifically with the needs of the child or teen, individually or in groups.

- Family-focused initiatives. Relating with the family unit as a whole.

- Parent-focused initiatives. Relating specifically with the mother, father, or both.

- Community-focused initiatives. Tackling the common problems of multiple families in the setting of the broader community.

The specific circumstances of the young person in need, the dynamics of their family, and their relationship to wider community context are all considerations in selecting the most appropriate approach from those listed above.

In order to open up generative discussion the working group began to imagine what could happen if anything was possible and we had unlimited resources. Given the bounded-ness present in our thought patterns it was useful to re-frame the issues in unusual and creative ways, resisting binary categories of "positive" and "negative". No space or community is abandoned as God-forsaken, and so we set about seeking the shalom possible in any situation. For example, where a child can't get to school, we ask if there are ways we can bring the school to the child? And who else in the environment might also then be brought in from the periphery to also gain access to these resources?

Using such techniques to free our minds from the ever-present shackles of rationalism and pragmatism a "reverse-dreaming" process was postulated. We endeavored to work backwards from the positive future we have imagined asking "How did we get here?"

Given the immediate context of the Summit, the working group began with the hypothetical future, imagining themselves returning to Bangkok in 2020 to discover that 50% less children were suffering exploitation. Returning again in 2030 they discover that the exploitation of children had been completely eradicated. The group imagined that the church, in its widest sense of the body of Christ in the city, had been the critical catalyst for bringing about this transformation. So what specific things had the church done then over these years? This problem, and the way it was framed proved to be an excellent catalyst for some highly engaging dialogue, highlights of which are included over the next few pages.

A Generative Dialogue Between Diverse Perspectives: Vietnam, China, Philippines, Bangkok

As the group considered the wisdom of Jean Vanier, that God's work is often about signs not solutions, we explored the implication that we need not exercise ourselves to exact a "perfect" answer. Rather our energies are given towards the release of a generous range of possibilities. Mostly we are only ever dealing with partial answers, which is why we need each other. With this open frame, we asked what the church might need to stop doing, and what it might need to start doing, and which of its present ministries and activities need to be enhanced in order to effect a dramatic transformation in the society within which it resides?

Perspectives from Vietnam and China

Perspectives were shared from working group participants who had travelled to Bangkok from Vietnam and China, both places described as "closed nations" by mission agencies.

> "In Vietnam we (the church) are very separate from the community. In Hanoi, I want to break down the barrier of Church and the community. We are often waiting for people to come to the place (the church), but we need to go to the community. We talk about the gospel, but don't care about the physical need of people. Now, NGO's can help materially, but cannot share the gospel. The Church share by their words, but not by action. NGO's can only share by action, because they will be kicked out if they share the gospel. This situation ought to stop.
>
> We see that there may be an opportunity to start something new. It would be possible for the Christian NGO's to equip the people in the Church to undertake compassionate ministry that meets vital needs but also is embedded with a gospel message. We could gather people in groups from NGO groups & Churches. In this way we could inspire a new wave of church outreach resulting in the making of many disciples.
>
> So in summary, what can the church keep doing in our country? Stay committed to sharing the gospel, but begin to do so using works as well as words."

As we listen to the perspective of the Vietnamese delegates we are struck by the concern for general systemic issues, which clearly have direct impacts upon the lives of children, but which point to the integrated approach required. Simply "targeting" children and young people (a highly contentious and dangerous phrase in any setting), will not satisfy either the sociological criteria for change, nor the gospel imperative for wholeness in communal, not just individual terms. Our vision of shalom calls for integration of word and action, and prompts collaborations between the agency of the people of

God and other agencies in the world.

Further work is needed in exploring and explaining the spectrum for recognizing gospel responses – beyond individual "two sidedness"[15] in which "repentance" and "decisions" are seen in isolation both from other relationships and community currents, and in isolation from what might be thought of as "sociological" or "welfare" outcomes. The primary engagement of ISUM participants with seeking shalom requires alternative language from that which churches and supporters may be accustomed.

In China the situation is similar, but with some notable differences.

> "China has so many problems but is not comfortable with having NGO's come in to solve these problems, especially those from western nations. There are House-churches, often small groups, and they face persecution. Then there are the government churches, which can be very big, and face little to no persecution. The House-church needs to stay committed to evangelism because it is working!
>
> By 2030, we would like to have churches where all can meet, with a special focus on Sunday schools for children and youth. Some House-churches have Sunday schools, but our impression is that kids tend not to be treated as being important. Additionally the conditions are not good, we don't have enough space and the teachers need teacher training.
>
> In China, we don't have slums. The economic outlook is so different. In fact we have a new problem, which is, parents spoiling their child. There is a big gender equality problem because families are only allowed one child and so they want to have boy, and they ignore the girls. On top of this parents are very busy, and don't see value in spending time with their kids. There is not a high-value culturally placed upon giving kids time to speak or encouraging them. There is so much pressure on children to be accepted by what they achieve in school, by their families. There is much verbal abuse, such as "you're so stupid." I've never heard anyone in China say "I am happy with my kids." With kids, it's not their fault. Therefore we need to teach kids to understand parents and respect them. The church needs parent training in Christian values.

---

15 Bill Prevette, Child Church and Compassion, Oxford: Regnum, 2012, p. 221; 263

An additional problem in China is the transiency. The cities are vast and each year about 1 million people move into the city and 1 million move out. It is very hard to have long-term stable relationships in this context. And yet we have a social responsibility to help people. The house church knows that there are family problems and marriage problems that need help. Too often these are ignored and we can't allow that situation to continue."

The voice of the Chinese participants brings an important corrective to the naïve impulses that see shalom for children and young people only in terms of eradicating poverty and valuing children. This is an important voice for the whole (global) church to hear. Seeking shalom for the urban children and young people of China becomes a call to speak and act against the instrumentalization of children in the aspirations of a society. Careful discernment in supporting parents in the role of parenting may draw from the resources of gospel-ethics and transform relationships of power and utility with shared and mutual grace and service. Neither child nor parent is enslaved to the other, but exercises the freedom of responsibility. Neither child nor parent is merely a utility to the other, but each is a gift of grace to the other. Neither child nor parent gains honor from the other, but neither is without honor, as the gospel values all as God's dearly loved children.

Seeking shalom in this context calls for courage to name what is present.

And of great importance also is the role of gospel communities in China not only to seek this shalom in their own context, but to speak prophetically to the Western church and culture in which the values of instrumentality, trophyism and aspirational mobility at the cost of relational responsibility and stability for families have been deeply embedded for centuries.

Perspectives from the Philippines

Those in the working group originating from the Philippines felt that the most important thing for the church to stop doing is dividing itself. So many of the institutionalized churches have fallen prey to division. This seems to be an enormous problem in the evangelical church and is a very poor witness to society. We must pray for a new spirit of unity. Many Filipino churches have also adopted the western leadership model where the congregation looks to one senior pastor and no one else contributes. The congregation go to stand-up / sit-down churches, where the leaders are responsible for all the work and activity. This is a direct result of the colonial history of the Philippines and we must not replicate it in the next generation. And yet the situation is perpetuated by western "sponsorship" and paternalism.

Historically, much of the Western mission agenda has been patterned on systemic and philosophical divisions.[16] The primary division of children as an "unreached people group", seen in isolation from family and community, culture and political realities has formed the backbone of western engagement in the majority world, via such sponsorship. Further divisions based on Western management ideologies[17] have replicated unhelpful patterns, which disintegrate children from community, community from leadership, and gospel ethical action from gospel articulation.

Much like the feedback given from Vietnam and China, the Filipino response identified the problem with separating evangelism from social welfare. There is a clear need to educate Christians in the ways that the gospel can be demonstrated as well as declared:

> "In terms of what we need to start doing we should devise methods of integrating churches. We should hold conferences like this (ISUM), as well as united prayer together as multiple churches. This would start to break down walls of suspicion between different churches. We should also encourage churches by profiling examples of the blessing that comes from giving to those in need, even when it is at a cost to ourselves. We know of a great example of a child that needed help, and was welcomed into someone's personal home at a cost to the people that took care of the child. These kind of stories need to be shared."

Perspectives from mixed East–West sub-groups:

> "We want to stop the thinking that all the good stuff happens in church and start in the community instead, with a people-focus, to grow community spirit. As we do this we should be asking 'How can the community take ownership of their young people?' This would probably necessitate a place to gather, some kind of urban community hub. We could envision a network of safe community HUBs scattered throughout many poor neighborhoods. In this way the church could

---

16 Bill Prevette, *Child Church and Compassion* (Oxford: Regnum, 2012), 31. Brewster (1997) described "children as an unreached people group" and raised no questions about the validity of the concept, the underlying mission pragmatism, or how these ideological concepts might be informed or critiqued by theology or alternate views of mission."

17 Bill Prevette, *Child Church and Compassion*, 39

enhance what it is doing already, and be holistic. It ought not be difficult to get churches involved because of the clear need for people willing to get out and build relationships.

In a way this is like fostering a village spirit within a large city. A village tends to have an established community structure, but in the city everything is so transient. So we need place that encourages the village spirit. By doing this children and parents of different families can begin to respect one another. It would be a culture of not just looking after your own kid but looking after everyone – a real community vision.

Our hope would be that a turn in this direction could contribute towards creating violence-free communities and families. Informal education using pictures could assist the promotion of the values of the community, amongst people who often can't read. There wouldn't need to be a lot of money involved, as local resources would be utilized. We see people in the community involved in running these places on a day-to-day basis. Everything that happens would be based on community needs whatever they might be, for example parenting workshops, sports, education, teamwork, daycare, arts & music."

And in another voice:

"The experience of my team here in BKK, is that there is a huge gap between the classes. There may be a possibility of mobilizing the Thai middle class but first their attitude toward the poor needs dealing with, as they do not want to personally spend time with the poor. Therefore the engagement with the poor is left to the foreigners who belong to mission agencies and NGO's. We need to get the middle-class locals included in solving the problems of their own city. A great way to begin would be by getting the local churches to pray regularly for local families and local neighborhoods – this would start to turn their attention outwards rather than inwards. " =

Approaching the end of this stage of the journey the sub-groups refined their thinking into a shortlist of shared priorities:

- The imperative to be conscious of constantly training a new generation of leaders and pioneers fully equipped to share the gospel in word and deed.

- Local community ministries must be held as closely as possible to the local church. Compassionate ministries amongst the poor are diminished in effectiveness if there is no opportunity for those being reached to be welcomed into the arms of Jesus and into the worshiping family of God.

- A shifting perspective on the modality of the church, with an emphasis upon the revelation that God desires to establish pioneers and leaders in all spheres of life. Once this has gained traction we could then move to develop ministries out in the community beyond current walls of the church.

- The conviction that it "takes a community to raise a child" calls us to establish stronger working models of this in practice, and multiplication of the model, spreading the idea more widely. Hence the idea of the community hub network - Christ-centered safe places scattered throughout urban neighborhoods.

The Bridge Children & Youth Resource Center is one such community center in Pattaya, Thailand that a Summit participant comments on:

> "Pattaya is one of the darkest cities in Thailand because of its blatant tolerance of prostitution. Although it is illegal, bars and massage parlors advertise sex on almost every street in the downtown area of this beautiful, yet exploited vacation town. The Bridge Children and Youth Resource Center is in the heart of downtown. The mission offers a safe place for children and youth to go within their community. The center is connected to a local Thai church, and is being facilitated by their youth, brothers and sisters in Christ, and operates as a big family. It is a community of children and youth, who receive and share the love of God in a real and tangible way. Those who come have an opportunity to express their creativity and develop their God-given gifts, surrounded by the love of God, and knowledge of Him. This is a place were holiness is held high, ministering to those that come to help, reconcile, and restore what was stolen."

Stage Two Summary

There is an intriguing connection between the practice of communication and the building of community. Even in the act of imagining of a better future for urban youth and children, sharing ideas and dreams with one another, we found we were weaving connections between one another across cultural and ethnic lines. There is a deep sense of the interpersonal and the relational here that is of great relevance to the development of urban children and youth.

This relational emphasis is also paramount in engaging children while they are young, to help them know and appreciate how valuable and loved they are – not because of what they do, not because of where they come from or even who their parents are, but simply because they are created by God. God takes delight in them simply because they exist. God is proud of them. They have intrinsic value beyond measure. They are made in the image of the living God.

Biblical Interval (3): A Reflection Upon The Gospel and Relationships

In chapter 2 of Paul's first book to the Thessalonians we hear a moving account of the way the apostle feels about his relationship with the community there that he spent so much time amongst. It is an unusual passage of scripture as it gives us some special insights into the close bond that existed between the one commissioned by God to reach out, and those who were reached. Intriguingly Paul refers to himself as both a mother and a father. Reading between the lines we sense that this community was probably at the lower end of the socio-economic spectrum as why else would Paul take the time to remind them that he worked bi-vocationally amongst them so as not to present them with a financial burden?

Perhaps most revealing though, for our dualistic contemporary Christianity, is the way that in verse 8 we hear him say that he, along with Silas and Timothy we assume, was delighted to share with them not only the gospel of God but their lives as well. And that this was because they had become "so dear" to him.

Once again, as in the Valley of Dry bones, we are presented with an issue of proximity. This time not simply physical proximity, although that is obviously a pre-condition, but it is amplified by a relational proximity. Here we have a wonderful example of the kind of closeness we should aspire to if we hope to be involved in the divine work of bringing transformation to a human life. This "proximity principle" stands as a stark contrast to the "professional distance" practised by many ministries and NGOs, be they Christian or secular. Not so with us, we are called to a higher standard of relationality.

Stage Three: Calls to Action and Recommendations for the body of Christ

> "The conditions among the growing underclass in the blighted neighborhoods of our cities can only be described as desperate. What is needed are charismatic leaders with an inspired alternative vision for the cities of our country, along with plans for translating their vision into concrete reality." (Tony Campolo, *Revolution and Renewal*)

The third stage of our gathering sifted and sorted the best of what we had generated over the previous two stages into a final grid of actions in order to reach a critical consensus about the recommendations we would make, that we believe will make a real and lasting difference to the shalom of urban young people if they will be put into practice by the wider church. These responses form the concluding section of this paper.

"How beautiful are the feet of those that bring good news." These oft-cited verses from Romans chapter 10 are preceded by strong words that resonate against injustice:

> "How, then, can they call on the one they have not believed in? And how can they believe in the one of whom they have not heard? And how can they hear without someone preaching to them?" (Rom 10:14)

Embedded in these few lines is the principle of apostolic sent-ness. We hold in view that we serve a sending God, a God with a mission in the world, a God who inspires, enlists and resources his people to effect new creation from the rubble of this fallen world. Therefore, our task as a working group would not be complete until we made commitments in line with our vision of the future city we desire to inhabit and share with all God's children.

Final recommendations from the working group

The working group concluded their journey of "Imagining a Better Future for Children and Young People in the Global City" by making a range of recommendations for the attention of the church in its broadest sense, that is, including local congregations of all shapes and sizes but also to Christian ministries and Christian activists. The recommendations related to three category headings:

What changes in practice can we embrace?

Where are the invitations to engage more fully?

What can we relinquish?

What changes in practice can we embrace?

- Continuing to think and act holistically, replacing (outdated) reductionist approaches to solving problems.

- Expanding our understanding of the gospel with a fuller integral vision of word and deed combined – social action and evangelism cannot be allowed to continue to exist as separate categories.

- Effectively and consistently communicating this fuller integral gospel amongst the body of Christ.

- Acting with greater compassion and humility when dealing with children and young people, honoring their innate gifts and allowing their voices to be heard.

- Choosing to strive for a future in which the church will be full of mentors, not full of programs. We can start by becoming less event-oriented.

- Giving parents confidence to receive help without feeling shame i.e. presently some families will not receive help as to do so is perceived to be an admission of their own failure as parents.

- Becoming more savvy about child-safety, ensuring that all adults in kids & youth ministry are suitable and accountable.

Where are the invitations to engage more fully?

- Affirming and partnering with families and communities in the roles they have as they are inherently involved in the development of their own children, even if this seems to make the task more complicated to the missioner. Our relationship emerges then naturally as we too are part of (not outside) the community that is naturally nurturing their children.

- Encouraging solidarity and collaboration amongst groups of parents to help each other, whilst recognizing the strong cultural factors that lead to the familiar stance of "they're not my kids so they're not my problem".

- Increasing our emphasis upon early intervention, seeking to identify and address problems before they get too big to fix.

- Modeling creative ways of partnering, seeking to work together and share resources.

- Developing our discernment around gender differences, exercising sensitivity to the possibilities of different needs that both boys and girls have at important stages of their life and development, alongside a concern for justice for all genders.

- Fostering peer group dynamics between children and youth of similar age cohorts in order to celebrate and support their innate ability to "look out for each other", turning this into a powerful driver of growth, development, education, and behaviors change.

- Alert to instances where the parents themselves have life-controlling issues, (relating to physical health, mental health, or addictions), and seeking opportunities for coaching children in skills alongside their parents to participate in building new healthy family patterns.

- Employing media and technology in creative and constructive ways, recognizing that this generation see these things as a central part of their lives.

- Focusing on people, above the task, the project or the initiative. Our primary call is to relational community with people.

- Remembering the universal returning yearning for community, common from East to West, from the wealthiest suburbs to the poorest slums.

What are we invited to relinquish?

- We can choose to relinquish the reflex of insulating ourselves and distancing ourselves in order to avoid some of the emotional pain involved in ministry amongst the poor and disadvantaged.

- We can resist the "rescue" urge that tempts us to remove children from their community to places and spaces where we feel comfortable. We recognize the integrity of meeting children in the context of their community rather than depending on a model of removing them to a "safe place", which could be several miles away from their home. We ought to be prepared for the challenge of taking up residential status in the community as incarnational neighbors.

- We repent of the individualist models of piety that have failed to recognize interconnectedness of life and the social aspects of the Christian life and which have undermined the larger vision of transforming the city together.

- We recognize that single "hit & run" events that have no connection with ongoing processes of community transformation do not conform to our vision of the sustained incarnational *missio Dei*, and the enduring work of the kingdom in our midst.

The three stages of our interrogation into the challenges to urban shalom and the seeds of hope within slum communities demanded biblical re-engagement, theological reflection, immersion experiences, story-sharing critical thinking and informed re-imagining.

The themes of social and theological integration, respect for sustained relationships, empowerment for children within their own communities, and holistic participation as community – child, young person, parent, adults – in the incarnational *missio dei*.

Of primary importance was the sense of proximity and incarnation, both as individuals or families and as church communities. The call to be in the midst, to be near and physically present, sharing in urban lives of poverty, risk, oppression, truth, love, and grace holds unwaveringly whatever our re-imaginings or strategies entail. In this we follow the pattern of Jesus. Our theology of child and our theology of Christ who came incarnate as child, connect with our own incarnate, bodily presence, and the presence of the body of Christ. Children and young people are thus incorporated into the bodily vision - not in abstraction, othering, or specialization - but as participants in the whole shalom of the urban context.

References

Adams, Kate; Hyde, Brendan and Woolley, Richard. *The Spiritual Dimension of Childhood,* London: Jessica Kingsley, 2008.

Allen, Holly Catterton and Ross, Christine Lawton. Intergenerational Christian Formation, Downers Grover: IVP Academic, 2012.

Brewtser, Dan. *Child Church and Mission,* Compassion International, 2011.

Bunge, Marcia. "The Child, Religion, and the Academy: Developing Robust Theological and Religious Understandings of Children and Childhood" *The Journal of Religion* 86.4 (2006), pp. 549-579

Bunge, Marcia. "The Vocation of the Child: Theological Perspectives on the Particular and Paradoxical Roles and Responsibilities of Children" in Patrick McKinley Brennan *The Vocation of the Child,* Grand Rapids: Eerdmans, 2008. pp.31-52.

Campolo, Tony, with Bruce Main. *Revolution and Renewal: How Churches are Saving our Cities* (Louisville: Westminster John Knox Press, 2000)

Cousins, Fry and Olivola. *Environmental Health Project, Activity Report 109, Health of Children Living in Urban Slums in Asia and the Near East: Review of Existing Literature and Data.*

Goodwin, David. *The World needs Children's Ministry Leaders: Lessons on Leadership from the life of Moses,* North Richmond, N.S.W. : Kidsreach Inc., 2008.

Jensen, David *Graced Vulnerability,* Cleveland: Pilgrim Press, 2005.

McLemore, Bonnie Miller "Children, Chores and Vocation" in Patrick McKinley Brennan, *The Vocation of the Child.* Grand Rapids, Michigan: Eerdmans, 2008.

Pegues, Beverly and Huff, Nancy. "A Call to Prayer for the Children, Teens, and Young Adults of the 10/40 window." Seattle: YWAM Publishing, 2002.

Prevette, Bill *Child Church and Compassion,* Oxford: Regnum, 2012.

Unhabitat Features: Twenty first session of governing Council report, Nairobi, Kenya, 2006. http://www.unhabitat.org/downloads/docs/4625_51419_GC%2021%20What%20are%20slums.pdf

Webster, Noah "Education of Youth in America," American Magazine (March 1788): 212. Quoted in Liberating the Nations, by McDowell, Stephen and Bellies, Mark. Charlottesville, Virginia: Providence Foundation, 1995.

Further Reading

Arles, Siga, ed. *Now and Next: A Compendium of Papers presented at the Now and Next Theological Conference on Children, Nairobi, Kenya, March 9-11, 2011.* Bangalore : Centre for Contemporary Christianity, 2011, accessible at http://www.hcd-alliance.org/resources/books/doc_details/112-now-a-next

Berryman, Jerome. *Children and the Theologians: Clearing the Way for Grace.* Harrisburg, PA : Morehouse Pub., 2009.

Buckland, Ron. *Perspectives on children and the gospel : excellence in ministry with children and their families.* West Gosford, N.S.W. ; Bletchley : Scripture Union, 2001.

Grobbelaar, Jan. *Child Theology and the African Context.* London : Child Theology Movement, 2012.

Herzog, Kristin. *Children and Our Global Future: Theological and Social Challenges.* Cleveland, Ohio : Pilgrim Press, 2005.

Jensen, David. *Graced Vulnerability: A Theology of Childhood.* Cleveland: Pilgrim Press, 2005.

Mercer, Joyce Anne. *Welcoming Children: A Practical Theology of Childhood.* St. Louis, Mo. : Chalice Press, 2005.

Miller, Bonnie. *Let the Children Come: Reimagining Childhood from a Christian Perspective.* San Francisco, CA: Jossey-Bass, 2003.

Tan, Sunny. *Child Theology for the Churches in Asia: an invitation.* London: Child Theology Movement, 2007.

White, Keith J; Willmer, Haddon. *Introduction to Child Theology.* London: Child Theology Movement, 2006.

A Movement of the Spirit: Fuelling Church Movements among the Urban Poor

Paul Cameron and Doug Priest[1]

Introduction

In 1700 fewer than two percent of the world's population lived in urban places. Beijing and London were the only cities that had populations surpassing one million. By 1900 an estimated nine percent of the world's population was urban. London was then the only "super-city" on the globe. In 1950 twenty-seven percent of the world's population lived in cities and seventy-three percent of the world's people lived on the land. By 1996 however, the world was growing by 86 million people a year and for the first time more than fifty percent of the world's population lived in cities. While the rural percentage of the world's population is declining, rural population is still growing in absolute numbers. The United Nations—which offers the most conservative growth estimate—projects that by 2025 over sixty percent of the world's estimated 8.3 billion people will live in urban areas.

According to the World Heritage Centre, by 2020 the urban population of Asia will be around 2.5 billion, having doubled in twenty-five years. By then more than half of the urban areas of the planet will be in Asia, and those urban areas alone will contain over one-third of the world's population. The same organization predicts that the cities of Asia will be growing twice as fast as cities in the rest of the world.

---

1 Paul Cameron and Doug Priest, who collated and edited this chapter, acknowledge the assistance of Michael Crane, David Jones and Trish Branken who acted as scribes for the Recruit, Equip and Sustain Working Group discussions at the Integral Urban Mission Summit, Bangkok, January 2013.

> For all the challenges of urban areas—traffic, pollution, noise, high cost of living, crowded and often substandard living conditions, economic disparity, stress, psychological overload, long hours of commuting, and violence—cities provide people in the developing world the best hope of education and income. People continue to be drawn to the city through migration and immigration…
>
> Surely, God has a purpose in this." (Glenn Smith)[2]

The urban poor are probably the fastest growing unreached people group in the world. It is of interest to note that among the 1.3 billion plus people living in urban slums, over the last decades massive church-planting movements have been initiated. There are green shoots in the asphalt. These are deeply spiritual activities, but at the same time they are not lacking in holistic engagement. They can best be seen as a movement of the Spirit.

So, how is God (or how can God be) fueling church movements among the urban poor?

This paper includes excerpts of working group conversations held in Bangkok at the January 2013 ISUM Summit. It contains some snapshots and pointers to engaging the question, "how can we be fuelling church movements among the urban poor?" The working group was facilitated by Viv Grigg, Doug Priest and Paul Cameron. Contributions come from the 20 plus workers (and "cheer leaders") from cities round the world as they engaged and interacted in immersion experiences in Bangkok, and participated in Summit working group discussions and workshops. The paper also reflects the group's actual experiences on the field, insights based on each person's learning, as well as ideas they shared from their own ministry experiences.

This then is a truly collaborative piece, with only a rare allocation of a responsible name. It is a piece that has been collated, and edited somewhat, by Paul Cameron and Doug Priest, with the invaluable initial assistance of Paul Rollett; but it has been kept raw, real, and personal wherever possible.

Some readers may find an answer or two to the broader, global question that framed the working group's thinking; but most will find or simply discover some responses to the question that will continue to inform all who are seeking to address it, wherever

---

2   From an article, *The Challenges of Urban Mission* by Glenn Smith, senior associate for urban mission for the Lausanne Committee for World Evangelization and executive director of Christian Direction in Montreal, Quebec, Canada (September 2006, found at www.lausanneworldpulse.com/themedarticles.php/480/09-2006?pg=all). This article has some valuable reflections, as does The Theology of the City, a piece by Tim Keller (albeit written with a Western ministry/mission perspective), that can be found at www.e-n.org.uk/p-1869-A-biblical-theology-of-the-city

they are located. These responses are offered with the understanding that to engage the question is difficult; to seek to address it is a struggle; but it is a question God calls us to struggle with, seeking as the sage of old, for "the wisdom of the poor (person) that saved the city."

Definitions

As we enter the conversation it is helpful to offer some possible definitions.

Church   A community of the people of God gathering in and around Jesus Christ whose collective Spirit-empowered life is centered on biblical practices of spiritual formation and discipleship and mission.

Movement   "A community that functions as a portal to the new world that God wants for his children. A Kingdom movement is a community of disciples who passionately seek the expansion of God's reign here on earth through the reproduction of disciples, seeking the transformation of whatever places they inhabit."[3]

"Missionary movements communicate the truth about God and salvation to others. They teach followers a new way of life that accords with that truth. The purpose of a missionary movement is that people accept the message, begin to follow Jesus, share him with others, and form new communities of faith that become partners in the spread of the gospel."[4]

Movements are started when there is *dissatisfaction* with the current state of play; a group of *dissidents* (or maybe only one) emerge who imagine another way; they *declare* that new way through a statement or manifesto which becomes the new *message and method* for the dissident group; and a *movement* coalesces around this new thinking and practices. Intentional care and action must be taken to ensure that over time the movement doesn't lose its way, suffer mission drift, become moribund, and solidify into a **monument** to past dreams and past dreamers.

---

3   A definition found in Mike Breen, *Leading Kingdom Movements* (Kindle, 2013, Location 68)
4   Found in Steve Addison, *What Jesus Started: Joining the Movement, Changing the World* (Kindle, 2012, Location 174)

	Church planter and movement theorist Steve Addison suggests there are several key characteristics of a movement.[5] They are each evident in the commencement, and need to be in the continuation, of a movement: White hot faith, commitment to a cause, contagious relationships, rapid mobilization, and adaptive methods.
Urban Poor	People who live in slum and squatter neighborhoods "that combine to various extents, the following characteristics (restricted to the physical and legal characteristics of settlements, and excluding the more difficult social dimensions): inadequate access to water, inadequate access to sanitation and other infrastructure, poor structural quality of housing, overcrowding, and insecure residential status."[6]
Fuelling	Any theological belief and practice, incarnational action, mission-focused activity, spiritual practice, community- and people-building process that is a sign, witness and foretaste of the Kingdom of God — God's dream for the world – and at the same time seeks and results in the welfare and "shalom" of the neighborhood; and any act of support, encouragement, empowerment, training, and development provided from external sources who share a common commitment to building church movements among the urban poor.

Hopes and Dreams

As the 27 participants in the "Fuelling Church Movements among the Urban Poor" Working group first met at the Summit, coming from 20 different organizations and 10 different countries, we noted the following hopes for the conversation:

- To intentionally create space for relationships. *To learn and listen*

- To observe and hear the experiences of Urban Neighbours of Hope (UNOH) in Bangkok. *We asked: how will this benefit formation? How will the transformational stories heard lead us to an integration of living and serving among the poor?*

- To share learnings and common conversations, and maybe create a library of

---

5 Steve Addison, *Movements that Changed the World* (Missional Press, Smyrna DE, 2009), 22-23
6 UN-Habitat, *Challenge of Slums*, p12; as quoted in Ashley Barker, *Slum Life Rising* (Melbourne: UNOH, 2012) 21.

ideas. *To discover synergies between different groups, new connections; commonality of followers of Christ in the world's slums, and their stories to be told*

- To hear God in the richness of our lives. *We were looking for the rawness/realness of living biblically everyday; a theology in the context of urban poor. To be in a relationship with Jesus is to be seeking to have a relationship with the poor.*

- To suspend our confidence of a theology "of the West" and open up to vulnerability to listen to the East and its theology within various cultures. *The dominant voice must actually be transformed by the voices from inside the slums. Urban missiologists must help the world to see itself transnationally. We need them, they need us, we need each other, we are one.*

- To hear what is God up to in the world, and be journeying with what God is already doing.

- To see the fruit of more workers on the ground; and to begin designing a plan leading that way.

- To help in "waking up" future leaders to be involved and to be ministering effectively.

- To find ways to release indigenous leaders/neighbors to be theologians. *To radicalize (and amplify the voices of) the nationals already doing the work on the ground. To address problem of outsourcing*

- To have opportunities to learn from the workers/ locals. *Field workers were empowered and encouraged to stand; practitioners will have the loudest voice here.*

- To see ministry to the urban poor have a higher place on the global and local missiological agenda.

- To discover adaptive responses to the increasing numbers of urban poor living in slums. *Are there different models for people to serve the poor? Do the exceptions make a new rule? We looked for deep engagement with practitioners but also for a platform that engages with the systems, governments, and structures that control.*

- The churches planted must be indigenous and empowering. *We must learn from history and not make the same mistakes again.*

Together we are seeking intentionality in the direction of the urban poor, following in the footsteps of our Master, Jesus of Nazareth.

Tensions

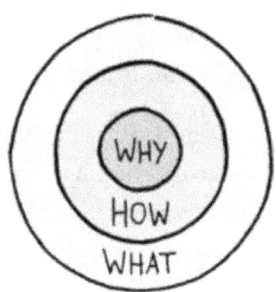

Simon Sinek has a good way of helping organizations and individuals focus on what can be described as its "core business" or primary mission. He suggests we should start with **Why**.[7]

It became quite clear at the ISUM Summit, in the immersion experiences, the workshops, and the Fuelling Church Movements among the Urban Poor working group sessions that there was a common commitment to the **Why**; it could be stated as to join in with the mission of God, the *missio Dei*, reconciling people with God and each other through Jesus Christ; living out God's dream for the world—his Kingdom, the space where Christ and his Way reigns, where justice, peace, joy, and shalom are increasingly manifest.

It became equally clear in the Fuelling Church Movements among the Urban Poor working group that there was a common hope and aspiration about the **What**; we all believed in the notion of the value of forming church movements in the urban slum context as an expression of the Kingdom, as a means of seeking the welfare and shalom of the neighborhood.

It must be acknowledged that it is the **How** that provides the challenge and point of debate; as it often does.

How do we do live out the Why, and be forming the What? Throughout this document readers may well see tensions between incarnation and proclamation; between community development and evangelism (or what has been caricatured as social gospel vs. evangelism); and whether we should start or end with ecclesiology (or "church"). This is a common tension, in whatever context we as the people of God are involved in mission. It is also usually a false dichotomy, and a draining polarization that can distract

---

7   See Simon Sinek's book *Start With Why: How Great Leaders Inspire Everyone to Take Action* (New York: Penguin, 2009)

from the mission of God (and the mission of the sent people of God, which is all of us). Maybe it is both/and, rather than either/or. Let's allow the reader to decide...

A. Immersion Experiences | The Context of Bangkok

In the immersion experiences participants looked for "one liners", for the unanswered questions, and for the questions that are not being asked. The responses are recorded here in the raw; with a view that as such they can inform a dialogue around the theme of Fuelling Church Movements among the Urban Poor.[8]

Immersion Experience 1 | Second Chance Bangkok

"Second Chance Bangkok" is a recycling shop started by some families in the Klong Toey slum along with the help of UNOH workers Chris and Jodie MacCartney. This initiative not only seeks to provide employment opportunities for people who have experienced barriers to employment, but it also provides an opportunity to reuse and recycle unwanted goods. Donations of second-hand goods are received largely from expatriates and are then sorted and sold from a store near the slum. This project helps fund school holiday programs for local children. See more at their website at www.scbkk.org.

The working group participants learned from this context:

- A "church movement" consists of anyone continuing the ministry of Jesus in their neighborhood.

- "Fueling church movements" is firstly the work of the Holy Spirit—it is a movement of the Spirit, manifesting the joy of Christ; it is expressed in connecting the suffering of our neighbors with the suffering of Christ.

- 80,000-100,000 live in this slum community Klong Toey; there are around 1 million slum residents in Bangkok; it is an urban village, a city of the haves and the have-nots

- Second Chance Bangkok (SCB), being part of Urban Neighbours of Hope (UNOH), seeks to operate out of Jesus' manifesto found in Luke 4:18-19.

---

8 The stories from two Immersion Experiences are recorded on these pages; a third Experience was with the Evangelical Church of Bangkok Care Group, but working group participants, while honoring the work of that Group, felt it was not truly a movement story relevant to the current discussion, and thus is not included here.

- SCB openly acknowledges that there are issues in just "handing out" resources; that operating an "opportunity shop" (or "thrift store") is but one solution; it is about creating opportunities.

- SCB is looking to serve and support the weak and the needy and the orphan and the widow, but also helping those in the neighborhood who are gifted and capable to use their gifts to help others, for the community's good.

- SCB is supported by expatriates, churches, embassies, word of mouth; in turn SCB supports at least 30 families through the opportunity shop.

- SCB is acting as a link between rich and poor; it is straddling two worlds by knowing and interacting with the wealthy and not feeling above them or that they are beyond God's love.

- A central value for SCB is an informal discipleship approach; SCB hosts a Friday night house church, as a weekly reflection of the often everyday and mundane aspects of community life, including worship. A "church" is forming .

- For the SCB community, most days are mundane and ordinary, and at times extraordinary; though the SCB may want to think strategically, it all comes back to one-by-one and the mundane, all discovered (and uncovered) as one commits to a neighborhood. *SCB is committed to smallness; to be faithful in our little way. Sometimes we can be tempted to do something significant, yet we are simply asked to be faithful.*

- The mundane includes prison and hospital visits; in Thailand tragedy is often the story of the prison system; young urban poor males are the ones stuck in the prisons because they don't have money to pay to get out. *One 65 year old man SCB had contact with had been in prison for 44 years; on release SCB drove him to his home a few hours away, and dropped him off in a hostile environment. SCB senses a call to respond to these situations with mercy. A few months later SCB had further contact with him, and invited him to work on translating Bonhoeffer. The man said "why have I not seen this before?" This man himself went through a beautiful conversion.*

- An ongoing challenge is working out how to balance "movement" and "walking slowly". There is a tension between the urgency of the task and waiting on the

Spirit, and discovering the right rhythms. One solution is working as a team, where some are about the big picture and others about the "daily grind". An underlying theme for SCB is "time" with rhythms of prayer and solitude, following Jesus who balanced work and ministry. We recognize the tension of time needed with neighbors and community life and forming links and partnerships along with time for solitude and prayer.

- In the slum the idea of "moving up and out" is always the temptation for people. The idea of staying (and making the choice to stay) is an important key to ongoing personal and community transformation, and it is usually seen as a contrast to what is expected, as a powerful, Christian counter-cultural act, standing against a possible idolatry of upward mobility; a commitment to staying within, an expression of the gospel as humility.

- SCB notes the challenge facing men in the community; "comfortable", "easy", and "convenient" are three Thai words commonly used by men; the best place to meet men is in a drinking circle; guys that do pick-ups for SCB refer to a team member as "boss", generally in Thai culture that authority is misused, but Jesus used it with gentleness and coming alongside, which becomes another expression of Kingdom values. *A participant shared that in Vietnam the connection has been with women mainly, with 300 "coming" to Jesus in one day through a crusade, but the next week none were "in church". Workers there note that it is more effective to do projects and come alongside people day to day; there is a need to walk with people over a long time; seeds of the Kingdom are planted more deeply when what is offered is more holistic, and not only "spiritual".*

- The challenge for the Summit (and Thai-based organizations) to deeply connect with local Christians is an indication that in Bangkok church life there are two circles: the holistic international circle and the Thai church circle (where pastors are good as a local "shepherd", but sometimes not much beyond that), with very little overlap. The question remains unanswered "how to find ways to be linking into existing Thai churches?" UNOH (and others) are seeking to be prophetic in this context, as another expression of the gospel, acting as "yeast" and a window to the Thai church, creating partnerships beyond boundaries and connections between local pastors and non-majority world workers, and the Thai church is starting to connect. *A point of prayer for leadership and partnership building revolves around the 5 fold ministry pattern of Ephesians 4; the apostolic, prophetic, and evangelistic roles are lacking in the Thai church, as in many Western contexts, and sorely needed.*

- SCB operates from an Asset Based Community Development model,[9] the reverse of the way that the world (and the church) usually speaks; replacing an emphasis on poverty and issues and problems, with the discerning, releasing, and empowering the assets of the people; a key to Kingdom-oriented community transformation is discovering people's strengths, and fueling movements through leadership development and training.

- Effective ministry is birthed out of relationships, not issues.

Immersion Experience 2 | Servant Partners

The Immersion Experience was located in Bangkapi district of Bangkok, facilitated by Kevin Walton (Servant Partners, Thai Peace Foundation) "The Thai Peace Foundation was established in 1998 to serve and empower the poor in Bangkok, Thailand. Its primary goals are to develop leaders among the youth and adults in slum communities; to facilitate community organization to address felt needs and desires; and to encourage personal and corporate stability and development through education, group service-learning opportunities, and reflective practices. We apply the "Action-Reflection" model of learning and progress in every area of our work. Thai Peace Foundation has established work in six different low-income communities, primarily in the Bangkapi and Bungkum districts." [10] The working group participants learned from this context:

- Initially two leaders had different visions (One, a focus on the poor at the grassroots; the other, a focus on the middle class and university students, including teaching English); the two split and expanded the two ministries; after two years, the former moved from a cell church model to a house church model; one important practice is teaching English to university students.

---

9 "Critical to (community) transformation is a participatory approach that builds on what people already know and assets they already have. This gives them confidence that they have worthwhile things they can share. (This can include) many other activities that show the people they have the ability as individuals and as a community to reshape their own lives and their neighborhood. People look at their neighbors with a new set of eyes through the use of Asset Based Community Development (ABCD) where the emphasis is on individual and neighborhood assets, not problems. At the center of change are individuals learning they have infinite value in their Creator's eyes…" *Neighborhood Transformation Overview*, p8, Collaborative for Neighborhood Transformation, Glendale, Arizona found at www.neighborhoodtransformation.net/. This piece also contains a community development action chart that has a number of transferrable principles.

10 Found at www.thaipeacefoundation.org/about/

- Activities have spread to another five communities in Bangkok.

- An initial provision of micro-finance had significant impact; families became believers as a result, the new disciples were growing in their faith, everything was growing and doing well.

- New workers arrived (offshore "missionaries" and a Thai woman working in community organizing), and new directions were taken.

- Evangelism initially took place in a government housing complex; the emerging house church model required a lot of wisdom and leadership.

- And, then after 6-7 years a privately owned complex was demolished and the community was scattered; 500-700 people had to find new housing; a savings program was created to gather funds for housing elsewhere; only 24 people stayed and saved small amounts for a year, but still they couldn't find land they could afford...they thought it was impossible; 4-5 leaders prayed together with the Servant Partner team who later returned home to tell the story; funds received were used to invite others back into the savings group; a management committee was formed: one person looking for new land, one going to a social welfare bank, one to find politicians; found a piece of land valued at 20m Baht [equivalent USD 0.65], the bank looked at the businesses and didn't find much to support a loan, no credit history and a loan was denied; person that found the politician found one who knew of a resources pool for sustainable housing for poor people...this gave the team the beginning of an understanding of the path they were on...

- Working with 70 families; saved 10% to buy land and started building houses on the 3 acres of land; everyone has the same area of land, with houses 4x6 meters, 2 stories high, good accommodation for a 4 person family.

- This is not the end of the story; carrying it out has been very difficult: connecting with various government departments; 14 houses built in 4 years; government froze funds for a year because 13m Baht budget was exceeded; another recent meeting started a new phase for utilities; this next phase will require new budget proposals, tightly maintained.

- The team also hopes to commence a church there; other house churches exist, a desire to form leaders in the communities, but this is very difficult, hard to facilitate growth; new believers are there but discipleship and leadership development is tough (church members did not want to come under the leaders); now clearly focused on discipleship and formation.

B. Workshop Inputs

1. Urban Poor Church Movements in India
Bishop Designate Aroon Kumar Das, Evangelical Church of India

Rev Aroon is serving in the Punjab. He started working with World Vision in 1981, having been touched by an experience with the poor and meeting a woman without bread for the day. This led him to give his life for full-time ministry. He went to South Korea for training, then returned to join the Evangelical Association. His wife was kidnapped because she was from a Sikh background. His life was under threat by Sikh militants. It was in the same month that his father died. Nevertheless he received a word from God to stay in his land and not to leave.

Rev Aroon now works with 25 pastors in his district (15 Himalayas, 10 Punjab); part of the Evangelical Church of India which is based in Chennai. It is an example of a mass church movement among the Malto, a largely Hindu people. There are 55 Malto evangelists, 563 elders, 79 ordained pastors and 12 Bible Schools. Their campaign, based around a theme "Every Community for Christ", the "Every Tongue and Tribe" community program and Church Multiplication Teams, each involved the sending out of teams of evangelists, with an expectation of 10-15 baptisms per month per pastor.

They are involved in preaching among multi-faith groups, sharing the gospel with established communities and among the Gujjar community. They are also facilitating church movements among sports people.

The process involves first finding a "person of peace" in the neighborhood or community, bringing them to Christian faith and training them to be a "pastor". There is then a focus on obtaining church buildings, by gaining free land from the government and building their own buildings, each designed to look like a Sikh worship center. Once a local group (or "congregation") has a building they will be recognized by the government.

Evangelism is often on the basis of questions like, "Do you pray?" and "Do you use the name Abba Father?" There are many other stories of conversion through preaching and proclamation. Most people coming to faith are poor, but respond because of their (or other people's) healings and seeing demons released.

A challenge is to ensure there is a true conversion taking place, and the complexity of discovering how to know people are actually coming to Christ, or as there are many gods, not simply adding him to their list of gods. Discipleship is vital; once they become a "follower", pastors then disciple the new believer to develop their knowledge of the one true God. Disciplers tend to use prayer more often than materials (other than the Book of Acts); this works to cleanse the new believers of the other gods that were in their life.

For Rev Aruun, the big question is how to get enough workers (church planters and evangelists; Master and Teacher trainers) and how to sustain them.

2. Multiplying Millions in Global Urban Poor Movements: Apostolic and Diaconal Movements

Viv Grigg, Urban Leadership Foundation, currently coordinating the global Encarnacao Alliance of Slum Movement Leaders

What are we fuelling? We are seeing the greatest migration in history. Half the world is urban; truly we are experiencing the beginning of the urban century. From 19-95% of the population of these cities are urban poor slum dwellers, squatters or as in Brazil, *favelados*. Two billion people have migrated to the cities in the last decades. There are now two billion people around the globe living in slums, sidewalks under bridges, on riverbanks, and in garbage dumps; there is a growing number of people working among the poor.

So what could be a healthy fuelling structure? First get a "church" in poor communities; second, make disciples; third, transform the community; and fourth, transform the city.

Part of God's current actions in missions is a multiplication of 50,000 workers from the slums to the slums. We have developed a global Encarnação Alliance of slum movement leaders who globally have been working on fuelling processes of grassroots training of church-planters with city learning networks and MA level training of movement leaders. The goal is to start with a movement of 10,000 people committed to stay in the slums 10-15 years; and an indigenous movement of thousands of churches (e.g. in Kolkata, Chennai and Sao Paulo slums).

The heart of the message is that this mission and ministry needs the anointing of the Holy Spirit. Having visited one hundred churches during a research project, I found that only three were formed by Christian community development. Rather churches were founded through healing, care and love; they didn't begin with structures, projects and programs from the West, rather an active commitment to release the oppressed and to be bringing the good news of holistic salvation to the poor. Too often holistic mission has come to mean large programs with foreign funding; it is a rich person's game with paid employees.

Fuelling church movements among the urban poor begins with evangelism. It then moves on to discipleship, to congregations forming through the gathering of larger groups. This results in socio-economic engagement of maturing churches to the coming of the Kingdom on earth; there's spiritual discipleship, economic discipleship based around tithing, social discipleship, and civic responsibility, which becomes public discipleship.

3. Training Workers with a Spirituality for Incarnational Ministry

Raineer Chu, Mission Ministries, Philippines and Asia Theological Seminary

Mission Ministries, Philippines (MMP) background[11]

MMP's Context
There are 586 slums in Metro Manila alone. These are homes of the poor. But they remain the frontier for evangelical mission work. The United Nations says that any person who lives on less than $US1.25 (Php58) per day is poor. In the Philippines, the poverty level is $US0.76 (Php38) per day.

27.6 million Filipinos (33%) live below the poverty standard.

12.2 million Filipinos (15%) live below the subsistence standard.

MMP's Activities
Mission Ministries Philippines Vision is to have "A sustainable church in every slum." To make the slum church viable, MMP plant holistic churches that meet the spiritual and physical needs of the most marginalized in the least reached slums. MMP partners with local churches to plant sustainable churches within two years. Usually a preschool, a drugstore cooperative, and a livelihood project help finance the church. All churches are planted in partnership with the local church to which the slum church eventually belongs.

---

11   As only a brief outline was recorded of this workshop, providing a rather sketchy but significant overview of the workshop theme, this background content has been included in order to see the significance of this short report in the context of the MMP mission and vision. Here is the foundation for the impact of MMP. The background is adapted from a statement found at www.mmphilippines.org/about-us

To date MMP has planted over twenty churches among the poorest of the poor in Metro Manila. It has livelihood programs providing job opportunities for poor families. It is developing an agricultural project teaching local communities the importance of stewarding God's creation. It partners with Asian Theological Seminary to provide contextual and biblical theological education for leaders equipping them to minister among the poor.

MMP's Distinctives

MMP's distinctives include: mobilizing labourers to the harvest working in teams; being a community that journeys in ministry and contemplation, with a mission to plant holistic churches in the poorest urban slums, in partnership with local churches.

MMP has had a significant impact over the years. It has:

- Created a social movement of early childhood programs in partnership with over 400 churches providing quality education to over 100,000 children. These children receive spiritual, mental and socio-psychological nurture and an environment of acceptance and love.

- Trained, mentored and provided jobs for over 2,000 teachers and administrators among the poor.

- Published preschool books for children in partnership with Christian professors from the University of the Philippines.

- Planted over 31 holistic churches among the poorest of the poor in Metro Manila who are able to sustain themselves. They receive leadership development training from MMP enabling them to set up their own schools and other community projects relevant in their context like livelihood and community drug stores.

- From the slums, MMP has mobilized dozens of workers to the harvest, workers without homes, without financial support, but full of the Holy Spirit, going out to the other slums to bring the gospel to their fellow poor. Most of the conversions in the Philippines, like the rest of the world, are happening among the poor. For more than 20 years now, thousands of those converts have heeded the call to mission, despite their poverty. We have found that the poor have less attachment to material possessions and are easier to mobilize. Today more than 60% of our staff are from the slums.

- Initiated the Certificate in Early Childhood Education in partnership with Asian Theological Seminary to equip teacher and administrators in establishing their preschools.

- Initiated the MA in Transformational Urban Leadership at Asian Theological Seminary equipping God's leaders on how to minister among the poor. This program is in partnership with Encarnacao Alliance, a fraternal network of urban mission leaders.

- Initiated the Doctor of Ministry in Transformational Leadership in the Global City at Asian Theological Seminary in partnership with Bakke Graduate University in Seattle.

- Success means the poor not only receive but are also empowered to give and the community is transformed. Success happens at two levels:

- At a personal level, success happens when the poor undergo a paradigm shift, moving from being the receiver to the giver because they know that Jesus (though he was poor) gave sacrificially.

- At the community level, success happens when the community becomes more united, organized, and mobilized toward a common goal.

Spirituality for Incarnational Ministry

Central to the Manila training conducted by MMP is retreating three times a year at a center of spirituality. The following process, presented in brief summary form, is developed from Carlo Caretto (1910-1988; a member of the Little Brothers of Jesus) on Spirituality.

From a Fallen world
1. Solitude. Face your demons, yourself and Christ. You can also sit together. Waiting in silence together, brings a bonding and deeper fellowship than when you talk. Learn to listen with your heart.

Journey
2. Prayer and worship is attending to God; being present to God.
3. Entry

Garden
4. Contradictions: God who heals; but they live with sickness
5. God who provides; but there is no food
Maybe God will let these people remain poor, even till the next generation.
6. Reading Scriptures from Bottom up

Slum as a Desert
Gospel
7. What you can live without: Freedom

Slums
8. Peacemaker: Advocacy

Living Counter-culturally

Brother Lawrence, in *The Practice of the Spirit of God*, brought spirituality to the poor. Loving God has to be a passionate desire to be in his presence; and in their presence (which in a very real way is also his presence...).

Prayer is vital to a sustainable and culture changing incarnational ministry. Consider for example a prayer breakthrough in Calcutta in India; in 40 years, 1 church started; after systematic and sacrificial prayer, in the next years, 700 churches. - That is a challenge to us all.

C. Immersion Experiences I Six Issues that Surfaced

As the working group reflected on their immersion experiences, and interacted with the plenary session and workshop input, it agreed on six issues that emerged from those experiences. Again these issues are recorded here in the raw, reflecting the diverse thinking and writing styles and cultures of people interacting with them, with a view that as such they can further inform a dialogue around the theme of Fuelling Church Movements among the Urban Poor.

1. Situational Challenges

This issue was summarized with these key words: Systemic Evil, Chaos, Messiness, Interruption, the Mundane.

- The obstacles and forces working against the fueling of new church movements in global urban centers that must be faced are found both external in the context of the city and internal within the church.

- The external challenges particularly of urban poor churches include economic, social, and spiritual dimensions. Spiritually, the church may often find itself as small emerging voice in a city dominated by other religious worldviews and spiritual forces that are resistant to the good news and oppressive to the point of forced resistance and persecution of the church. This is particularly the case in the 10-40 window in cities among Hindus, Muslims and Buddhists. The spiritual challenges include the realm of spiritual forces of evil and demonic oppression seen in the spirit of idolatry, materialistic greed, worldly lust, and human brokenness, addiction to vices, injustice, and oppression. In this context the spread of the gospel is a declaration of spiritual war against these forces and powers. Those who first express interest in Christ in a community may often be the most broken and needy requiring significant release, healing, and restoration before being prepared for leadership. These challenges also present opportunities for demonstrating the power of the gospel.

- Socially, the lifestyle of city dwellers is often busy, rushed, and stressed with limited time for other relationships or pursuits. There are also myriad of other competing interests and pursuits in the city that are fighting for their time, money ,and energy. City dwellers may also often be living isolated lives without a strong sense of community and therefore urban ministry is challenged to connect with people who often do not even have a relationship with their immediate neighbor.

- Economically the church among the urban poor are stretched and challenged in sustaining its own needs and activities, much less how to fund and sustain church planters. Full-time staff and property are usually out of the reach of new emerging urban poor churches.

- While the external challenges are multiple, we agree with Ray Bakke in saying that the greatest challenges are often those that are internal within the church. This can begin first with the challenge of sustaining the hope, energy, and spiritual integrity of leaders. So often movements are held back or diminished by the lack of leadership or the moral failings and resignation of existing leaders in the face of these many challenges. Recruiting and developing new workers and servant volunteers is a continual need. Other internal challenges have to do with the mindset of the church that may be resistant to collaborating with even other Christian churches and agencies much less non-Christian neighbors. When there is not a holistic mindset, the church does not want to address economic and social issues impacting the lives of the people around them. In separating itself from worldly forces churches can have a fortress mentality creating barriers to involvement in community and even relationships with those most needy and open to the gospel might be avoided.

Other Challenges include:

- Leadership within
- Leadership quality
- The lack of men participating and in leadership in the Thai context
- Economic support of house church leaders
- Finding culturally correct style of evangelism among urban poor in different contexts
- Multi-faith population in city – resistant to gospel
- Being a Christian is a challenge
- Persecution
- Resistance to the gospel
- Recruiting workers; slow decision-making of church "systems"
- Brokenness/dysfunctional nature of the urban poor (opportunity for transformation, but…)
- Oppression and injustices
- And specifically in Bangkok:
- Sustaining hope
- Facing the demonic
- Lack of responsiveness in Buddhist culture

2. Relational Engagement

This issue was summarized with these key words: Friend, Relationship, Trust, Encouragement, Partnership, and Servanthood.

Three areas to do with Relational Engagement as it relates to Fueling Church Planting Movements in the Slums are dealt with here.

The first has to do with the interaction of proclamation as it relates to relationships. The group discussed how this might be the best place for proclamation to occur. However, *how* the proclamation takes place is important. It was agreed that proclamation must be done with meekness and humility, and within the cultural context; and that the best way for this to happen is through relationships. Many groups are dealing with broken people and engaging needs, and thus can't (and possibly shouldn't) just "proclaim" the gospel; fuelling church movements among the urban poor seems very different from traditional church movements in the West. It is important for there to be a high emphasis on building trust (connecting with the deep level needs of the other; which can be more meaningful with the urban poor, and tougher with the middle class).

The group acknowledged what can sometimes be seen as tension between Presence Evangelism, Proclamation Evangelism, and Power Evangelism; yet each are important aspects of a whole.

Rev. Aroon in Northern India presents a great case study for relational engagement. In order to preach the gospel amongst the Sikh people throughout Northern India, in both the rural areas and urban centers, they have to first establish relationships with the people, or at least one person from the community, before the gospel can really take root. Often this comes through finding a person of peace[12] in a village or community, someone who takes particular interest in the message being preached, or wants to learn more (after which a longer season of discipleship with this one person typically follows). Other methods of building relationships with the various people groups and communities where Rev. Aroon serves are in the forms of sports outreaches, youth camps, and even parties. While proclamation in word is always present in one form or another, the relationship piece is necessary for roots to begin being established in individuals and communities.

The second theme discussed was the difference of relational engagement for both locals (insiders) and foreigners (outsiders). The group concluded that its experience is that in the Asian context in particular (this is a generality, and not always the case), while the Asian will say hello and welcome the foreigner (particularly Caucasian), they

---

12   See Luke 10:1-12 for a biblical basis for this process.

will typically know that that person wants to change their religion. In order for that person to understand our message and not simply dismiss us (often the struggle is that Christianity and Western culture are connected, so in the rejection of Western Culture, Christianity is also rejected), a relationship must be built where trust is formed, needs are (typically) met, and the foreigner lives as close to the local people as possible (in location and lifestyle, incarnationally). In some ways this could be understood as pre-evangelism, or better yet as a form of evangelism in and of itself—a medium that matches the message we bring. This can also be important for the local missionary or Christian, but our experience has shown this need for developing trust to be much more important for the foreign (particularly Caucasian) missionary.

To illustrate, Thais, even more so than other Asians nationalities, are very diplomatic in their relationship and friendships with foreigners. This means that their "yes" does not always mean yes, and their "no" does not always mean no. There is a large importance on saving face and keeping one's respect. When a foreigner comes in, the Thai person will save face, often times agree with the foreigner (or even receive Christ), even if they don't really believe the message being brought, but if no relationship is formed, there will be no real transformation of lifestyle, religious beliefs, and action.

Thirdly, and as stated above, building trust is central to effective mission, and trust is not usually built over night. It takes time. It takes being involved in the mundane. It requires deep patience, and the capacity to see beyond the immediate to the long-term prophetic Kingdom hope of an ideal humanity manifesting imagination as a sign and foretaste of God's dream for the world, the Kingdom.

In every context, churches form from signs and wonders (97 of 100 churches in 12 countries around the world in the research study underlying the book, *Cry of the Urban Poor*). Meeting people's physical and social needs and community development projects alone don't form churches; signs, miracles, dreams, direct Holy Spirit leadership, and the actions of people being Jesus to the other in various ways do. However while some may say that "for the "missionary" to start a community project, it usually stops the flow of the gospel", to the group it is clearly an overstatement, constructing an unhelpful polarity between actions that are holistically integrated in the life and ministry of Jesus, and in the life and activities of the early church, as described in Acts; actions that are as much (or in certain contexts more) a "sign and wonder" and an expression of a prophetic Kingdom hope as anything else.

3. Sustainable Character

The issue was summarized with these words: Commitment, Longevity, Stickability, Courage, Faith, Bravery; and in 3 levels: Individual (faith, commitment, courage), Team/group (unity, tolerance), and Organizations/inter-agency (collaboration, common vision).

Sustainable character needs to be intentionally nurtured with spiritual disciplines or practices.

With sustainable character, people of God can face situations that are challenging over long periods. This relates to the Thai issue of facing challenges.

To illustrate: Evangelical Church Bangkok has been working for more than ten years in a village. Now they are working together with families. Now the leader is a friend of the Imam, with exchanges between mosque and church; a very beautiful expression of Christ's presence in the community.

4. Intentional Living

The issue was summarized with these words: Simplicity, Discipleship, Alternative Community

In order to fuel church movements amongst the urban poor we must be intentional, i.e. deliberate, pre-meditated, pro-active, and initiating action in the following areas.

Intentional ministry, furthermore, will be incarnational, relational, formational, and missional:

4.1 Incarnational

John 1:14 is instructive. "The Word became flesh and moved into the neighborhood." As a result, we feel called to realize the need for:

- Jesus is our model. Jesus is the one we are to follow. Responding to his call "follow me…"

- No templates, pre-conceived strategies or methodologies.

- Being vulnerable. Being immersed into the real life of people. Journeying and walking alongside people. ("When in Rome, do as the Romans do.")

- Build meaningful relationships. Build trust.

- Be dependent on the generosity of the people, especially from those whom you have built meaningful relationships with. (Be the person of peace)

- Be a learner first.

One particular way of Jesus is that he moved into the neighborhood. For the first time in history, God can be pinned down in a certain geography and lived in time. This signals us to the call to particularity. Whether we are to stay put or are called to relocation, all of us are challenged to particularity.

This is the strategy (if there ever was one). Often times, we come to people with our pre-conceived strategies, methodologies, and templates. But with Jesus, the main strategy is to move into the neighborhood. He lived with the people. Jesus started his public ministry at the age of 30. This makes you wonder as to why Jesus would wait that long. He could have started in his teens. If God's plan to save the world through him is urgent, then why the long wait?

There has been a lot of talk today about "urgency" and the need to "win the world" for Christ and "hasten his coming back". We mobilize our young people to be part of the mission force and put them to a "fast track" training so that they can be deployed right away. We put so much emphasis on "efficiency", thus creating all sorts of discipleship method and systems to "save the world".

But God holds the timetable. While it is good to have a sense of urgency with the task set before us, we are reminded that God has his own timetable. So for this matter, humility and patience and being a learner is of utmost importance.

Dietrich Bonhoeffer once said, "the first thing we owe people is our hearing." At the heart of incarnational living is to immerse us in the lives of the people; to know them and listen deeply to their pains, hurts, hopes, and aspirations, we are to identify with them. Part of this incarnational process is to become vulnerable ourselves, to become dependent on people; to be recipients of the hospitality and generosity of the people; to be constantly building meaningful and authentic relationships as we journey with people and seek to be in solidarity with them.

Incarnation therefore teaches us to become learners first. And with this learning, we then better understand how we could respond to particular issues our neighbors are facing. This is the heart of what it means to live and think contextually.

It is also interesting to note that Jesus preferred the margins over the center of society. He went after the lost, the least, and the last; he spent much of his time with the outcasts of society; he dined and ate with people of dubious and notorious backgrounds; he developed a reputation of being a friend to prostitutes, tax collectors, and sinners. Again this signals us to the movement of "downward mobility".

Values that we intentionally develop as part of incarnational ministry include:

- Humility
- Submission
- Trust
- Servanthood
- Love
- Relinquishment
- Solidarity
- Identification
- Active listening

4.2 Relational

As well as being incarnational, we seek to be intentionally relational. We are inspired by the truth that:

- Jesus' lifestyle was to connect with people and build relationships.
- He established and built a grassroots movement of followers. It was a more "organic" community that became a prophetic statement against the whole Jewish religious institution.
- He intentionally lived together with his disciples.
- Through this community, Jesus showed what it looks like to actually live out the whole of Scriptures. He reinterpreted the law and showed what that interpretation looks like in the lives of the community he formed.
- It is about loving God and loving your neighbor.

With these relationships, Jesus established and built community. It was a community that exemplified what it means to live under the reign of God; a community that demonstrated love, forgiveness, reconciliation and healing; a prophetic community that was counter-cultural, living the upside down Kingdom life; Jesus intentionally lived together with his disciples.

Values that we intentionally develop:

- Friendship
- Acceptance
- Reconciliation
- Forgiveness
- Love
- Compassion
- Mercy

4.3 Formational

A further significant framework for us is to be intentionally formational. Again Jesus is our ultimate example:

- Jesus intentionally discipled 12 people.

- Jesus was creative in his discipleship process. He taught using everyday life examples. He acted together with his disciples, and modeled other things for them. (e.g. Feeding the 5000).

- He involved people and his disciples in doing ministry.

- He taught by example (e.g. servanthood).

- Jesus intentionally demonstrated to them the importance of spiritual disciplines (e.g. before dawn he goes up to a hill and pray, going to synagogues as was his custom, etc.).

In his formation process Jesus demonstrated to us the power of the few. For the kingdom to come, we don't necessarily have to become the majority, but be the overwhelming minority. In Mark 4 Jesus used the metaphor of the mustard seed to describe the influence of the kingdom. In other passages, he used salt and light, metaphors, which continue to highlight the power of the few. As stated by a Summit plenary social anthropologists are suggesting that it only takes 5% of a total population of people to rise up and effect transformation.

Jesus used every moment in life as a teaching tool; every moment became a teaching event. Most importantly it was in the context of doing life together that important teachings were truly conveyed. This alerts us to think of discipleship in terms of community life. We may want to rethink the way we do discipleship in our time. Discipleship today tends to be more programmatic and "assembly line" (everyone is expected to be on the same assembly line and get out at the end of the line as the same finished product.) It presumes a one size fits all method. Also, discipleship tends to be top-down. The discipler is seen to be the "expert" and a repository of knowledge and wisdom. The disciple is expected to simply submit to that authority over him/her. But Jesus was unique from his contemporaries. His approach was different from the normal Talmid-Talmidim (Discipler-Disciple) relationship of the rabbis.

Jesus' way of formation is an empowering way. Jesus involves his disciples in his ministry; they do things together. He sees to it that the disciples are keen on observing things he is demonstrating (e.g. healing and casting out demons). Jesus also shares the ministry and empowers the disciples to also do what he is doing (preach the good news, heal the sick, and cast out demons). This is one reason why his disciples would inquire of him after their own mission on what they did well or what went wrong. One example is when the disciples came back from a short-term mission rejoicing that demons were cast out. On another occasion they inquired why demons were not cast out. And on another instance asking Jesus to teach them how to pray, since they have observed that the power of Jesus came from his prayer time and spiritual disciplines. One may also notice that during the Last Supper in the Gospel of John, Jesus washed the feet of the disciples to teach them an important value on servanthood and humility. Jesus made sure that the teaching would truly be etched in the hearts and minds of his disciples. He did this by assuming the role of a servant that washes the feet of his masters.

So, as stated above, Jesus never came to be "over" people or to "lord it over them"; but he came "alongside with." His way was about companioning and journeying together. Brian McLaren captures this well when he said: *"Jesus was short on sermons, long on conversations; short of answers, long on questions; short on abstractions and propositions, long on stories and parables; short on telling you what to think, long on telling you to think for yourself; short on condemning the irreligious, long on confronting the religious"*.[13]

Also, part of the formation of the disciples was the life of simplicity. Jesus lived a simple life. Simple enough that total dependence on the Father is absolutely necessary. He had no clutter and no baggage. His was a life that was characterized by faith rather than certainty.

The reality is we can never live out the "Christ-life" on our own strength and will. We can never, on our own serious efforts be able to live out our call to Christ-likeness apart from the very life of Christ (John 15: 1-8; Galatians 2:20) through the enabling of the Holy Spirit (John 6: 63; 14: 15-27; 16: 5-15). The key to a "Christ-life" is not simply to imitate the ways of Christ, but to be empowered and indwelt by his very life through the Spirit.

Essential to this kind of life is our partaking to the divine life of the Trinity. God as community of persons invites us and includes us to partake in this divine fellowship or communion (2 Peter 1: 3-4). It is in that communion that we are conformed and transformed in the image of God. Jesus himself demonstrated that communion in his life on earth. He was constantly in touch with the Father and fully dependent on the Spirit's leading (Mark 1: 12, 35). Jesus' exemplary life and powerful ministry emanates from that communion.

Spiritual formation, therefore takes seriously the need for authentic human transformation by providing practical ways to keep our souls in touch with the very life of Christ so that our lives reflect and emanate his character. In short, spiritual formation is how we become more like Jesus (Acts 4:13). Spiritual formation answers the question, *"How can we abide in the presence of God in such a way that it produces the character of Christ in us?"* This kind of spirituality therefore is the motivation and shape of a life of following Christ in the power of the Holy Spirit. It is characterized by Contemplation – Action cycle; and it is three directional: Attentive to God, Attentive to the world, and Attentive to self.

A consistent challenge of Father Richard Rohr is for Christians to be active contemplatives and contemplative activists.[14] Thus the emphasis is not just about

---

13 Brian McLaren, *More Ready Than You Realize: Evangelism as Dance in the Postmodern Matrix* (Grand Rapids: Zondervan, 2002), p15

14 This is a paradox described well in the history of the Rohr's Centre for Active Contemplation. "The name was chosen because it expressed the paradoxical nature of the Center's purpose: standing in a middle place, at the centre of the cross, where opposites are held together. We believed that action and contemplation, once thought of as mutually exclusive, must be brought together or neither one would make sense." For more see www.cac.org/about-cac/history

personal piety but it is about Christian community. Companioning and journeying with others. This is a spirituality that challenges us to a continuous and ongoing openness to God and to a needy world.

Values that we intentionally develop:

- Creativity (discipleship happens every time people are just doing life together; a more informal, but just as rich, discipleship).
- Spiritual Disciplines/Practices (e.g. solitude, confession of sins, prayer, contemplation, study of scripture, etc.).
- Simplicity (a simpler lifestyle).
- Community.
- Participatory empowerment (e.g. community hermeneutics).

4.4 Missional

Finally, we seek to be intentionally missional. In his teaching of the early disciples:

- Jesus formed them so that they may do what he is also doing; to preach the gospel of the kingdom, cast out demons, and heal the sick.
- Jesus shares his mission with the disciples.

This section now brings us into full circle. Each of these categories do overlap, the Missional aspect is well integrated with the Formational aspect and being Incarnational. It is a "Missional Spirituality" that is developed; it is a way of life and not just projects; it is the way of Christ and not what we decide; it is through the Spirit and not self-effort; it is in community not through a solo effort; it is being discipled and not simply busy; it is for the world and not for ourselves.

Missional Spirituality in other words is a participation in the Missio Dei and the saving mission of Jesus to bring about God's Kingdom on earth. It is based on the conviction that action and involvement in the world constitute a path to holiness and to union with God. This calls us to continuous and ongoing openness to God and to a needy world. We are to be intentionally willing to respond, move/relocate/incarnate, be downwardly mobile, and to learn, identify, serve, suffer, and endure.

Further the Creation mandate of Genesis 1 gives us the trajectory towards restoration and will realize its fruition in the new heavens and the new earth of Revelation 21-22.

The Great Commandment gives us the inspiration to love our neighbors as we love ourselves. We are called to respond to the least, last and the lost (Matthew 25). Jesus said that the world would know that we are his disciples by our love for one another. We are to love others as Jesus loved us.

The Great Commission commands us to go and make disciples of nations; it's not just about making individuals as disciples but that nations and societies and *"ethnes"* and cultures will be discipled. The goal is not just to seek that everyone will become "converts" to Christ, but that whole societies will be greatly influenced by the values of the Kingdom, thus manifesting the "shalom" of God in the world.

Values that we intentionally develop are:

- Integral Mission (Word and Deed/ Word-Works-Wonders/ Proclamation and Demonstration/Evangelism and Social Action)

- Becoming a witness. We are witnesses to the fact that Jesus is Lord and that all authority in heaven and earth has been given to Him. We witness to the Lordship of Jesus in all aspects of our being (both the spiritual and the everyday affairs of life).

- Becoming contextual and indigenous.

5. Empowering Local Leaders

The issue was summarized with these words: Indigenous, Contextual, Local Leadership, Ownership.

It is an imperative to identify and develop, release and empower local leaders from all classes and castes, to make training more accessible to all, and to provide ongoing training, mentoring, and discipleship as needed. Care must be shown in the development of the content of training, so that it provides:

- A balance of proclamation and presence.

- Networking and unity between national and international leaders.

- Practical training (e.g. economic discipleship, drug and alcohol issues, mental health etc.).

- The establishment of trust and rapport.

- Skills to discern the longevity and timeframe of leadership and their tasks; developing the spiritual practice of patience. (e.g. In Second Chance Bangkok a woman, raised in Bangkok, having had a complex life, worked on a cruise ship, later studied and through engagement with UNOH team members her worldview began to shift, her skills and strengths were identified, empowered and released, and now she manages the Second Chance Bangkok op shop/thrift store. She became a person of peace and recognizes (and rejoices) in being called to the slum community and won't leave though she has that option).

- Resourcing (e.g. a Bible translation, not just in the language of "the King", but in the language of the people).

6. Prophetic Hope

The issue was summarized with the words: Ideal Humanity, Imagination, Signs.

The previous five points engage this issue in a range of creative and challenging ways.

However, prophetic hope does involve social action **and** evangelism; and for that conversation of balanced discovery, these texts are useful:

- Isaiah 68, Kingdom life as miracles of the mundane, in addition to signs and wonders.

- Isaiah 65:17-22, a Christian prophetic community.

- Luke 25, the Parable of the Good Samaritan—making the street safe, and, for developing a theology of interruptions.

- John 1:14, Embodying the Word out on the street.

- Matthew 25, raising a possible difference between the "Protestant" and "Catholic" ways, when we feed the poor, we are feeding Jesus Christ.

Conclusion

As noted in the Introduction the urban poor are probably the fastest growing unreached people group in the world. These reflections from this ISUM working group celebrate some of the Kingdom-announcing green shoots in the asphalt that this people group lives on, which, as noted, is best be seen as a movement of the Spirit.

The reflections simply give a few clues about how, in different contexts, God the Father, God the Son, and God the Holy Spirit is fueling (or beginning to fuel) church movements among the urban poor.

The whole process reminded working group participants that deeper and more relevant responses to the question will best be discovered by those who read the paper and interact with it in their own neighborhood or mission context, wherever that is. Hopefully some readers will discern that while engaging the question is difficult, and seeking to address the question is a struggle, it is a question that God calls every follower of Jesus to struggle with, as together we seek there to release (or unleash…) the missional imagination of God.

Again, this can only ever be a movement of the Spirit, realized to the full as a result of sacrificial and Spirit-led prayer and action; for the future of the people of God in every context is within the people of God, because the Holy Spirit is within the people of God.

We look forward to hearing future stories of the way this movement of the Spirit will be manifest as through God the Father, Son, and Spirit fuels church movements among the urban poor.

Joining God in the Challenges and Opportunities of Multi-faith Cities

John Baxter-Brown, Sharmila Blair and Rosalee Velloso Ewell

1. Prologue

Cities are places where both vices and virtues are seen in bold. This ISUM working group was well aware of such realities as we struggled together to explore the dynamics of living and dialoguing in the context of multi-faith cities. We met and interacted with people from diverse religious backgrounds and examined the implications for witness and collaboration in such varied places as health clinics, refugee camps, urban slums, and business offices.

Though this working group was not structured around particular bible studies or biblical texts, it is helpful to examine some of the key issues through a biblical lens. The scriptures remind us of our own stories and how we have been brought into the one great story of God's redemption of all of creation. They further challenge us to see anew the ways in which we are called to participate in God's mission in this world, working alongside people of such varied backgrounds and traditions, seeking to serve and to embody the good news in the city. The text of Mark 5 is one such text that we offer here as a way to set up both some of the methodologies and findings of our group.

St. Mark presents the reader with three snapshots of Jesus' ministry. The author takes some care to record the context in which the different stories occur, what Jesus did and, in particular, the impact Jesus had and the people's reaction to him. We can draw some inferences about the nature and the breadth of the Gospel from these three narratives. In the first snapshot Jesus encounters a demon-possessed man in the region of Gerasene and delivers him from this affliction, resulting in the man being found "clothed and in his right mind" (Mark 5:15). The next two snapshots are intertwined: Jesus is on his way to the house of Jairus, a local religious leader, when he encounters a woman who had suffered from a long illness. While Jesus is busy healing the woman, Jairus' daughter dies. The final snapshot is of Jesus restoring Jairus' daughter back to life.

Two themes emerge from this chapter: (1) the authority and power of Jesus and (2) the breadth of the gospel. First we see that Jesus has power over evil; he has power over disease and illness, and he has power over death itself, hinting towards his own forthcoming resurrection. The early church recognized the importance of acknowledging Jesus' power and authority in the first Christian creed: *Jesus is Lord!* It is an assertion that Jesus Christ, the Son of God, holds ultimate power and authority over all things. It is also a call to all Jesus' followers to accept the Gospel as the ultimate narrative on which to base doctrine, theology, and practice. Jesus showed mercy (5:19) gave peace (v.34): although not explicit within Mark 5 it is clear that He was motivated out of compassion and love (see, for example, Matthew 9:36). Secondly, the text shows that the Gospel extends to all of creation: it is for men and women caught up in evil, for people who are suffering from illness and disease, and for children and their parents. The breadth of the gospel is for those excluded from the community (the demon-possessed man), for those within who are also outcasts (the woman), and also for those in positions of power and influence (Jairus). Everyone is in need of God's free and saving grace. Transformation is for all.

2. Process and Methodology

To explore these themes of how we understand Jesus' authority and our witness to him in multi-faith contexts, a small group of conference participants used four different methodologies. These consisted of:

(i) three immersion experiences, described below

(ii) two seminars, with one based around the document "Christian Witness in a Multi-Religious World"[1] and the other exploring stories and issues in evangelism

(iii) group work

(iv) sharing of the rich experiences of group members.

What follows is a reflection based on these methodologies and our time together.

---

1 World Council of Churches, Pontifical Council for Interreligious Dialogue, and World Evangelical Alliance, "Christian Witness in a Multi-Religious World: Recommendations for Conduct" (28 June 2011), accessible at http://www.oikoumene.org/en/resources/documents/wcc-programmes/interreligious-dialogue-and-cooperation/christian-identity-in-pluralistic-societies/christian-witness-in-a-multi-religious-world

3. Immersion Experiences

We begin with a description of the three immersion experiences. The main purpose of these visits was to introduce participants to different contexts and examples of service in multi-faith cities. Secondarily, the immersion visits stimulated theological reflection and food for thought as we discussed the issues later. We went with a posture of humility, hoping to see, listen, and learn about the ways God is at work in such varied settings.

A. Wat Klong Toey Nok Temple

Thailand is a predominately Buddhist country, with over 90% of Thai people adhering to the Buddhist faith. During this temple visit we spent time interviewing a Buddhist Monk and meeting people at the temple grounds. It was a time for cultural observation, as well as dialogue and interfaith understanding.

One of the aspects of Buddhism that struck us most has to do with the focus on prayer and the inner life. The monks are to be commended for their disciplined and prayerful life. At the same time, such focus on interiority seemed to make them immune to the injustices and poverty of the city around them. It is not that they were blind to it or thought ill of doing something to improve the situation of beggars, for example, but there was no sense that we are called to be bearers of justice or healing in this world. In the context of this particular temple, the religious life was not viewed as something that one takes up in order to serve God and others, but reflects more a duty that one has to oneself in order to improve or "be promoted" in the next life.

Christian virtues such as compassion or forgiveness were viewed in purely individualistic or self-gratifying forms, such as "I forgive someone or I give alms to the poor so that I get rewarded in the next life." The shadowy flipside of this is the belief that someone is poor or ill or disadvantaged in some way because of a past sin or wrong committed in a past life.

Despite these obstacles, those living at the temple seemed open and willing to collaborate with people of other faiths and to discuss ways to improve life in the community. Though their beliefs about and sense of social justice seemed lacking, their practices showed us the importance of discipline, the need for mentoring of young people, and the impact a prayerful life has on the individual.

B. Bangkok Breast Cancer Centre

The Bangkok Breast Cancer Support Group (BBCs) is a small group of dedicated expatriate volunteers who have been actively involved with breast cancer education and support in Thailand since 1999. Founded by Dr. Kris and Kunying (Lady) Finola Chatamara, BBCs serves low-income communities and poor women by facilitating diagnostic testing, breast-cancer screenings, and cervical cancer screenings. If anything abnormal is detected during clinical breast examination, BBCs arranges for counseling and free treatment.

Fundamental to the success of this center is the cooperation with the local community—integral to such initiatives is the willingness to work together with community leaders to maintain integrity, but also more importantly, to avoid reinventing the wheel. Going into a community alone as an outsider has its downfalls, such as being subject to the whims of the local mafia. It can also jeopardise the validity of the project. Trust has to be established first. Due to distrust there is a risk that people will simply not cooperate. It is therefore important to seek out a local native speaker from an organization, such as is the case with Finola Chatamras, co-founder of the breast cancer hospital. Her visits into slum communities are not undertaken alone, but together with an organization. Collaboration such as this allows the ministry to flourish. In her case this is the mobilization of women from slum communities into the breast clinic for treatment and assessment. Going into slums together with a local native speaker from a community organization is a tremendous asset in order to build trust, maintain integrity, and, more practically to get the numbers of patients on the day.

In addition to collaborating with local leaders, BBCs has also had an enormous impact on the medical community, mobilizing doctors and nurses to donate their time and expertise to the center. It has become so well known for its quality and high standards that its services not only attract women from the poorer populations, but also from the wealthier classes. The greatest challenge is the education and encouragement that the volunteers must pass on to the patients because of the stigma and cultural barriers surrounding issues of women's health.

What was most striking in terms of how the center reflects its multi-faith setting was the prayer room. In it we did not find a generic "lowest common denominator" type of room, but a place carefully designed to welcome and create particular spaces for worship and meditation. One could pray as a Christian in a church space, as a Muslim in a mosque, or as Buddhist in a temple. At the same time, there were spaces created for sharing and dialogue, for asking questions and learning about one another. This was not a place where philosophical arguments were stacked up against one another to see which religion is best, but a space where women and their families could grieve, question, comfort, and hope for healing.

C. The Bangkok Refugee Centre (BRC)

The Bangkok Refugee Centre (BRC) is an agency devoted to helping refugees and asylum seekers living in urban Thailand. Asylum seekers and refugees are some of the most vulnerable and desperate individuals in the world. Many must rely upon the care of others to persevere and survive. Refugees and asylum seekers in Thailand are no different from those found elsewhere. The aim of BRC is to ensure that all asylum seekers and refugees enjoy personal security and a basic quality of life. This work is carried out in partnership with UNHCR as the guiding partner and with other NGOs working to help this target population. The hope is to enable urban refugees to live their lives with greater dignity and to keep hope alive in the midst of their struggles. The facility is located in inner Bangkok and is open to a target group numbering at least 2,000—young and old, single and members of families, male and female from many different countries.

Paramount to such ministries is the need for a holistic theological framework. In the case of Friar John and the Bangkok Refugee Centre, this means caring for the person's immediate presenting needs: for food, a place of acceptance, welcome, and being treated with dignity. A respect for a person's personal faith is also important so that clientele know that they are valued and accepted for who they are as human beings, not just potential Christian converts. They need to know they can partake of the service with no strings attached. This also means caring for the person's psychological, physical, social as well as spiritual well-being.

The different levels of trauma of the people serviced at BRC was striking. People without a country, without family, completely uprooted from anything familiar, and then tossed into yet another unknown—where will they go from here? The inter-faith issues within such contexts are enormous because not only does it need to beware of how it engages with those of other faiths, but the refugees themselves must find ways of dealing with one another. Furthermore, they must learn to live in such temporary settings, always with the shadow of knowing they are in competition with each other—each one vying for a placement, for asylum, for home.

Learning points from the Immersion Experiences

• **Indiscriminate love and acceptance.**
We noted that both in BBCs and BRC the staff were accepting of any individual or group that came to them for help. This was irrespective of religious affiliation, ethnicity or, indeed, any other categorization. For example, BBCs counts among their clients the least, last, and lost of the women from the slum districts of Bangkok to the Queen of the country in her palace. All are served.

• **Building personal relationships, not just service delivery.**
A key factor, which is closely linked to the first, is the need to build personal relationships with the clients. The BBCs and BRC are both Christian ministries. Core to maintaining their Christian identity is the need to love people and treat them with the dignity that they deserve as people. The only methodology necessary for this is to build relationships. Related to this and seen as one of the challenges is the patience and the time required for such relationships of trust and respect to be developed. It was not overnight that the founders of BBCs were trusted and able to carry out their work in the slums—it took a long time, and often, such a wait can be discouraging on the staff and frustrating for the leadership.

• **Christocentric focus.**
Both BBCs and BRC maintain a strong and clear focus on Jesus. This was seen in several different ways: (i) the motivation of the staff is directly linked to their faith in Christ; (ii) there are opportunities for prayer and worship for staff and others; (iii) the ethics and the conduct of the centers were very Christ-like and shared an ethos that the good news of the gospel must never be imposed, but can be shared in many ways—in words, deeds, and character. It is often through the unspoken witness and acts of love that Jesus is made known.

• **Avoid mission drift**
Focus on the specific need and serve as a signpost to other service provider. "Mission drift" is where an organization strays from its original aims into another area of work. It is easy to do especially in a context such as deprived urban centers where the level of human need can be acute. However both BBCs and BRC have avoided this by staying focused on their goal of serving women and refugees, respectively. Therefore,

when someone comes to them with a genuine need, but one that does not fit into the particularities of their mission, they can act as signposts, pointing the person to other agencies that can offer further help and support in that area of need.

- **Work with local personnel whenever possible.**

Fundamental to any urban mission is interacting and partnering with local communities. This helps to build links with the people and it also develops within the community a sense of ownership for the project. In the case of the temple, there was a sense both of its significance and importance within the community, but also the passive ways in which it interacts with the people—it is more of a one-way street in that the person in need must come to the temple, to the monks for assistance and prayer. The temple is static and its servants do not go out to the people, but instead wait for them inside.

- **Ecumenical collaboration is essential.**

All around the globe we know of too many examples where Christians have argued or fought amongst themselves thus causing damage to the ministry and harm to their collective witness. It is essential that we remember that we are Christ's witnesses together before a watching world. What does the world see when it sees Christians? In multi-faith contexts this is even more important because so often Christians are a minority group and therefore must work harder to work together and to collaborate so as to strengthen the witness (cf. John 17).

- **Long term commitment is required especially in Christian-minority contexts.**

Once more this learning point reminds us of the need for patience and grace. In the visits we made and in stories shared within our group, one major challenge was to think about what such long-term commitment looks like when the community in which one lives is itself transient. This is the case for the BRC but also for those working with trafficked women, with male and female prostitutes or with the homeless. A missionary might live for many years in the same neighborhood, but the people of that place come and go, sometimes overnight. What does witnessing look like in these contexts? How can we talk about continuity, about building trust and developing friendships? Our group could not answer all these questions, but even in light of the discouragement behind them, there is hope and grace that somehow God works through even the shortest encounters and that justice is indeed in the hands of a just God.

- **Cities are messy, especially in multi-faith contexts.**

There is no formula for being God's people in the city. The city offers us its own gods, its own temptations to draw us away from belonging to one another, away from shaping and living in community. The city often gives its inhabitants the illusion of control, of being able to sort out one's own destiny, whereas the bible teaches us we have been chosen by God, set aside and enabled to work for his justice. Doing so in the city is messy, complicated, frustrating, and rewarding.

- **The human need to have a place to belong.**

Even during the temple visit, this human desire to be a part of something bigger was striking. It reflects a deep need to belong, to know one is loved and treasured for who one is. Whether rich or poor, healthy or not, all the people we met on these visits reflected to us different ways of belonging, different ways of trying to meet this basic human need. From a story in Jakarta we learned of the importance of a name, of calling the children by their names, and the meanings of such names. This built confidence and pride in people whose entire lives were shaped by neglect and oppression.

- **The challenge of evangelism in a Buddhist context.**

All the sites we visited were in Bangkok, situated within the Buddhist context of that city. This led us to ask questions such as (i) what in our service, such as health care, actually challenges the dominant worldview that "you are caring for me to get to heaven, to gain merit for yourself?" (ii) how do we talk about forgiveness and justice within a context where such terms mean something totally different? (iii) what or where is the prophetic role of Christians within this context?

- **Inter-faith conversations.**

One way to begin answering the questions above has to do with building inter-faith conversations and friendships. We noted that despite many differences, there are issues that people have in common that can serve as starting points for friendships. When different people are brought together over a common issue or challenge, brought in a safe space and shown indiscriminate love, they might open themselves up more freely to discuss and dialogue and maybe through these, they will learn about Jesus. One concrete example of this was an online course for teenage refugees, Christians and Muslims, who shared the desire to learn and to work on computers—it was their common need and the challenges they faced together that opened spaces for conversation and friendship.

4. Seminars

There were two seminars within this track of the ISUM summit.

A. Seminar I: Partnerships across faiths – an examination of the document "Christian Witness in a Multi-Religious Context."

This seminar functioned as a workshop to explore issues around the ethics of our witness. What are the modes appropriate for Christians in the ways we share our faith, especially when we are engaged in activities such as disaster relief, caring for orphans, working in hospitals, etc?

We began the seminar by sharing a bit of the context of the document so that participants could understand why these issues were so pertinent to thinking about matters of conversion and evangelism today. The final text of "Christian Witness" was made public in June 2011. It was the result of a 5+year process that included Christians from all around the globe and from many different traditions. Officially, the document was a collaboration between the World Evangelical Alliance, the Roman Catholic Church (Pontifical Council for Inter-faith Dialogue) and the World Council of Churches.

It arose out of the need to say something simple but powerful about the Christ-like character of our witness. Due to the growing number of anti-conversion laws and persecution in many parts of the world, Christian workers needed a tool, an official document that stated simply that as Christians we are not called to practice proselytism; we do not buy converts or enforce our views. Rather, it is the joy and the duty of every Christian to proclaim the good news of Jesus, but such a message must never be imposed. The document begins and ends with mission, and sees prayer as central to all that we are and do as Christians. This is fundamental as we seek better and more wholesome ways to interact, to develop friendships, and to look at the challenges of living in multi-faith cities.

The seminar at the ISUM summit focused on examining some of the main questions and paragraphs in the document and discussions arose about how to apply these to particular contexts. Since its first recommendation is to study and use the document for one's own context, we offer the main parts of the text below.

****

Christian Witness in a Multi-Religious World: Recommendations for Conduct[2]

Preamble

Mission belongs to the very being of the church. Proclaiming the word of God and witnessing to the world is essential for every Christian. At the same time, it is necessary to do so according to gospel principles, with full respect and love for all human beings.

Aware of the tensions between people and communities of different religious convictions and the varied interpretations of Christian witness, the Pontifical Council for Interreligious Dialogue (PCID), the World Council of Churches (WCC) and, at the invitation of the WCC, the World Evangelical Alliance (WEA), met during a period of 5 years to reflect and produce this document to serve as a set of recommendations for conduct on Christian witness around the world. This document does not intend to be a theological statement on mission but to address practical issues associated with Christian witness in a multi-religious world.

The purpose of this document is to encourage churches, church councils, and mission agencies to reflect on their current practices and to use the recommendations in this document to prepare, where appropriate, their own guidelines for their witness and mission among those of different religions and among those who do not profess any particular religion. It is hoped that Christians across the world will study this document in the light of their own practices in witnessing to their faith in Christ, both by word and deed.

A basis for Christian witness

1. For Christians it is a privilege and a joy to give an accounting of the hope that is within them and to do so with gentleness and respect (cf. 1 Peter 3:15).

2. Jesus Christ is the supreme witness (cf. John 18:37). Christian witness is always a sharing in his witness, which takes the form of proclamation of the kingdom, service to neighbor and the total gift of self even if that act of giving leads to the cross. Just as the Father sent the Son in the power of the Holy Spirit, so believers are sent in mission to witness in word and action to the love of the triune God.

3. The example and teaching of Jesus Christ and of the early church must be the guides for Christian mission. For two millennia Christians have sought to follow Christ's way by sharing the good news of God's kingdom (cf. Luke 4:16-20).

---

2   http://www.worldevangelicals.org/resources/categories/index.htm?cat=67 .

4. Christian witness in a pluralistic world includes engaging in dialogue with people of different religions and cultures (cf. Acts 17:22-28).

5. In some contexts, living and proclaiming the gospel is difficult, hindered or even prohibited, yet Christians are commissioned by Christ to continue faithfully in solidarity with one another in their witness to him (cf. Matthew 28:19-20; Mark 16:14-18; Luke 24:44-48; John 20:21; Acts 1:8).

6. If Christians engage in inappropriate methods of exercising mission by resorting to deception and coercive means, they betray the gospel and may cause suffering to others. Such departures call for repentance and remind us of our need for God's continuing grace (cf. Romans 3:23).

7. Christians affirm that while it is their responsibility to witness to Christ, conversion is ultimately the work of the Holy Spirit (cf. John 16:7-9; Acts 10:44- 47). They recognize that the Spirit blows where the Spirit wills in ways over which no human being has control (cf. John 3:8).

Principles

Christians are called to adhere to the following principles as they seek to fulfil Christ's commission in an appropriate manner, particularly within interreligious contexts.

1. **Acting in God's love.** Christians believe that God is the source of all love and, accordingly, in their witness they are called to live lives of love and to love their neighbor as themselves (cf. Matthew 22:34-40; John 14:15).

2. **Imitating Jesus Christ.** In all aspects of life, and especially in their witness, Christians are called to follow the example and teachings of Jesus Christ, sharing his love, giving glory and honor to God the Father in the power of the Holy Spirit (cf. John 20:21-23).

3. **Christian virtues.** Christians are called to conduct themselves with integrity, charity, compassion and humility, and to overcome all arrogance, condescension and disparagement (cf. Galatians 5:22).

4. **Acts of service and justice.** Christians are called to act justly and to love tenderly (cf. Micah 6:8). They are further called to serve others and in so doing to recognize Christ in the least of their sisters and brothers (cf. Matthew 25:45). Acts of service, such as providing education, health care, relief services and acts of justice and advocacy are an integral part of witnessing to the gospel. The exploitation of situations of poverty and need has no place in Christian outreach. Christians should denounce and refrain from offering all forms of allurements, including financial incentives and rewards, in their acts of service.

5. **Discernment in ministries of healing.** As an integral part of their witness to the gospel, Christians exercise ministries of healing. They are called to exercise discernment as they carry out these ministries, fully respecting human dignity and ensuring that the vulnerability of people and their need for healing are not exploited.

6. **Rejection of violence.** Christians are called to reject all forms of violence, even psychological or social, including the abuse of power in their witness. They also reject violence, unjust discrimination or repression by any religious or secular authority, including the violation or destruction of places of worship, sacred symbols or texts.

7. **Freedom of religion and belief.** Religious freedom including the right to publicly profess, practice, propagate, and change one's religion flows from the very dignity of the human person which is grounded in the creation of all human beings in the image and likeness of God (cf. Genesis 1:26). Thus, all human beings have equal rights and responsibilities. Where any religion is instrumentalized for political ends, or where religious persecution occurs, Christians are called to engage in a prophetic witness denouncing such actions.

8. **Mutual respect and solidarity.** Christians are called to commit themselves to work with all people in mutual respect, promoting together justice, peace and the common good. Interreligious cooperation is an essential dimension of such commitment.

9. **Respect for all people.** Christians recognize that the gospel both challenges and enriches cultures. Even when the gospel challenges certain aspects of cultures, Christians are called to respect all people. Christians are also called to discern elements in their own cultures that are challenged by the gospel.

10. **Renouncing false witness.** Christians are to speak sincerely and respectfully; they are to listen in order to learn about and understand others' beliefs and practices, and are encouraged to acknowledge and appreciate what is true and good in them. Any comment or critical approach should be made in a spirit of mutual respect, making sure not to bear false witness concerning other religions.

11. **Ensuring personal discernment.** Christians are to acknowledge that changing one's religion is a decisive step that must be accompanied by sufficient time for adequate reflection and preparation, through a process ensuring full personal freedom.

12. **Building interreligious relationships.** Christians should continue to build relationships of respect and trust with people of different religions so as to facilitate deeper mutual understanding, reconciliation, and cooperation for the common good.

Recommendations

The Third Consultation, with participation from the largest Christian families of faith (Catholic, Orthodox, Protestant, Evangelical and Pentecostal), having acted in a spirit of ecumenical cooperation to prepare this document for consideration by churches, national and regional confessional bodies and mission organizations, and especially those working in interreligious contexts, recommends that these bodies:

1. **study** the issues set out in this document and where appropriate formulate guidelines for conduct regarding Christian witness applicable to their particular contexts. Where possible this should be done ecumenically, and in consultation with representatives of other religions.

2. **build** relationships of respect and trust with people of all religions, in particular at institutional levels between churches and other religious communities, engaging in on-going interreligious dialogue as part of their Christian commitment. In certain contexts, where years of tension and conflict have created deep suspicions and breaches of trust between and among communities, interreligious dialogue can provide new opportunities for resolving conflicts, restoring justice, healing of memories, reconciliation, and peace-building.

3. **encourage** Christians to strengthen their own religious identity and faith while deepening their knowledge and understanding of different religions, and to do so also taking into account the perspectives of the adherents of those religions. Christians should avoid misrepresenting the beliefs and practices of people of different religions.

4. **cooperate** with other religious communities engaging in interreligious advocacy towards justice and the common good and, wherever possible, standing together in solidarity with people who are in situations of conflict.

5. **call** on their governments to ensure that freedom of religion is properly and comprehensively respected, recognizing that in many countries religious institutions and persons are inhibited from exercising their mission.

6. **pray** for their neighbors and their well-being, recognizing that prayer is integral to who we are and what we do, as well as to Christ's mission.

****

B. Seminar II: Ethical Evangelism with Vulnerable Peoples

This seminar was built around the text of Luke 5:1-11, often called *The Miraculous Catch of Fish*. As part of the narrative we find Jesus in a boat that is full to sinking of slippery, flapping fish and Peter saying, "Go away from me, Lord, for I am a sinful man." Jesus, however, does not leave but tells Peter that "from now on you will be catching people". And it was Peter (and his colleagues) who "left everything and followed him".

Luke uses the word *zogreo*, translated as "catching people". It is not the normal word for fishing – *aleeis*, which is used by Matthew (4:19) and Mark (1:17), is the more common term. *Zogreo* is a compound word from zoos meaning "alive" (from which we get the English word, "zoo") and *agreuo*, "to hunt or catch."

> "Thus, there is a subtle but significant difference: Peter has been fishing and the fish are gutted and eaten: they die. Luke, however, is saying that Peter's future purpose is to catch in order to give life. This places a different emphasis upon the concept of 'catching people' which is a metaphor for evangelism in this passage."[3]

---

3 John Baxter-Brown, "Evangelism through the Eyes of Luke 5:1-11 and holistic evangelism for the 21st century: Towards life, justice and equality ... but not as we know it", *St Francis Magazine*, 8:6 (December 2012) 742, 732-748, accessible at www.stfrancismagazine.info/ja/images/stories/SFMDec2012-Evangelism-JohnBaxter.pdf, accessed 8 July 2013.

Such a concept creates an ethical framework in which our evangelism must take place because the agenda for evangelism is set by Jesus, the Lord. This agenda includes the purpose of evangelism which in turns shapes both the choice of methodology and the ethical constraints that are placed upon our practices of evangelism. This is brought particularly into sharp focus when working with people in vulnerable situations or people who lack power. For example, women and children are usually among the most vulnerable people in society; likewise, those facing various forms of disaster or poverty are often in positions of powerlessness. The challenge required of us, as followers of Jesus, cannot be how can we exploit circumstances to win converts?; rather, we must ask ourselves and our Lord, what does it mean to give life, and life in all its fullness, for these people? We have the example of Jesus himself as he healed people, cast out demons and confronted evil; as he faced down the powers of imperialism and defeated them through the Cross; as he rose on the very first Easter Sunday; as he forgave and befriended, fed and feasted with the last, the lost and the least.

We explored these themes through the life of Jesus and through the stories of those in the seminar. We examined both our own conduct but also the conduct of other Christians whose practices can often be misunderstood by other Christians and by those of other faiths. The concern is that unethical evangelistic practice actually undermines the very gospel that is being promoted. Some examples of this are the so-called prosperity gospel theologies, the exploitation of vulnerable people in disaster-relief contexts, and the misuse of wealth and power of the Western Church. Another related concern is the danger of unethical practices by people or churches who have good intentions. Thus we are challenged to think about (i) our discernment processes, (ii) how we encourage our Christian brothers and sisters to reflect on their practices, and (iii) the ways our interventions or actions might be perceived by others, even when we have the best of intentions.

The primary importance is to be a follower: if we lose sight of Jesus, we lose the very source of our power and life and love and become empty, noisy and futile. It is not that we need Jesus because we need His presence with us to do the ministry; rather it is that if we have His Spirit within we cannot help but become engaged in evangelization. And so we need to bring ourselves before Him, to be with him and follow him and listen to him say, "Go and do likewise."

5. Epilogue

It is fair to say that the ISUM summit raised more questions than it answered—questions about how to build or participate in community-building ministries when the very nature of the city pushes against such sharing in one another's lives; questions about finding Jesus even in the darkest places and learning to be light and salt and bread to those we meet along the way. How to embody Christ in multi-faith contexts remains an ongoing challenge that requires of the church continual discernment and prayer so that we hold firmly both to the authority of Jesus, acknowledging his Lordship, and the breadth of his love for all creation.

Though our time together was short, the process of listening to one another, hearing the stories of those we met during the immersion experiences, sharing in struggles and joys—all of these were as important as the final outcome or any answers we might come up with. Witnessing to Jesus, no matter what context, is, in the end, about persons and being in relationship. It is learning to live together in ways that might counter the ways of the world; in places of death, it is sharing life, and life in its fullness (cf. John 10:10).

Recruit, Equip and Sustain Christian Leaders in a New Urban World

Lynette Leach, Scott Bessenecker and Andrew Menzies[1]

The last decade has seen a significant response in the number of practitioners involved in urban mission around the world. Today the need is urgent for the broader church to take collective action to motivate and mobilize a strong contingent of Christian leaders who will commit to living incarnationally in poor urban communities. This is already happening which is a sign of hope for neighborhoods to be transformed with the good news of kingdom justice and mercy. To respond to the challenges brought about by the massive rise of urbanization in the world, recruiting people to follow Jesus into tough urban contexts cannot be ignored. Once recruited, they need to undergo appropriate preparation and equipping. To be sustained in their vocation and call to faithful discipleship, and ministry for the long journey requires supportive networks. Recruiting, equipping and sustaining Christian leaders is vitally important for kingdom transformation to be accomplished in an increasingly urbanized world.

Introduction

A gathering prompted and inspired by the Spirit, where every experience was geared to responding faithfully to God's heart for a growing urban world—this is what characterized the Integral Urban Mission Summit held in Bangkok in January 2013. Active participants in urban mission from every continent were drawn together with an urgency to do whatever it takes to alleviate the destructive cycle of injustice and poverty and to be agents of hope and transformation in slums and poor neighborhoods.

Faced with the overwhelming statistics that over a billion people live in urban slums today, and that by 2030 the number could double to two billion, Summit participants were challenged about the need to recruit, equip, and sustain Christian leaders to help extend God's reign among the urban poor.[2] Trying to grasp the magnitude of what is

---

[1] This chapter was originally published as an ISUM Summit Briefing Paper (#2).
[2] Ashley Barker, *Slum Life Rising: How to Enflesh Hope within a New Urban World* (Melbourne: UNOH, 2012), 20.

required to meet that need can lead to a sense of powerlessness to be able to make any significant difference. Abstract numbers can blind us to the seriousness of this rising surge, so reality must be confronted through the experience of individual people.

Ashley Barker relates an incident he had when his response took him by surprise, despite having lived since 2002 in the Klong Toey slum. One day as he rode his motorbike past a woman sitting eating in the doorway of her plywood shack, he was engulfed by the signs of poverty and the smell surrounding her: no water, no power, rubbish, human and animal faeces scattered around. They exchanged smiles but as Ash rode away he was overcome by her misery and what he describes as an inadequate response. Haunted by this encounter, he calls attention to the need to take poverty personally in community. This woman represents a kind of futility in "a stinking ocean of poverty", yet she is one human life, made in God's image, in the midst of thousands.[3] For her life and her neighborhood to experience transformation, and for that to be multiplied in similar settings around the world, it will take a significant movement of Christians responding to the call of Jesus to follow him into the hard places.

This paper reflects the energy and commitment of Summit participants who are vitally concerned with recruiting, equipping and sustaining Christian leaders for a new urban world. The structure mirrors the themes which the working group had as a focus: Recruit, Equip, Sustain. The guiding questions which shaped discussion and responses were:

> [1] Where do we see seeds of hope for urban shalom in recruiting, equipping and sustaining Christian leaders?
>
> [2] What are the challenges to urban shalom?
>
> [3] What are our calls to action to the broader church to recruit, equip and sustain Christian leaders for urban work?

Collective action arising out of the Integral Urban Mission Summit was identified as an important outcome so that the time and cost invested in participating in the Summit would bear fruit for mission. Reflecting on Shane Claiborne's statement in his Summit message on the Good Samaritan story, "We cannot make poverty history until we make poverty personal", the working group applied the same principle to identify calls to action or recommendations to the broader church. The group recognized that we cannot expect

---

3 Barker, *Slum Life Rising*, 102-103.

the broader church to take action unless we are prepared also to take action personally. So we identified an action or a step we could each take in our own ministry when we returned home as a result of being at the Summit. Sometimes recommendations can be vague and general, so the challenge was to identify specific actions that would galvanize the broader church to recruit, equip and sustain Christian leaders in their vocation.

The spheres of recruiting, equipping, and sustaining workers, although having distinct priorities and emphases, overlap, and inform each other. As you read this paper, look for those links and be open to the Spirit guiding your responses.

1. Recruiting Christian Leaders

Summary Statement

Jesus commands his disciples not to pray for the harvest—that is already plentiful: "But I say, wake up and look around. The fields are already ripe for harvest" (John 4:35). He asks his disciples, rather, to pray for workers to attend to a ripe harvest (Luke 10:2). The call upon Christ's disciples to pray for the release of workers, as well as to attend to the harvest themselves is clear. In a world that is 50% urban and a church that is still catching up to that reality, the need to recruit Christian leaders for the new urban world has never been greater. The urban world is ready and waiting for a greater manifestation of God's kingdom. In many ways, the urban mission field is a fruitful place and there are signs of hope that Aslan[4] is on the move. Something is stirring in the majority world church as, despite limited resources, pastors and missionaries in poor communities are being mobilized to bring kingdom transformation to the world's megacities.

There is also movement in the more affluent west, as young Christians raise their voices and invest their hearts in ministries that address injustice, oppression, and urban poverty. Still, significant challenges lie ahead for mobilizing Christian leaders into urban poor communities. The gap between rich and poor is massive, the consumerist spirit and the prosperity gospel run unchecked, and the complexity of ministry in dense, urban communities that are marked by extreme poverty requires a special leader.

This section of the working group paper will review the signs of hope and the challenges, then suggest some action steps toward recruiting and mobilizing women and men to participate in establishing the kingdom of God among our urban, poor neighbors.

---

4 Aslan is the central character of C. S. Lewis's *The Chronicles of Narnia* series; the lion of The Lion, the Witch and the Wardrobe; and intended by C. S. Lewis as a Christlike figure.

Signs of Hope

i. Youthful altruism

In the West there is a noticeable rise in concern for injustice activism and a desire to address the issues surrounding urban poverty. This is being expressed in a variety of ways, including scores of young people re-locating to high crime, high-poverty locations within Western countries. In Canada, for instance, an organization called Move In has mobilized more than 200 households of mostly young people to buy or rent property in some of the most deprived neighborhoods in the country in just three short years. Organizations like the Eden Network in the UK and The Simple Way in the US are seeing a similar movement of altruistic young people re-locating in order to "be the change they want to see in the world."[5] Throughout the so-called developed world young people from affluent backgrounds are making the downward journey to plant themselves in neighborhoods marked by drugs, prostitution, and poverty. The ISUM Summit itself, with 200 participants, represented a sign of hope as people from around the world gathered to pray, trade stories, think, and write about the work currently underway in poor communities.

ii. Majority world rising

Likewise, majority world believers are mobilizing to address the situation in slum communities. Viv Grigg, during a seminar at the ISUM Summit,[6] said that ten years ago a word was given that God was going to raise up 50,000 workers from among poor communities as servants to their poor neighbors. Grigg now estimates that there are easily 50,000 pastors and missionaries from among the urban poor who are ministering in slums around the world. Another member of our group, Nigel Branken, who lives with his family in Hillbrow, an inner-city high-rise slum in Johannesburg, commented that affluent youth are expressing interest in experiencing life and service among the poor. In his neglected suburb, youth from Germany are volunteering and serving among the poor. Some poor youth who have been able to move out of their community are returning in order to work for kingdom transformation. He shared a story of a former street child from Hillbrow who, after attending Bible College, has returned to the community to serve on Nigel's team reaching the homeless. Simply hearing about or seeing the Spirit of God moving among the marginalized who, themselves, are ushering

---

5   Quote attributed to Mahatma Gandhi.

6   Viv Grigg co-facilitated a working group at the ISUM Summit, "Fuel Church Movements Among the Urban Poor".

in transformation, is a sign of hope that is attracting others to draw near to Christ as he brings healing to poor communities.

iii. The testimony of history

We take courage that God has consistently sparked revival and change on the margins of empires. Whether slaves and women in the first century, Welsh coal miners in 1904, or 21st century Dalits in India, God loves to move powerfully among those deemed "least" by the powerful. God has mobilized young people by the droves to move to places considered geographically, sociologically, culturally or spiritually distant from their places of origin. St. Francis of Assisi was 26 when he began to attract other youth to his radical life of simplicity and service. Teresa of Kolkata was 18 when she became a missionary.

Aslan is indeed on the move. Christian young people are hungry for deep, lasting, and holistic transformation among our poor neighbors. Majority world pastors and missionaries are remaining in or returning to slum communities to shepherd churches, witness to the resurrection, and advocate for godly change. We are buoyed by the testimony of history as we recall God's propensity to move powerfully among the world's margins.

Challenges

i. Class division

Yet we are not naïve about the obstacles to mobilizing workers to serve alongside our poor neighbors. We live in a class-divided world. Perhaps humans have always lived in class division, but the current manifestation of class division seems to be deepening and widening. The statistical estimates are disturbing: 99.9% of the global population possesses less than 20% of the world's wealth while the other 0.1% enjoys more than 80%.[7] This gap between rich and poor can make mobilization difficult. In order to recruit people among both rich and poor some kind of relationship is needed. The rich, who are often out of touch with the situation among the poor, are likely to misunderstand the reasons for global urban poverty or to underestimate the need. Those in poor communities will also need the encouragement, advocacy, and resources of the rich in

---

7   Henry, James, "The Price of Offshore Revisited: New Estimates for Missing Global Private Wealth, Income, Inequality, and Lost Taxes" Press Release, Tax Justice Network, July 2012, 5, http://en.wikipedia.org/wiki/File:Global_Distribution_of_Wealth_v3.jpga accessed on 5 March 2013.

order to return or remain in their communities. The deep chasm between the world's rich and poor presents a challenge to mobilization.

In addition, mission agencies have for too long presented a truncated gospel. This may be due, at least in part, to the division between rich and poor. Many western Protestant mission agencies have historically been run by and populated with missionaries who come from middle class or wealthy backgrounds who have had an inadequate understanding of God's mission to bring not only people, but systems and structures under the authority of his Son. Protestant mission agencies and missionaries have sometimes assumed conversion and church planting is all that is needed in order to bring transformation to poor communities. Many in poor communities, for their part, have accepted this class division as well. Father Paul Uwemedimo, a participant in our group, said that in Nigeria a poor community may expect as a point of pride that their priest will live in relative luxury. Our class-divided world has added fuel to unbalanced power dynamics and a patron-client relationship. Many mission agencies simply are not equipped to recruit the right people because of a faulty paradigm under which they operate.

ii. Prosperity gospel and consumerism

The prosperity gospel and its western counterpart consumerism are deceiving Christian communities into believing that the pursuit of wealth and possessions is acceptable among believers. Western believers have been sold a sufferless Christianity which suggests that following Jesus does not involve sacrifice or hardship and that ministry among the poor, when it occurs, should be done from a comfortable distance. In addition, a messianic complex can make it difficult to recruit young people who are convinced that they are the answers to the world's problems rather than the risen Christ. The call to incarnational ministry among our poor friends has never been so counter-cultural in a comfort-obsessed western church. Likewise, in many poor communities in the majority world, the call to remain in or return to those communities runs against the grain of Christian teaching on prosperity which suggests that God wants his people to succeed by possessing large amounts of personal wealth and then move out of poorer areas. While it is true that God's heart is for sufficiency, even abundance among all those made in his image, the emphasis on possessing large amounts of private wealth has obscured God's intent for communities to enjoy shalom. Whether due to theologically errant teaching or cultural pressure to assimilate, a large obstacle to recruiting believers to walk alongside poor communities is their love of money.

iii. Recruiting the right people

Many believers living in poor communities should seek greater financial stability, education, and serving as a kingdom ambassador in the world of government, business, academia or the sciences. While all are called to radical hospitality, concern for the marginalized, being satisfied with daily bread, and giving generously—not all are called to remain in slum communities or return to them after they have been able to move out. In the same way, many who have grown up in relative affluence must pursue a simpler lifestyle and grow tender-hearted toward those who survive on much less, but not all are called to relocate long term to a developing world barrio. Recruiting the right leader to live and serve full-time among the world's destitute can be difficult. Some whom we might not expect to be called and equipped to leadership in urban poor areas may grow into the very person a poor community needs, while others who seem an "obvious" fit for service among the urban poor may end up causing unnecessary harm to themselves or others because they simply were not cut out for leadership among poor neighbors. The process of careful discernment and calling within the church and youth or mission organizations, and the need to create safe testing places and times for believers to discern a call, is critical.

Calls to Action

i. Discipleship

Like so many things in life, recruiting leaders to the new urban world is not so simple. The church, indeed, must give voice to the urgent needs in our communities and call people to respond, but it is not enough to just present some statistics about the needs in the megacities and issue a call. Nor is it as simple as giving people short term experiences of building relationships and walking alongside our neighbors on the margins, yet the church must continue to do this as well. The primary need is for steady, holistic, life-on-life discipleship. We need mothers and fathers of the faith to take the long, faithful walk alongside fellow believers, helping them to develop a better understanding of holistic kingdom transformation and helping people discern their role in that transformation. The church in the slums as well as the church in the wealthy suburbs needs to recapture a vision of shalom and disciple each other into positions of bringing shalom to the desperate places on earth. Some of those places will be urban poor communities.

Ralph Winter's differentiation of modality (rooted local church) from sodality (missionary band) has been helpful in identifying one way of accomplishing the church's mission.[8] But it may have served its purpose in the development of post-World War II mission agencies. A new ecclesiastical paradigm is needed to help every Christian understand their missional call in bringing kingdom shalom and then methods are needed to equip all believers to do so without a strict separation between missionaries and non-missionaries.

ii. Focused short-term opportunities

While some have been recruited to a life of cross-cultural service simply from reading Scripture or going to a missions conference, most of those serving in poor communities today have been called through relationships and experiences. Even those from the majority world need clarifying experiences of serving in slum communities to discern a call to return or to remain. They also need relationships with those who live missionally on the margins (whether local or expatriate) to confirm their calling. To do this we need to see careful opportunities carved out, which will expose people to a discernment process on the margins shepherded by those who live and serve there.

Focused short-term opportunities for people who have lived outside slum communities need to be carefully crafted to avoid poverty tourism or solidifying dangerous power dynamics between the poor and non-poor. Whether the participant lives 10 kilometres or 10,000 kilometres from the community, these experiences require solid orientation and deliberate preparation for everybody involved. Those exploring the possibility of a life of service among the poor need to enter the experience with the expectation that God will speak to them about their future relationship to live and serve in that setting. Their goal is to hear from the Spirit of God in regard to calling more than it is to provide any long term benefit, though experiences should be crafted so the participant makes some contribution to a community. Those in the community should have significant say over how the visitors enter and contribute.

These experiences should call participants to a clear next step. For instance, after a one to four month experience in a marginalized urban community, expatriates should be challenged to commit to two years of incarnational service. Those living in or near the community already should be invited at the conclusion of a service experience to commit to another step in their level of involvement. Those who are not called to long-term incarnational ministry on the margins (or "insiders" called to move out of a slum community) should be encouraged to live simply and give generously wherever they end up. Those discerning a call to at least two years of incarnational service should be given

---

8 Ralph D. Winter, "The Two Structures of God's Redemptive Mission", Perspectives on the World Christian Movement, edited by Ralph D. Winter and Steven C. Hawthorne (Pasadena: William Carey Library, 1981) 178-190.

tools to test that call within their community and explore options.

While short-term mission has numerous pit-falls, it can be used as a valuable discernment tool which can be leveraged to make modest contributions to a community. We must not underestimate the power of an outsider simply giving time to listen and stand alongside our friends on the margins if only for a period of weeks. Creating points of solidarity can radically bless both parties.

iii. Effective equipping and sustaining

Of course recruitment is futile if those living and serving in the new urban world are poorly equipped and not well sustained. Part of good recruiting is creating the structures which will properly equip those serving in urban poor neighborhoods and help men and women to thrive in this challenging setting. Many of the missionary biographies from the past include the critical place of someone living the missional life that influenced the potential recruit with their lives and stories. We need to help those who are thriving in these settings to tell their stories and invite relationship with those who are considering the possibility of a life on the margins.

While Viv Grigg estimates there are currently 50,000 workers (almost exclusively majority world residents) serving in the slums, many, many more are needed. We are hopeful that this working group paper will help churches and mission agencies to spawn discussion on how to best recruit, equip, and sustain a new wave of urban leaders.

2. Equipping Christian Leaders

Summary Statement

A passion for working in urban poor communities is a vital element for Christian leaders in their response to God's call. The recruiting of such people and the harnessing of their passion in their subsequent preparation is clearly a challenge. To send workers to tough urban contexts without adequate preparation, hoping that they will learn "as they go", is to invite disillusionment and potential damage for workers and neighbors. It is understood that ongoing learning and equipping will occur for urban workers in their mission settings, but this needs to be built on training, formation, practical application, theological reflection and immersion experiences. The Equip working group spent the first session together identifying areas of hope in the equipping of leaders for urban work. The second session considered challenges and barriers faced by urban leaders. The group then identified creative calls to action that incorporate various ways of equipping Christian leaders for a new urban world.

Signs of Hope

i. Broken systems create opportunity for change

There is opportunity for good things to arise out of broken systems in both church and world. Einstein said that the definition of insanity was continually doing the same things, yet expecting change. Similarly, many people doing "the daily grind" in church and society know that life could be more fruitful and meaningful if they stepped out and made a positive change.

There has been plenty of magnification and exposure of broken institutional systems in the church and the world in recent years. For example, the effects of the global financial crisis and resulting insecurity in most parts of the West led to disillusionment and dissatisfaction. Similarly the exposure of sexual abuse and generally declining trends in church have made people realize that many parts of the old system are broken. Circumstances such as these can provide the seedbed for changes in leadership patterns and practices with hopefully a closer examination of biblical patterns and principles, as they apply to contexts of urban poverty.

ii. Mentoring and discipleship

There is wonderful scope for new possibilities as the emerging generation purposefully seeks relational systems. This means that there is potential for change towards newer, more relational and mentoring paradigms in leadership development. Potential leaders do not have to have hurdles placed in front of them to "sift" out those who are suited to living in poor communities. Potential leaders can examine and pursue models and examples from wider settings which contrast with "one-size-fits-all" models formerly sought by denominations and mission agencies. This means that there is potential to impact beneficially those who are emerging in leadership transition and succession; we note that it also might not too!

The working group cited the following as factors that are regarded as necessary by emerging generations for the equipping of leaders:

> [1] authenticity: the involvement of urban mission practitioners in the training of emerging leaders gives credibility and substance to what is taught;
>
> [2] mutuality in mentoring between the mentor and mentoree: the mentoree benefits if the mentor understands the challenges of life

and discipleship in poor communities from personal experience; shared experiences between mentors and mentorees provide inspiration and learning for both;

[3] accessibility: the trend for on-line learning, off-campus training, immersion experiences in urban mission contexts, and seminars and workshops facilitated by practitioners has opened up possibilities for emerging leaders to access training and formation readily;

[4] vulnerability: emerging leaders develop their understanding and become more effectively equipped to enter poor communities when practitioners who are involved in the equipping are transparent about the highs and lows of incarnational living in poor communities, and are prepared to be honest about their own experiences;

[5] increased possibilities for deep listening and hearing: listening to those who are immersed in poor communities and learning from them is a valuable feature of equipping emerging leaders;

[6] democratization of knowledge: the spread of knowledge and ease of access to information and research has become widespread in the digital age, reaching people in many contexts through technology. Knowledge is no longer the sole domain of the professional academic sector. A blend of academic and on-the-job training facilitates the equipping of emerging leaders.

Equally, the working group hopes that there is less "Pollyanna-ism", that clear cut answers and "experts" are viewed suspiciously (the healthy side of scepticism), and that a genuine inquiring stance is encouraged. Alongside this, a deep-seated suspicion of the effects of colonialism is recognized.

The emerging generations of activists and missionally-oriented people, together with the leaders who arise among them, are all deeply affected by globalization. This, at least at some level, is bringing in a common language and set of expectations and preferences across nations and cultures. This could intensify the pressure for changes in models and practices in the equipping of leaders, if there is a widespread swell in that direction, thus encouraging greater practical discipleship as greater proximity, training, and mutual learning in equipping is embraced alongside emerging leadership. These hopes are based on assumptions that there is a continued increase in "on the job" training and relational equipping. One participant expressed this as a flattening of the generation gap.

Equipping models and methods that become more "hands on", and oriented toward closer proximity and relationship, could suit a majority world urban poor setting. This could potentially place less emphasis on the distant and removed Academy and more emphasis on learning and formation on the ground in the local context.

A story was shared in the group of an example of how common language and culture among globalized young people in Singapore was an advantage in interaction and conversation with sex workers. The younger workers made a much easier connection with the sex workers because of shared language and being part of the same youth culture, compared with the older staff members who came from a more "separatist" and pietistic church culture common to their generation which made it difficult for them to relate effectively across the generations.

iii. Emerging majority world missions movements

There has been a tremendous change in the location, focus, and orientation of Christian workers in one single generation. There are fewer traditionally oriented missionaries and significantly more chaplains, counselors, aid and development workers, community development staff, nurses, doctors, engineers, all of whom are cautious of colonization by the sending (usually western) culture. The group noted concerns about the rise of short-term mission trips where the sent are not well trained and equipped in the practical and real limitations of such a venture. However, notwithstanding that, the general trend towards cultural sensitivity, holistic concern for integral mission, and development of nationals is a sign of hope. There are stories from every continent where broken western approaches to mission are being replaced with vitalized and "bottom up" (grass-roots) local models. More prevalent is the emerging indigenous and local concern about integral mission. We know that while the western church and its missions-systems are generally in decline, Christianity is now a majority, non-western faith that is thriving in many parts of the majority world.

iv. Stories of the kingdom showing signs of thriving in slums

Slowly, churches, mission agencies and aid and development organizations are awakening to the current reality of urbanization. They are awakening gradually to the strategic nature of people movements and demographics resulting in the estimate that a majority of the world's population will be living in urban slums by the middle of this century. They are awakening also to the differing dynamics of slum life (compared to traditional, rural settings) and its place in the industrialization of economies. Increasingly, stories are being told widely of the kingdom thriving in slums.

In the midst of this, Viv Grigg estimates that around 50,000 new urban workers have been mobilized since 2002. The working group noted the diversity of people and roles within this trend. The former "one-size-fits-all" generalist missionary has morphed into a vast and wide assortment of workers, activists, entrepreneurs, community developers and researchers.

v. Awareness of dreaming among people in the slums

The working group noted many stories and examples of people actively improving their circumstances in the midst of slum life. From a bird's eye view a slum can look all the same, but when inside the community in the alleys, homes and shelters of perhaps 100,000 plus people, some are doing better than in the village from where they came. We note that certainly not all people in a slum are doing well, however the nature of slum life compared to village life affords possibilities. Some rise through crime while some rise through micro-business and cottage-industry opportunities. The main sessions at the ISUM summit presented by Dr Ruth Callanta, Founding President of the Centre for Community Transformation in Manila, and Dr Sonny Tha Nyan, General Secretary YMCA in Yangon, provided examples of this. The story of the Klong Toey Football Club founded by Dr Ash Barker is a different example. We know that many of the world's best footballers emerge from the particular pressures of slum life with the passion, skill and temperament required for elite sport.

vi. Other

The working group noted some further areas of hope:

[1] There is a new creativity emerging as part of the potpourri of globalization and a digitally connected and sharing world;

[2] There is greater freedom to change and question;

[3] People can be inspired and engaged by compelling messages and images. This can mobilize people to take some form of action at far greater speed due to the digital communications revolution;

[4] Younger Christian believers seem to be more concerned about social justice and integral Christianity. The old divide between the evangelical and social concerns of the church, though still present if looked for, seem strange to younger Christians. "How could they ever be separated?" many younger Christians ask.

Challenges

i. The move to mentoring and equipping mode

Can established leaders, particularly those with a western mindset, make the adjustment to a more relational, mentoring, vulnerable mode of equipping when often they did not receive much modeling of this? Can they learn with and from the emerging generation, like the biblical examples of the little boy taking blinded Samson's hands to put them on the pillars, or David demonstrating a new, lighter method of warfare?

The working group noted the challenges and barriers for emerging non-western leaders in this process. Often cultures and institutions have strong hierarchical and deferential cultures, influenced by "face" and "shame". These factors can mitigate against the relational mentoring mode and democratization of knowledge.

The western need to *fill the gaps* with knowledge and information was seen as a challenge and obstacle to indigenous leadership taking on greater roles of equipping. Often this western trend is fuelled by too much pressure and urgency to achieve targets, thus missing other important qualitative aspects of integral mission. Westerners need to leave space – for God, and for majority world leaders to take their place in the responsibility of equipping.

ii. Formal education

The working group noted the propensity of formal education towards too often being remote, disconnected, irrelevant, abstract and inaccessible for potential students. One aspect of this for teachers and prospective students is accreditation. The working group noted the bias away from professional academic life for the teacher and researcher if concern is for the urban poor. Real practicalities like status, title, classification, publishing, influence and security in the wider Academy all require devotion of time, energy and physical presence by staff, usually at the cost of the development and training of urban poor leaders.

The group noted that faculty simply have to attend to the situation of the urban poor through spending time in the context of the urban poor, yet few colleges and universities easily permit this. We noted the limiting approaches of rote learning and deference in educational settings in some cultures.

Finances too are an issue. The western model is very expensive. It involves potentially a big debt burden on western workers and holds a large "no entry" sign up to majority world people. These issues all point to the challenge and question of whether training and equipping modes can be shifted to models which are more practitioner based and accessible, and are in closer proximity and relationship to those who are responsible for equipping and those who are being equipped.

To what extent may practitioner based approaches be already in deployment in majority world urban poor settings? On this point, we recognized that most of us present at our working group sessions, and certainly with voices being heard, were western world people. How in touch are we with what is happening on the ground in majority world settings?

iii. Barriers faced by poor urban leaders in accessing equipping

Rationalist western approaches to equipping and learning present a difficulty for the majority world. There is need for greater narrative and story approaches in learning settings which would connect and communicate more naturally with poor urban leaders. The gap between them and predominantly western equippers is wide. This limits effective training and learning. How can you mentor people if not among them? There is a great need for incarnational living and training. Another factor was noted by a majority world member of the working group who spoke of the continuing negative legacy of colonialism resulting in genuine questions about the real motives of expatriates which affect the level of trust. Language barriers pose difficulties in communication. English is the *lingua franca* of many trainers and equippers, including ISUM participants.

Availability of resources and training in mother tongues is often rare.

Poor urban leaders are time and cash poor. The sheer instability and transitory nature of existence in urban slum life or in poor communities in western cities is a major issue. Kendi Howells Douglas, Professor of Cross Cultural Ministries at Great Lakes Christian College Michigan US and a member of the working group, conveyed a first-hand example about her house church in Lansing, Michigan, switching focus and location to share life and worship with the urban poor. She noted that there were many "three month-ers" in her community. They were people who were moved on every three months from rented accommodation for failure or inability to pay rent. This affects their capacity to be able to develop and maintain deeper relationships.

The time and energy to survive daily life when in poverty makes it very difficult to be ready to invest in learning, leadership, and in thinking differently. Fear may prevent potential workers from taking on leadership particularly when it is likely to involve the need to challenge existing power structures and cultures.

Calls to Action

i. Move to "mixed mode" of Academy and local learning

We need to develop relationships between formal education providers and urban poor practitioners to facilitate a greater mixed mode of learning and equipping that combines the Academy and "on the job" training in the relevant local context. An example of this is what has been developed between Great Lakes Christian College (Michigan, US), Stirling Theological College (Melbourne, AUS) and Urban Neighbours of Hope (UNOH). Networks like ISUM provide a place of discovery and brokerage for such mixed mode partnerships to be fostered and developed. Such partnerships can only develop if the leadership of the Academies and urban mission agencies see it as essential and are willing and co-operative to make it happen.

ii. Encourage a more intentional mentoring and relational paradigm of equipping

More experienced practitioners need to be paired with less experienced practitioners in the context of open, vulnerable, and authentic relationships. The length of these placements and mentoring relationships must be realistic, recognizing that there is great value even in a short, intensive exposure to the realities of urban poverty. However, more effective equipping and testing of call for those planning to do cross-cultural work needs longer time-frames for preparation, which naturally leads to greater value in the local urban poor context, especially when equipping includes deeper understanding of factors such as language, culture, needs, longings, and systemic patterns.

A group member, Ranu from the Punjab India, gave a detailed account of very intentional training and development that has the aim of raising up a large cadre of missional church planters within the context of his own denomination. It was notable that we had few people in the working group who were engaged in a church planting context working with existing indigenous churches. This paper does not present a critique of what perspectives are lacking in regards to indigenous church planters, recognizing that our working group did not and could not reflect or contain wider perspectives.

iii. Encourage development and formation of clusters for mutual learning

Clusters for mutual learning can operate in various styles and patterns ... just as long as they happen. We see no reason why everything is oriented to individuals just because western society is individualized. The synergy of co-operating together, sharing knowledge, encouraging each other and learning from each other could have great benefit in the equipping of urban poor leaders and those from affluent backgrounds who have been challenged to be equipped to work with the poor.

iv. Apply western Christian resources to the education of the world's poorest

Western Christian teaching institutions, denominations, mission agencies, para-church groups and churches ought to find creative, responsible and meaningful ways to dedicate annually a significant amount of their resources, including investments, scholarships, teaching time, libraries, properties and information technology, as a starting point towards the education and training of the world's poorest, and as an example of Christian stewardship and commitment. We recognize that this is a great challenge set against all sorts of systemic blockages and pre-existing commitments, however the immense disparity between teaching and training resources in most western church settings and those in urban poverty settings must be named and challenged as a fundamental Christian ethical and moral issue.

The calls to action presented by the Equip working group offer resourceful and innovative ways of addressing the challenges of equipping leaders for a new urban world. They take seriously what is needed in poor communities for urban shalom and what is needed to prepare, equip and develop leaders who seek to co-operate in God's kingdom work among the poor.

3. Sustaining Christian Leaders

Summary Statement

When the initial enthusiasm and passion to respond to the call to follow Jesus is tested by tough challenges in urban mission contexts, where do Christian leaders find resilience, nurture, encouragement and care to stand firm? When faced with situations of dire need in neighborhoods affected by poverty, what sustains workers in their vocation? The working group that focused on sustainability considered this important issue, recognizing that mission agencies and leaders who do not give attention to this, will pay a price in burn-out, exhaustion, cynicism and, sadly, sometimes having to withdraw from their ministries. Faithful discipleship and ministry for the long journey is both invitation and challenge. The Sustain working group discussed signs of hope and challenges for sustaining Christian leaders in an urban world. Calls to action center on what the broader church ought to consider in ensuring that leaders have appropriate support.

Signs of Hope

i. Leaders as models

Courageous people engaged in courageous projects, loving what they do, are a sign of encouragement for other leaders. Ministry is not a job to them, but a passion and calling. The lives of leaders who have sustained their vision for many years inspire other leaders to continue, especially when they see evidence of older workers who have served faithfully for a long time and have not succumbed to cynicism and negativity.

ii. Lives transformed

Transformation of lives in local urban communities is a constant source of hope for leaders as they see God bringing positive change to people's lives. Seeing the fruit of their ministry as broken people minister to other broken people gives hope. Jeff Smith, a working group member from Alaska who is part of Adventures in Mission, related an experience in South Africa when a homeless man, who had developed a friendship with Nigel Branken (who leads a ministry in a slum in Johannesburg and who is mentioned in Section 1 of this paper), led Nigel and Jeff to other homeless people and began to pray over them. An immersion visit during the summit to the Overseas Mission Fellowship (OMF) Khannayao church planting team in Bangkok enabled the group to meet an older Thai woman who started a church in her home after only two years of being a Christian. This showed how the gospel can be spread simply and it gave hope to leaders, some of whom are working in difficult circumstances and unreceptive places. The OMF church planting team works specifically among urban poor communities.

iii. Healthy spirituality

Dependence on God, rather than self-dependence, sustains people and their work through personal and corporate times of prayer, Scripture, sabbath and reading, to name a few ways. Without this, ministry with the poor can seem like aid and development work. In challenging urban poor contexts, faced with relentless need and calls for action, spiritual disciplines may fall away. Maintaining a healthy spirituality was named as a common priority among the working group members.

iv. Mission agencies taking missionary care seriously

There has been a resurgence of churches and mission agencies accepting responsibility for involvement in the care of missionaries and partnering with leaders in the field. Leaders who face the reality of their struggles and are prepared to be vulnerable could receive support through counseling. An immersion experience during the summit enabled participants to visit the New Counseling Service (NCS) in Bangkok which was established in 2002 and provides a range of counseling services for missionaries and local people in all walks of life, Thais and foreigners. Debriefing opportunities particularly following situations of crisis are necessary so that leaders can process their responses and deal with the fatigue and emotional pressures that can build up.

Richard Glazier is a working group member and urban missionary at The Well Bangkok, which provides supportive ministry and friendship to women involved in the Thai sex trade. He gave an example of how a network of supportive relationships upheld him and his family at a time when he contemplated leaving ministry in Bangkok and returning to England, feeling defeated and depressed. He answered the question, "What prevented us from being among the avoidable casualties of ministry?" An integrated safety net of intentional relationships between friends, his sending church, and his mission organization helped him and his wife to build a sustainable rhythm of life.[9] Annual appraisals, debriefings of emotional and spiritual issues arising from their work, monthly conversations with the leadership of the sending church which fed into prayer offered by their home church, and spiritual direction were put in place and changed what had become an unmanageable situation. He emphasized the importance of this kind of network for all urban missionaries.

---

9   Rhythm of life refers to a healthy pattern of life and mission that includes attention to the physical, mental, emotional and spiritual components of life, and practices and disciplines that contribute to a person's sense of well-being and capacity to thrive.

v. Team support

Being part of a team prevents isolation, even though team challenges are also a reality in some contexts. A sustainable rhythm of life that draws teams of leaders together in a common vision and purpose through community living, Bible study and worship, and shared ministry times in their communities, has become a uniting, sustaining and integrating factor among workers in various missions. Times of celebration together for teams and with their neighbors in communities are important too. Communication is vital for healthy team relationships and for connection beyond teams. Various forms of communication, for example, Skype, Facebook and email, have made it easier to connect leaders and their support networks, where ideas and issues can be discussed openly and promptly and leaders encouraged with positive feedback. Networks of support are more accessible as connection with families, friends, and supporters can be immediate.

vi. Opportunities like the Summit

The group strongly affirmed the Integral Urban Mission Summit as an experience of hope which energized them. The investment of time and travel to attend, the informal conversations, and learning from each other, reminded leaders that, "It's not just me doing this," and, "I'm not crazy!" Realignment towards their original vision, when leaders might have been lacking evidence and experiences of hope, has sustained them and re-ignited their dream through texts like Isaiah 58 and 61. Supportive relationships developed beyond national boundaries and across mission agencies, facilitated by common purpose and understanding of life in urban poor contexts.

Challenges

i. Team dynamics

Achieving unity or a healthy team dynamic can be challenging. Relational conflict within teams or neighborhoods can be a source of pain and may not be dealt with effectively. Conflict, jealousy, and competition are a reality at times. Changes in team structure, for example an increased number of workers joining a team, can present challenges. More energy, time and resources are needed to sustain larger teams. A regular common rhythm of life practised by the team can be a help. Regular team communication, as well as personal and social communication with fellow workers, can fall by the wayside if the team culture is not geared to this. An independent spirit in workers makes it difficult for team bonding and can harm the influence that a team has in the neighborhood if neighbors witness tension in the team. Immaturity of workers needs careful handling by team leaders, who ought to provide newer and younger workers with a safe space to grow and mature, while encouraging and helping them to be able to withstand the rigors of life in a complex urban context. The "transient" volunteer, who is in the field for a short term, can deplete the energy and time of long-term workers in a team. Yet, volunteering has its place as a means of informing and exposing people to urban contexts and the possibility of volunteers deciding to train to become mission workers. Pioneering work without a team to support leaders presents a challenge when establishing new work and developing trust and relationships with neighbors, even if a pioneering spirit is strong in the leader.

ii. Balancing an active-contemplative approach

An activist mindset, which most leaders in urban mission contexts probably have, can be a challenge to sustainability. Activists are more inclined towards action, finding solutions, trying to fix problems and start projects, than attending to their inner needs or participating in individual counseling or group therapy sessions, which could be beneficial in addressing problems rather than ignoring them. Building in some regular reflective time in their life could balance this. Yet, it was recognized by the group that workers who can accept responsibility, who are reliable, and who can take initiative when needed, are an asset in mission settings. The concern is about unhealthy extremes of obsessive activism which may lead to burn-out.

iii. Discouragement

Not seeing the fruit of their work or not seeing results quickly enough, particularly when fighting against big systems and structures, can be very discouraging and may even result in leaders giving up those systemic struggles or even the work itself. The celebration of small victories can be important as a way of addressing this problem. Spiritual discouragement stems from a lack of intimacy with God and will drain leaders of their energy and fruitfulness. This can include being so caught up with doing things FOR God that they forget to spend time WITH God. Leaders are called to a relationship with Christ first, before being called to the work of Christ.

iv. Crisis of faith

When leaders experience a crisis of faith, the John 6 moment becomes a reality: "Are you going to leave too?" The following factors can result in a crisis of faith and leadership:

[1] when tragedy, brokenness, or overwhelming situations occur in the lives of leaders or in the lives of those around them;

[2] ill-preparedness of leaders, when they have not been adequately equipped or there is not enough ongoing equipping or pastoral care of workers supporting them through their trials;

[3] an under-developed or warped theology of suffering which gives rise to a triumphalist view of the Christian life and therefore disillusionment when struggles happen. Incarnational living will mean that workers are subject to the same difficulties and similar anguish as their neighbors. Leaders may not have understood the call to lay down their lives for Christ and his call to suffer for the sake of the gospel;

[4] burn-out occurring through any of the above, or through not dealing with difficult issues as they arise. Trying to cope with this by attending group meetings, which are intended to be encouraging but may instead include "hype", ignores or avoids the issue rather than addressing it through effective individual counseling;

[5] isolation in lonely places away from mentors and spiritual guides who might provide conversation, wisdom, debriefing and prayer, can contribute to leaders losing their faith in Christ;

[6] supporters who believe in good works rather than faith in Christ himself cause leaders to place value on works and projects in an effort to maintain good relationships with supporters so that they do not lose their funding;

[7] poor boundaries around work and rest periods may lead to exhaustion and lack of adequate, intentional time being focused on maintaining a healthy relationship with God, and healthy personal relationships with team workers and local people.

v. Adjusting to local contexts

It can take time for workers to understand cross-cultural challenges and ongoing cultural differences. This might be addressed by preparation before going into cross-cultural settings and by regular debriefing during mission experience. Sometimes inhospitable and unfriendly attitudes from other Christian workers already in the field can result in strained relationships, unhealthy tension, avoidance or direct conflict. This can be hard to cope with, particularly for newer workers who might have expected to receive support from their team or missionaries around them. If this is coupled with a lack of community within the home church from which Christian leaders come, combined with a lack of encouragement, interest or understanding from members in the home church, leaders can feel very isolated.

Calls to Action

i. Develop a culture of discipleship

Discipleship must be taken seriously by the whole church - discipleship that is ongoing and life-long at every stage of a believer's life. This means every Christian being discipled - and every Christian discipling someone. It is the lifeblood of sustainability and healthy mission. Every Christian, every grass-roots worker, every leader needs to be engaged in discipling.

Mentoring plays an important role and if every church and every mission agency prioritized mentoring and discipling relationships, a strong discipleship culture would develop. This would address the problem of many churches in the western world declining in vitality and numbers. It would also result in urban missionaries, when they move into neighborhoods or communities, realizing the value of discipling and being discipled.

The sending or supporting church, or mission agency, needs to be proactive in offering to identify suitable mentors for urban missionaries in the local context and holding them accountable for seeing that mentoring happens. In situations where it is difficult to locate appropriate mentors, there are mentors who are able to provide Skype mentoring, supplemented with face-to-face mentoring when visits are possible.

ii. Set up peer community cluster groups

Before engaging in overseas cross-cultural mission, or local neighborhood mission, workers need to have experience in local peer community clusters, which include coaching, mentoring, accountability, service opportunities, and learning and working together in teams. As part of this, sharing learning about life and ministry is important, providing grounding for urban missionaries.

This highlights the fact that sustainability in mission has a long-term focus and is influenced by how well prepared and equipped a worker is before they are engaged in mission. It is too late to address this when crisis happens. This aspect indicates the link between recruiting, equipping, and sustaining workers.

iii. Provide exposure to various aspects of mission

A call to greater exposure to the various aspects of urban mission together with better preparation and ongoing learning about cross-cultural life as well as being informed about poverty contributes to a realistic understanding of what is involved in long-term sustainability. For example, an understanding of compassion fatigue including symptoms and responses is one aspect that could help mission workers in their on-going learning. Training in leading teams before commencing mission work, or "on-the-job" training in building healthy teams, would provide support for leaders. There is a need for increased and ongoing sharing of wisdom and experience from missionaries, workers and leaders who have spent many years in their contexts. They are a source of mentoring, encouragement, teaching, and advice.

iv. Provide pastoral care for urban missionaries

A difficulty was noted in situations where the director of a mission group is also the one responsible for pastoral care. Workers are sometimes hesitant to voice their concerns to the person to whom they may also be required to report and who may be responsible for their appraisals. Ideally, the two roles should be separate. Pastoral care needs to be proactive and intentional, not only offered when a crisis occurs. Mission agencies ought to be open to recognizing when workers may need to be offered leave in exceptional circumstances. Workers are not cogs in a missional machine, able to be easily replaced. Their health and well-being is to be valued.

v. Encourage interdisciplinary interdependence

Interdisciplinary interdependence between churches, colleges, and mission agencies is needed. Another way of expressing this is "networking", where different Christian organizations, movements, churches, and disciplines working in a particular area (either geographical or groups holding similar values) could assist one another, providing support, advice, practical help, and combined efforts in community work. This could lead to partnership across denominations, church groupings or disciplines which could result in a more combined, integrated effort into respective areas, leading to a greater unity against the powers that be and institutional structures. It addresses the mindset expressed in the attitude, "You in your small corner and I in mine", which contributes to independent thinking and ministry, whereas the synergy of workers combining their efforts in joint projects is more effective. An example of interdependence was mentioned in Section Two of the paper which noted the relationship exchange that has developed between Great Lakes Christian College, Stirling Theological College, and Urban Neighbours of Hope.

A local example of interdependence was noted by Trish Branken, a working group member who lives in a poor community with her husband and family where they have established a ministry called Transform (Hillbrow, Johannesburg). Recently a Lutheran church minister and his volunteers joined Trish and Nigel on their weekly street outreach into Hillbrow visiting the homeless. The church minister later joined them at a meeting with lawyers and the homeless about recent police brutality on their streets. Hearing about the opening of Transform's Learning Centre and its limited computer space, the minister offered space for adults to learn in his much larger computer center at the Lutheran church across the road. Co-operation and sharing of resources builds community spirit and enables positive outcomes to be achieved. It is indicative of the way that Jesus would want resources to be shared for the benefit of all. Generosity of spirit among urban missionaries and local churches encourages interdependence.

Sustaining Christian leaders in their vocation in the new urban world is not an optional extra on the agenda for mission groups. It is a sign of hope that more staff are being appointed to intentional ministries that have the care, support and sustainability of missionaries as their focus. Each Christian leader in an urban setting ought to develop a rhythm of life that is appropriate for their sustainability. The responsibility for ensuring that leaders are able to endure and thrive is a shared one, between the leaders themselves and the mission agencies, churches, and groups who are the sending bodies.

Conclusion

How has the Spirit been guiding your thoughts as you have read about what is happening and what needs to happen in the domain of recruiting, equipping and sustaining Christian leaders in an urban world? As you reach the end of this paper, is there a response stirring in you sparked by your eagerness to be involved in recruiting, equipping, or sustaining Christian leaders in their vocation?

It was inspirational for the working group to meet the elderly Thai woman, just two years old in Christ, who leads a small church plant in her home in Bangkok (mentioned earlier in this section, Signs of Hope). As she told her story, it was evident that she loves to share her experience of how God changed her life. The healing of her husband through prayer is a feature of her testimony to people in her neighborhood about how God can help them. She is sustained in her leadership by a local Christian College who sends interns to her every weekend to assist her. These young interns are gaining experiences that call some of them into ministry. The elderly woman plays a key role in discipling and mentoring the young women who are assigned to her as part of their Christian College practice and experience. The interns spoke about the positive influence that this elderly woman has on them through her faith, seeing how she handles difficulties in her life, witnessing her peace and patience, her study of the Bible, and her persistence in prayer.

This humble woman's response to the need in her own neighborhood for a church provides a model of the kind of leadership required in a multitude of different urban settings. As she equips interns and is equipped herself through prayer and Bible study, as she is sustained through the presence and work of the interns at weekends, as the interns are recruited and equipped to go out to do pioneering work and other forms of ministry after their College study, there is hope for urban shalom being realized even in small, mustard seed ways. The hope of transforming urban poor neighborhoods depends on faithful responses, like this one, to God's invitation to recruit, equip, and sustain Christian leaders.

References

Barker, Ashley. *Slum Life Rising: How to Enflesh Hope within a New Urban World*. Melbourne: Urban Neighbours of Hope, 2012.

Henry, James. "The Price of Offshore Revisited: New Estimates for Missing Global Private Wealth, Income, Inequality, and Lost Taxes." Press Release, *Tax Justice Network*, July 2012: 5. http://en.wikipedia.org/wiki/File:Global_Distribution_of_Wealth_v3.jpga

Winter, Ralph D., "The Two Structures of God's Redemptive Mission", *Perspectives on the World Christian Movement*, edited by Ralph D. Winter and Steven C. Hawthorne (Pasadena: William Carey Library, 1981) 178-190.

Additional resources

Recruit:

Dunn, Richard R. and Jana L. Sundene. *Shaping the Journey of Emerging Adults: Life-Giving Rhythms for Spiritual Transformation*. Downers Grove: IVP, 2012.

Richardson, Rick. "Emerging Adults and the Future of Missions", *International Bulletin of Missionary Research*, Vol. 37, No. 2, April 2013.

Stiles, J. Mack and Leeann. *Mack and Leeann's Guide to Short Term Missions*. Downers Grove: IVP, 2000.

Equip:

Arbuckle, Gerald A. *From Chaos to Mission: Refounding Religious Life Formation*. Geoffrey Chapman/Cassell: London, 1996.

Bakke, Ray. *The Urban Christian: Effective Ministry in Today's Urban World*. Downers Grove: IVP, 1987.

New Urban World Journal. International Society for Urban Mission. Contact: www.newurbanworld.org

Sustain:

Calhoun, Adele Ahlberg. *Spiritual Disciplines Handbook: Practices that Transform Us*. Downers Grove: IVP, 2005.

Palmer, Parker J. *The Active Life: A Spirituality of Work, Creativity, and Caring*. San Francisco: Jossey-Bass, 1990.

Pohl, Christine D. *Living into Community: Cultivating Practices that Sustain Us*. Grand Rapids: Eerdmans, 2012.

Interviews with Urban Missionaries

Mari Muthu, Natagamon Roongtim (Earth) and Mary Kamau[1]

Interview #1:
Mari Muthu, YWAM, South India

Q: Which communities do you work in and what sort of work do you do?

We work in three slum communities; one is all lower caste people, the people here have lots of problems like alcoholism, drugs and family difficulties. I have a team of people, there are 14 of us. In the slums we try to have one on one meetings and prayer meetings in people's homes. We have had difficulty finding the right teachers and many of them have dropped out.

The other community is a gypsy community. They move all the time and they are very poor. Many of these people are illiterate and their whole life story is a mess, there is a high level of alcoholism and family break ups, so we are trying to bring God's kingdom into their lives. Among the gypsies we have a tuition program for the children as there are a lot of children who don't want to go to school so we try to bring them all together and give them free tuition.

We also work with the begging community. In India it is a big problem, in every big city we see hundreds of thousands of people who beg. There are many reasons why people beg and many types of people who do. It is common for people with leprosy, the blind, handicapped, and also the old and neglected to become beggars. We call them often and give them haircuts and showers. We give them food, clothes, and also spend time with them and tell them about Jesus, when they are in need. For example when they are sick we take them to the hospitals and provide them with medical care, we also bring them special things and celebrate with them, that is our ongoing ministry. We try to meet them almost every day on the streets to find out how they are doing.

Those are the three communities we work with in my city.

---

1 This chapter draws on three of the interviews at the January 2012 ISUM Summit.

Q: Why are you involved personally?

The main reason is because Jesus changed my life, and the Bible says what you do to them, you do to me. We believe it is everybody's responsibility: a Christian must show the love of Christ in action. That's the main thing we do. Secondly we see their lifestyle and it's so sad so we do our best to lift them up so they can live a normal life in society.

Often we think that we can just help these people, but we have found that they also want to help others, they volunteer to build their own community. For example we have a person who is living on the street, he is a hair barber, so we call him when we have people in need, and he offers to cut their hair freely, so that is a big encouragement to me. I find a lot of hope in that.

For a long time the church in India has distanced itself from these people, but now there is a change, a move, for people to participate in ministry like ours.

Q: What are some of the challenges you face?

Sometimes you invest a lot of time and energy and you don't see the result. That can be very discouraging. We also struggle to find the resources to help the families, we always need more resources, and so that is another big challenge.

There is also the challenge of working with the other faith based mission groups but for me the key thing is partnership. If we all come together and share what we have without selfishness, we can all work together, which helps us not give up. We can do much more together as the body of Christ, we all need to stop worrying about our differences and work together then we can bring shalom, peace, God's shalom.

We have to be willing to keep sacrificing, to keep giving up things. If you want to see communities change, lives change, we are to sacrifice our comforts, our normal life, there is always a cost to pick up the cross to follow Jesus.

Interview #2:
Natagamon Roongtim (Earth), Disability Activist, Thailand

Q: Can you introduce yourself and share some of your story?

My name is Earth, I live in Bangkok. I work as a Thai translator to earn a living. This year I started working with an international organization in disability and inclusivity development.

Q: What is it like to live with a disability in Thailand?

I have lived in Bangkok for many years, and I have seen many people with disabilities here, but they are not able to go outside. People would like to believe there are not many people with disabilities, but statistics say there are more than 50,000 people on the registration system. There are many others who are registered in other provinces but come to Bangkok to find work, so that number should be higher.

There is a broad range of people with disabilities. You can have those who are born with disabilities, those with hearing impairment, visual impairment, autism, and physical impairment. And there are also people with learning difficulties who have different needs. When you are talking about people with disabilities there is great variation both of disability and need. People with disabilities are like everyone else they are all unique.

We face many challenges living in our society. A long time ago, people thought we should be put in an institution or in some kind of home so we will be easy to take care of. But the reality is we don't want to be separate, we want to be with others, living in communities. But the buildings, the transportation and the way that communities are built make it difficult for us. They are not accessible, in a sense. And that causes a lot of unnecessary and unfair expense. For example I myself pay more than 10,000B a month for taxis, because I can't use a bus. That is not because I am lazy or because I want to always travel in taxis, but I can't get into the bus or get out again.

It affects all people with disabilities but especially people who are poor or have less resources. For example, if you want to get an education, or go to school, the school is there, but how do you get there? Or the school is there but the textbook is a printed book not braille so you can't read it, even if you work very hard. You just touch the book and it is nothing. You need more accessible ways, changing the form of the textbook, the form of the building, the form of the vehicle. Then you can use it. It is also important that you are able to use it for an equal price but usually it is more expensive. So if you don't have many resources you end up staying home and it is hard to be independent, you don't even realize you can be more self-reliant. You have to depend on your mum and dad and when your mum and dad die you have to move in with your sibling. And it's not really a meaningful life to totally depend on others all the time.

Q: What are you currently working on?

I have started an independent living center with my friend. We believe that it's good to learn from other people with disabilities. I have learnt a lot of techniques from my friends with disabilities. For example I often have to work out of my house and I stay overnight in a different place. I have to use a different wheelchair for taking a shower. But it's not easy to take two wheelchairs in a taxi. My friend told me, "Earth, you put the plastic over your wheelchair like a raincoat, then you can take a shower." So I tried it and it worked well. These kinds of skills are not taught in the rehab centers or schools, but we can learn them from other people with disabilities.

We developed the independent living center to share resources with people with disabilities; how you live your life, how you manage, how you negotiate with your parents to allow you to gain independence and try new things. It was a big challenge for my mother when I told her I want to travel in a taxi by myself. "Why don't you wait for me, or my sister, to go with you?" she said. I told her, "I need to live my life", and that was not easy for my mum to hear. She is very scared that the taxi driver would harm me, which is a concern for many people, but especially for the families of people with disabilities. But overprotection or love should not be a reason to stop your children being able to take a risk, a good risk, in life. She was crying, but she said, "Ok! I called you a taxi; call me when you get there." It was the first time I travelled alone.

I still have some limitations. I do not travel alone at night time, I just go in the daytime. If I have to go at night time I go with someone else, but that is my choice. I have more freedom, but I still consider my family as well. When my mum passes away she told me to continue working for independent living, train other people with disabilities and share with their parents so they can have hope. She wants me to show them that their children can go on in life and they can have a good life.

I need someone to carry me to take a shower. And it has been a concern for many years for my family, who is going to help me when they die? This is an issue for many families. So we are doing a lot of work training personal assistants. Now you can actually pay for that type of assistance. We would like to encourage the government to subsidize this service. That way families can be sure there will always be someone to help their children do the basic activities needed to care for them, like taking a shower and brushing their teeth. There are people that need very basic assistance so that they can continue their work.

Q: Can you share some stories of hope?

One of the times I did some counseling for the center, I spoke to a group of mothers with kindergarten level children with disabilities. I noticed that when the mothers see adults with a disability like me, they find hope. I saw that many were crying, and I told them: "I can speak on behalf of your children with disabilities and say that you as the mother are very important."

You know there are mothers who want to see that their children start walking like other children, but their child has cerebral palsy and will not be able to walk. I tell them: "I cannot walk either, but mum is still mum and children are still children. You can have a good life, and you can encourage your children to develop to their full potential. They can have a good job, and earn their own living."

I hope that in me they see that it's possible to have life even with a disability. I can be a role model for people with disabilities. I can live by myself, I can give money to my parents, I can marry and I can have children. I think all of that is possible. Other people have that, other people can travel by plane and so can I. I go out. I don't worry what if people look at me. I'm ok, I'm someone. That brings me hope and I want to share that hope.

Q: What are some of the challenges to bringing peace to your city?

It is very good when people understand about accessibility and how they should modify or create the environment that can be used by everyone. People are changing, putting the ramps on the building, starting to provide information in audio form – that is good. But sometimes people still hesitate; they as, "Why do we have to do that? We have limited resources and not that many people use the different forms of access. Can't we just keep the old buildings and carry you sometime?"

They don't want to put the ramp on because it is expensive but they are happy to carry you. So sometimes people hesitate to make the changes because they don't understand it is not about how many people you serve, but it is about the need for full participation. The government also sees this as a low priority, they have many things that are more urgent and all need resources. But I think making the environment usable for everyone is very important. A ramp is not only for people with disabilities or wheelchair users, children love to run up them, elderly people and people with luggage find them helpful. Many people can benefit from accessibility in the city. The research shows that if you plan for it in the beginning, it only costs 3% more. It is not expensive. Normally if you use 100B for this, you use 103B for that. It is affordable.

Q: What is your call to action for the church?

Many people say that they welcome people with disabilities. But we need more than just a smile and for you to say, "come in please, come we welcome you". To become a society that welcomes people with disability, you need to provide accommodation and make things accessible.

I'm looking for a church with an elevator. And I'm look for a place where we have the words of God in many forms, not only on paper, but in other forms too. In sign language, video, audio, plain language – then we can understand the word of God in simple ways, so we can all access it.

Q: Why are you doing this?

There are many times when I feel like I don't help anyone very much, but I can listen to them. I share my story, the way I manage my life, and they learn from it. And I share the resources that I have. They are able to then work things out for themselves. But the thing that encourages me the most in my work is I think that God put this desire in my heart.

When God puts someone in your heart he keeps reminding you. And God gives me strength, God's love makes it possible to give love to myself and my friend. So I believe that God needs to work with me every day to make me able to work with others.

I see myself walking along with them, we walk together, that is the point.

Interview #3:
Mary Kamau, Missions of Hope, Nairobi, Kenya

Q: Can you introduce yourself and paint a picture of your community?

I am Mary Kamau and I work with Missions of Work International in Nairobi in Kenya. This is an organization that is reaching out to orphans and vulnerable children in the Mathare Valley Slum community. As we work with the orphans and vulnerable children, they give us an entry point to their families. We are able to build relationships with these families. We are also able to come up with empowerment programs with these families, so they are able to get to know Christ in a holistic way as we meet their physical, as well as spiritual needs.

The Mathare Valley is a community that consists of over 800,000 people in an area of about half a mile wide and three miles long. It's very, very crowded. Most of the families live in houses, they call them houses but they are actually shacks. The average house is ten by ten feet, the biggest is ten by twelve. Most of the families don't have running water in their homes, they may have access to community water points outsides. They have running open sewers.

Children in this community do not have opportunities to get quality education. Many of these children start going out to the streets of the city looking for ways to survive. This is why Missions of Hope started a program where we provide educational opportunities for these vulnerable communities. In this community there is a lot of crime, a lot of prostitution. There is also a lot of alcoholism.

Q: What work are you involved in?

Missions of Hope has a number of different programs. One of the programs is providing education opportunities to orphaned and vulnerable children. The children come to our centers every morning, as they come they learn the love of God in the morning. We use the Kenyan school curriculum to provide the education for them. We also have feeding programs for these children, while they are at schools because we want to retain them in the schools, and we don't want them to go out to the streets for food.

Besides that we have two boarding schools, one for boys/one for girls, where children from 6th grade up to high school are able to attend. They are able to get a better school environment and able to study for the national exam. What happens in Kenya is that after primary school and 8th grade, all the students sit for a national exam – this determines who continues to go to school. And then in another 4 years they have to sit for another national exam which determines who goes to university/college. So it is important to have an environment conducive to study for these exams so we have started these two boarding schools.

Besides educating the students we are also able to walk with their families as we reach out to them and share the love of Christ, giving them opportunities to receive Christ.

There are some families, where the guardian or other family members are living with HIV/AIDS. And we have an HIV/AIDS program where people who are HIV positive, are able to join classes and support in these programs. They are able to live positively, even if they are HIV positive.

We also have a micro-finance program, which is a way of training and helping these people to start businesses which enables them to earn a living. This way they don't engage in antisocial behavior, like prostitution, drugs, alcoholism and such. We also have a skills training program, where we provide hands on skills training; like beadwork, hairdressing and beauty school. We also have a sewing workshop and offer training in knitting and crocheting. This means people can make things with their own hands. Recently we have started a welding workshop, especially for the men in the community who want to gain other skills.

And while we are doing all these things we are also reaching out to them with the love of Christ. And as they receive Christ we have discipleship groups, growth groups, and this is where they are able to attain spiritual growth. We are able to introduce them to churches that we are planting in the different communities where we are working. Then recently we also started an agricultural program in our boarding schools, because we have a lot of land in our boarding schools. In this agriculture project we are teaching the kids farming skills so they can grow food. We are able to use the food we grow in our feeding programs. Recently we started a water plant program, we are bottling water from one of the wells that we have in our boarding schools. So there are different things we are doing in our organization, but all in all we hope to integrate both spiritual and physical ministry to the people of Mathare valley.

Q: Where do you see seeds of hope?

When we first began, the children here didn't have much hope. They looked very helpless. They didn't think they would even get an education. In Mathare valley, and other slums in Nairobi, the number of children who graduate from primary to high school is usually less that 5%. However, today because of the ministry that is taking place more children are attending school. Other people and organizations have also come into the community because they have seen that it is possible to make a difference. These children and communities can get an education and they can break out of the cycle of poverty. It used to be that no child was able to go beyond 8th grade. Most children did not even complete 8th grade. But there is hope now because that system is changing. And as they get to see that it is now possible for them to go to high school, it is now possible for them to live a different life, it is really giving them a lot of peace and it is really teaching them that God really loves them. And the more we are seeing that, the more we are seeing people giving their lives to Christ. They now have hope, not only for a better life here, but also hope for eternal life. And that is what I see in this community.

Q: What are some of the challenges to Shalom?

One of the challenges that I see in this community and other similar communities is that the needs seem very overwhelming. Everyone who steps into Mathare Valley thinks it is not possible to do anything. It is not possible to make a difference, because the needs are so great. There are so many people in need, and so many needs. And it is really challenging to choose what needs we are going to focus on.

The other challenge is the people themselves think they cannot make it. They have always thought their lives are meant to be that way, and so when you come in and tell them there is hope in Jesus, some of them find it hard to believe. We found this especially when we first started the programs. It was really tough to break through, but I have seen that it is still possible, and when they have seen the progress their children are making in school that has really given them hope that it is possible and they have found hope in Jesus Christ.

Q: What is your call of action to the church?

Most of the time people are afraid to step out in faith, they are afraid that the needs are so overwhelming and they wonder what difference they could possibly make. But I would encourage everyone who knows Christ that if Christ is enough he is greater than the one who is in the world.

So the call to action for these people would be to step out in faith, regardless of all the discouragements that are there, regardless of all the challenges that are there. Just step out in faith, and know that because you have Christ you carry the hope of the world. So that person who is in need, even if it is just one person, that you make a difference in their lives, it is worth it – just step out in faith and just trust in God – and just offer hope to that person. And that is my encouragement to anyone who knows Christ.

Q: How did you end up doing this work?

God loves me so so much. And personally I take it as an honor and a privilege to be part of what God is doing in Mathare Valley. I didn't know that such a place existed. I didn't know that that kind of poverty was anywhere in this world. For me poverty was the life I lead myself in central Kenya. In a polygamous family of 22 children, that is what I knew as poverty. But when I went to this community as a student I realized that I had so much that I could offer. I had already found Jesus Christ, he had already loved me and revealed himself to me. And I knew that just offering these people Christ, who had given me so much hope was good enough. And I stepped out in faith, and I will not take credit for anything. But I give glory to God who I have witnessed working in these people's lives over the years. And I just thank God for what he is doing.

Lessons from the Good Samaritan

Shane Claiborne[1]

I thought that when it comes to reading Scripture, most of us know there's 2000 verses that talk about God's care for the poor and the marginalized... so I decided that we're just going to walk through each one of those!

Actually I thought, it might be fun to do something a little different, at least for me. I don't know how many of you do *Lectio Divina*? It is an ancient way of reading Scripture. It's hundreds of years old and it's where you contemplatively and prayerfully read it three or so times together and take different things out of it each time. This is a variation of it. What I want to do this morning is read a text that is pretty familiar to us from Luke's Gospel. I want to offer a retelling of it in two instances, one from our neighborhood and one from outside, which might invite us into the story today. We'll have three different readings from Luke's Gospel [verses 30-36], the good Samaritan:

> In reply Jesus said: "A man was going down from Jerusalem to Jericho, when he was attacked by robbers. They stripped him of his clothes, beat him and went away, leaving him half dead. A priest happened to be going down the same road, and when he saw the man, he passed by on the other side. So too, a Levite, when he came to the place and saw him, passed by on the other side. But a Samaritan, as he traveled, came where the man was; and when he saw him, he took pity on him. He went to him and bandaged his wounds, pouring on oil and wine. Then he put the man on his own donkey, brought him to an inn and took care of him. The next day he took out two denariie and gave them to the innkeeper. 'Look after him,' he said, 'and when I return, I will reimburse you for any extra expense you may have.' 'Which of these three do you think was a neighbor to the man who fell into the hands of robbers?"

---

1   This chapter was originally published as an article in *New Urban World Journal* (November 2013), 37

As we listen to the story just as Jesus told it, some things that jump out at me are, first of all, that it's one of the most scandalous stories, where Jesus is like, "I've got one for you, the religious folks walk by, and then a Samaritan!" And then everyone is like, "Whoa a Samaritan," the one that they don't even talk to, the one they shun; that's the one who listened into the ditch and brought the beat up person out.

According to Sister Joan Chittister, constantly in Jesus' teaching you can see that he is challenging the chosen and including the excluded. That challenge to the chosen, it seems like the most likely candidates were the religious folks, but they do nothing. The Samaritans who were shunned both partly because of their race, religion, and how they thought of God—they were ostracized in the whole community, they are the ones celebrated as the heroes of the story. As I think of that, there's also something that is to be said, one of my elders said, "If the devil can't steal your soul, he might just keep you busy with church work!" We don't know what the religious folks were doing; maybe they were late to a trustee meeting or going to serve in the soup kitchen, but they were too busy to be interrupted. It occurs to me that that is the case so much of the time; we are too busy to be interrupted and this story—and half of the gospel—is about being interrupted and about our patterns. For example, when Jesus is on his way somewhere and somebody pulls on his shirt or they say, "My sister is dying," or, "We just ran out of wine at our wedding, can you help a brother out?" That interruption is what the gospel is made of and it's what this story is about. The strange thing is, people get beat up at the most inconvenient times, don't they? The call is that we have to allow ourselves to be interrupted by injustice and pain. And yet as we continue this work we have less and less space for interruption; we get our rhythms and schedules down, our programs and nonprofits and NGOs; and our work has a space, a category, a compartment; and yet the Spirit moves inside and outside of that, so we always have got to be ready.

In our community in Philadelphia, it started with an interruption. I'm thankful that we were students in the suburbs, studying theology, and, all of a sudden, we saw on the front page of the newspaper that there were groups of homeless families living in this abandoned cathedral in Philadelphia. They were getting evicted. The story explained that they were given 48 hours to get out; if they weren't out of this abandoned Catholic cathedral, they could be arrested for trespassing on church property. And we were interrupted. Something in us didn't feel right about that; there are those times you throw your hands up at God and say, "Why don't you do something?" and he says, "I did, I made you! Get out!" You're the one passing the person in the ditch. Maybe you're the answer to your prayer.

What also strikes me in this verse is that this story would not have been told if the Samaritan had not been walking down the road where people get beat up. So often we move our lives away from the suffering of the world, we don't want to walk down the roads where people get beat up. Yet that's what the gospel is all about: Jesus moving into the neighborhood, and a neighborhood where people said nothing good could come. Jesus knew suffering from the moment he entered into the world until he died on the cross. He entered into the pain and the suffering. It's that story that calls us to an inertia different from the pattern of the world, to move out of suffering; the gospel calls us into it.

There's so many ways we can insulate ourselves from people who get beat up in the ditch. Subtle ways that sometimes even our programs and charities become ways that we no longer encounter people but that we run stuff. That call to the personal, is what I love about the work that so many of you are doing. I love the title of Ash Barker's book, *Make Poverty Personal*. We get all excited about making poverty history, but we can't do that until we make it personal. Until we have the courage to respond, and walk in the places that people get beat up and everyone and everything will tell us to move out. There is a great song by a guy in the States, by Derek Webb, where he says, "Thanks be to God, I am finally able to move up and out of Jesus' neighborhood." He's talking about how, this upward mobility, as one preacher said, "We better be careful, if we are climbing our way up the ladder to success, we might pass Jesus on his way down." The call is to those places where people get beat up, where there is pain and suffering. Every one of those responses in Matthew 25 about the least of these, they are personal responses: when I was hungry, you fed me; when I was a stranger, you welcomed me; when I was in prison, you visited me. We always have to keep that call to make poverty personal at the heart of what we do.

The other thing that a friend pointed out to me about this story is about the person in the ditch. He has been stripped and left unconscious. My friend who is a Bible scholar says there are the two ways you can identify people: (1) by the clothes on their back, you can see where they are from; and (2) by their language and their dialect. So you have a person who is stripped of their identity, left in the ditch, which leaves us with this: we have no idea who this person is who got beaten up except that they are a human being, a child of God, of unbelievable value, and precious. We don't know the person's religion, sexual identity, who he or she voted for in the last election… just a human being beat up in the ditch. Our call is to respond.

What I love about the way that the Samaritan responded is that he took his time and his own donkey (everything he had), and put the guy on it. That call is to take whatever we have and offer it to God and to the suffering of the world and say, "God do something, with what little we have, we give it to you." I love how Beatner said we have to take our deepest passions and connect them to the world's deepest pain. Whether it's a donkey or a cooking degree. That's what we are to offer up to God, and we see it used to heal and to redeem; we see God work through the gifts that we have. So these are the things that jumped out to me with the first reading.

On to the second reading of this text: I want to offer it to you from the context of our little world in Philly. It was about midnight a couple of years ago when we heard the gunshots ring out; they sounded really close. My friend and I were nearly asleep and we jumped up, came out the front door, only to see a young teenager fall on the steps with bullet wounds in his body. We didn't know what else to do but hold his hands, whisper to him that he is precious, that he is beloved. I prayed the Lord's Prayer with him. He's just shaking and we're waiting for the ambulance to come. Finally it does; he's put in the ambulance. The next morning we find out he died. Something happened in our neighborhood: we've had a lot of gunshots, we've had a fair amount of murders, and this one shook everyone. Stuff started happening. It's amazing because within weeks, we had a movement of neighbors and advocates calling attention to the problem of gun violence in our city. There have been news stories calling our city "killedelphia" as we had almost a homicide a day, over 300 gun murders, this year. This is an epidemic in our country. We have over 10,000 homicides a year largely to gun murder, and it's the largest killer to young people and teenagers—second to car accidents. As you look at that, there comes a point where we deadlift this young man off the streets, but part of God's integral mission is that we begin to ask questions: what is causing people to end up beat up on the road to Jericho? Let me offer Martin Luther King Jr's words as we think of that: "On the one hand we are called to be the good Samaritan on the road side, but that may be only an initial act, one day we come to see, maybe the whole road to Jericho needs to be transformed so that men and women will not be constantly beaten and robbed as they make their journey on life's highway."

True compassion, says Dr. King, is more than flinging a coin at a beggar, it's not half hazard and superficial; it comes to see that an edifice, which produces victims, needs restructuring. Amen.

That reading offers us the sense that we are to respond to those who get beat up, but after you see so many teenagers get shot and killed, you start to say, maybe the whole road to Jericho needs to get rethought; maybe we need to ask where are the kids getting the guns. We saw that in our city, there are a few notorious gun shops, selling irresponsibly, just a few blocks from our house. They were notorious for selling over 200 guns that were tracked to violence on our street. Those are places where we need to pray for God to move. We began prayer vigils outside the gun shops. 400 mayors said that the gun violence would change; we weren't trying to shut the gun shops down. We were just saying that we want the business to look more responsible; some did. If they changed their practices, we had a celebration; if we didn't, we had a protest and continued praying. This was one that refused to make these changes, a couple of them in Philly.

One of the most powerful services, on Good Friday, the kids in our neighborhood carried a cross to the gun shop, and hundreds of us gathered outside of the gun shop. Our teenagers carried the cross and they sat it outside of the gun shop on Good Friday. We connected the suffering of Jesus on the cross to the suffering on our streets. We listened to the gospel reading of the women weeping at the foot of the cross, and we heard women and men share their testimonies and stories of seeing their kids shot on the streets of Philly. There was something powerful that happened. We had good preaching too, he said it might be Friday now, but Sunday is coming. In the end of the story, Jesus triumphed over the sting of death, all that is evil, ugly, wicked in the world; he rose to show us that love conquers death and hatred. This one woman, as she had tears rolling down her face, said to me, "I get it. God understands my pain, because he watched his own son die a violent death." I thought, that's good theology. This is the God who comes in and enters our pain, walks our streets, moves into our neighborhoods, and understands deeply the oppression that our friends suffer everyday.

It occurred to me that what's so beautiful now is that many of the faith community throughout the United States are now raising attention to this issue. Many deeply committed out of their faith imagined what would God's kingdom look like if it came to their neighborhood. It looks *not* like 300 young people getting killed in a year; what would it look like if God's most perfect dream came in our neighborhood?

One of those gun shops in Philly came a time when the religious community said we cannot just continue to let business as usual happen and they bowed down on their knees and gathered in front of the gun shop, literally putting their lives and bodies in the way of the flow of guns, they were eventually arrested, and for a nonviolent Martin Luther King Jr-type demonstration, they were brought to court in Philly. What was amazing was that it was in the paper. Schools were let out so kids could see justice at work. What was amazing was that through the course of the trial, each one of these religious leaders from all different streams of faith, shared why they did what they did. And that gun shop went on trial.

And that's what Dr. King said, our job is to expose injustice that it becomes so uncomfortable that people have to respond. So the judge found all the religious leaders not guilty. In the ensuing days the gun shop owner was found guilty to trafficking illegal guns, his license was revoked, and the shop was shut down. It is a beautiful story.

We are also people of restorative justice, so we still believe that a gun shop owner can do different. He can run a paint shop. In the end, God moves in the midst of this, and it's when we respond. In that story, it wasn't the religious folks, but the leaders in our city who stood up and said we will not allow our young people to continue to end up in the ditch. There are all kinds of different demons and principalities at work in our neighborhoods. This is not the story of every neighborhood. In fact most the world seems to be doing better at this then the United States. I think of Ray Bakke, the great urban theologian, who said that we talk a lot about exegeting Scripture, but we've also got to exegete our neighborhoods. We've got to read them with the eyes of the Spirit, to see where is God at work, and where the devil is at work. As we exegete our neighborhood, gun violence is one of the principalities and powers we wrestle against. It is a spiritual battle; it is a battle we take on to the streets; we pray outside of the gun shops; we teach our kids non-violence; and ask, "Where are they getting the guns?"

Finally, the third lens through which I want to invite you to see the story of the Good Samaritan is an experience that I had that transformed the way that I read this story. I think when we read stories we often have different eyes that we look at the story through. I always read the story as if I was the person that needed to lift the person out of the ditch. But then through this experience I began to see the story through the person in the ditch, rather than the person responding. It was right at the beginning of this story, almost exactly ten years ago, when I was inspired by the Christian Peacemakers Team, and other doctors and nurses who had gone to Iraq to voice concern about the bombing and the war, and also a real missional innocence to go: "God loves you, we love you no matter what the United States government does to your country. We want to be with you through that." So we were there and we had no real idea that we would be there during the bombing, but we were in March 2003, ten years ago. It was the shock and awe campaign: the bombing of Baghdad. We were there and I encountered some of the hardest things I had ever seen in my life. During the bombing, we lived there and volunteered at the hospitals. I also experienced things that spun my world upside-down. There was one worship service with Christians from all over Iraq and the Middle East. They had come together, we sang "Amazing Grace" in Arabic. Bishops from all denominations read a statement from the Christian church to all Muslim people saying,

We want you to know that we love you; we come from the same dysfunctional family of Abraham and Sarah; we're praying for peace.

I was so moved; tears were rolling down my face. And I went up to one of the bishops and said "This is amazing, I can't believe there are so many Christians here," and he said very gently, "Yeah, this is where Christianity started; that's the Tigris River and the Euphrates over there, you heard of them? The Garden of Eden is right down the street, bro!" As we were leaving Baghdad, which is where the Samaritan story comes to play, we're driving through that desert road from Baghdad to Amman, Jordan. Hours and hours of that sandy desert, it's surreal. Bombs were falling, bridges were down, cars on fire. In this little entourage coming out of Baghdad, our car hit something in the road that popped the tire of our car, spun us off the road, and flipped our car over. All of us were injured. I was one of the least injured, and I had a separated shoulder. I was trying to gather us together. The car was on the side. Two of my friends had pretty bad head injuries; we get everybody somehow to the curb, and we're sitting there as planes fly over, and wondering what do we do now. So we pray. I'm convinced that part of why so many of us Christians don't see God at work, or see miracles in a very visible way, is because we are rarely in a place where we really need a miracle. This was one of those. We said, "God, you're gonna have to do something in this desert, my water bottle is almost empty." My two friends were very deeply injured. As we're praying, we see the first car coming down the road. It was the first car to come past us. It stops and these Iraqi guys come out and I try my best to explain in broken Arabic why we were there and what was happening. They smiled, wrapped their arms around us and put us in the car and drive us to the nearest town. As we get to this town, called Rutba, a small town of 20,000 like the town I grew up in, in East Tennessee, it's big news. The whole town gathers and they see that one friend was going into shock, who needed to get to the hospital. When we get there, the doctors are waving their hands in the air, screaming "Why, why is this happening!"

They start naming everything that has been bombed in their town; one of the bombs hit the children's ward, so the whole hospital was shut down. They couldn't take us in there. They see our hearts sink, but they smile and say, "Don't worry, we'll still take care of you." So they set up a little shanty clinic for each one of us. We had a bed. As they started taking care of us, folks start bringing gifts, blankets and food, and I'm so moved by all of this that, as we finally wrap it up, I start thinking I've got to thank these guys. My American mind thinks, money. So we collect Iraqi dinar and take it to the head of the hospital and say, "We just want to thank you," and he says, "Then what is this? Keep your money and say 'Thank you.' We don't want your money, we just want you to know we love you. Just tell people the story of what we did for you, that's all you can do to repay for us." So we've been telling that story for almost 10 years. It's been so inspirational for all of us, that my friends started a community in North Carolina called Rutba House to practice that same hospitality to lift people out of the ditch. It's always been our dream to go back. So a couple of years ago we got to go back—it's not easy to travel from the United States to Iraq. We get back to that town and we are given the most amazing welcome to that town; it's like we were kings! They said, "We don't get a lot of visitors and we haven't had anyone visit us without guns since you were here before," and then they said, "You've got to know that there are a few people that might want to hurt you, but only a few, so we will protect you." And I'm like "That does not fit into my theology, but so grateful for your hospitality." As we are there, it's so amazing. We share stories and we meet the doctors that had saved our lives 10 years ago; some of them came a long way to see us.

As we're sharing, the mayor of the town comes and says, "This is beautiful! This is what changes the world, we need a sister city between Rutba and the U.S.!" and I'm like, "Philadelphia! It's the city of love," and the mayor is like, "No, no, it's also a big city. We need a little town to be our sister city, have you ever heard of Durham, North Carolina… the only city I've ever been to in America. It reminded me of Rutba, I wonder if we could ever become a sister city of Durham, NC." The Spirit moves in ways I can hardly even imagine. I don't have a theological container for it all—that's what the story's all about: we can't put containers around God, certainly the church is God's primary instrument for bringing in the kingdom and yet God is not confined to Christians. If we read Scripture, God is at work. God can work through pagan kings and brothel owners, Samaritans, and politicians, and anybody in the world. So we pray that we would be the people that God would use. One of my friends even said, "There's that old story in the Old Testament where God speaks to Balaam through his ass, his donkey, and he said God spoke to him through his ass and he's been speaking through asses ever since." If God should chose to use us, we shouldn't think too highly of ourselves, and if we look at someone else and think God could never use them, we better think twice, because God is big and God is bigger than the confines of our imagination.

So as we find ourselves now in that story after a few ways of retelling it, I don't know if you find yourself seeing the story as the person beat up in the ditch, when all the religious folks have abandoned you, or the religious folks who are on their way somewhere or fearful and pass by on the other side, or maybe you're the Samaritan who is worn out because you have lifted so many people out of the ditch, or maybe the innkeeper who has helped from a distance. It's my prayer this morning that we would allow God to move in us, that we would pray that God would give us eyes to see those who are wounded, beat up, and that he would give us imagination to collaborate with the innkeepers and those who have tools that we may not have on our own. Because it's the story of community, that's what this gathering is about, we can do more together than we can on our own, we need each other, we see God move where two or three of us come together. There are 38,000 different denominations in the church, and yet Jesus' prayer is that we would be one as God is one. That is my prayer this weekend as we gather: that we would feel that unity, that we would feel God speak to us and among us, that we may not all see everything through the same lens.

Let me close with one of my mentors [Dr. John Perkins], who said:

> We've all heard that saying, give someone a fish and they'll eat for a day, teach them to fish, they'll eat for the rest of their life. We've also got to ask: who owns the pond? Why have gates been built up around the pond? Why is there pollution in the pond that has poisoned the fish? Why does a fishing license cost so much?

So that's the work of integral mission: it is responding to people who are hungry, and offering food. We have brothers and sisters in the neighborhood that are hungry, so obviously we're going to share food. We're also going to try to create jobs, so they can provide for their own families and have dignities in themselves. And we're also going to ask the questions of the systematic stuff, the principalities and powers that are landing people in the ditch over and over... that's what it means to be the church. All of us may not do everyone of those the same, but we can see more fully as a body than any of us can on our own. May we be one as God is one.

Prayer:

Oh God, we thank you for your word that invites us to see you and your movement in the world, and to see our world with new eyes.

We pray that you would continue to meet with us this weekend, that you would speak to us through one another, through your Spirit moving in the midst.

We pray that we would be people who interrupt injustice and allow ourselves to be stirred with compassion when we see someone who is hurting.

We pray that we would indeed be integral in the work that we do and seek your spirit with all that we are, and know that your hands are bigger than our hands. And yet also know that you want our hands and want our gifts and you want our passions.

So let us see the kingdom that is within us and among us, and let us seek your kingdom on earth as it is in heaven.

Give us the eyes to see you at work in the world and the courage to respond.

We love you Jesus, in the name of the Father, Son and the Holy Spirit, Amen.

Authors

Elizabeth Waldron Barnett children and families in community has been at the heart of Beth's service in pastoral, local mission and denominational consulting roles as a practitioner, teacher and resource writer. She is currently completing a doctorate in New Testament, reconsidering the marginalization of "child" in Pauline literature and the discourses of maturity, development and power.

John Baxter-Brown was born in India, but has lived most of his life in the UK, apart from a recent span of nearly three years when he lived and worked in Geneva. He was there as Consultant for Evangelism for the World Council of Churches, and currently he is consulting for other global Christian organizations in evangelism, mission, ecumenism, youth ministry and church relations. He is an author and editor and part of the World Evangelical Alliance Theology Commission. Throughout his career he has blended holistic evangelism with youth ministry, and a commitment to working for Christian unity. So far he has two degrees in theology and is working towards his PhD. He is married with two teenage daughters and two dogs and lives in Wiltshire, England.

Scott Bessenecker is Associate Director for Missions for InterVarsity Christian Fellowship and sends 3,000 university students each year as servants and learners around the world. He is the author of *The New Friars: The Emerging Movement Serving the World's Poor*; *How to Inherit the Earth: Submitting Ourselves to a Servant Savior*; and editor of *Living Mission: The Vision and Voices of New Friars*, and *Quest for Hope in the Slum Community*. Scott has been walking alongside several organizations focused on incarnational ministry among the poor as an advocate, an encourager, and prophetic voice. Scott claims to possess the world's largest international cigarette collection owned by an Evangelical non-smoker. He and his wife, Janine, have three kids and he blogs at https://urbana.org/blogs/least-these

Sharmila Blair has been serving with Urban Neighbours of Hope for ten years. She, and her husband Peter and their young daughters Divya and Ashlyn live in Dandenong in Melbourne, the most culturally diverse municipality in Victoria in Australia. Sharmila teaches English as a second language to new arrivals, including many asylum seekers, and their home is a place of hospitality and welcome. She also helps facilitate a women's discipleship group supporting women who come from backgrounds of sexual abuse and mental illness. She also enjoys rapping in her spare time, highlighting issues of injustice in her neighborhood, and engaging the broader church.

Aimee Brammer works with Chab Dai Coalition and has called Phnom Penh, Cambodia her home since 2009. She is part of a national & international team that facilitates collaboration between anti-trafficking stakeholders in Cambodia. Alongside several networks and forums she advocates for the protection and rights of Cambodian migrant workers and has played a role in building a cross-border referral network with partners in Malaysia. Currently she is completing a research project exploring the influencing factors and programmatic shifts to addressing exploitation and trafficking in Cambodia over the last decade. In her free time she enjoys running, drinking coffee with friends, and travelling in Southeast Asia. She blogs at aimeeandcambodia.wordpress.com and can be contacted at aimee.janee@gmail.com.

Amy Brock-Devine, M.Ed., is a missionary who has served in Argentina, China and the US. She currently works in Bangkok, Thailand with YWAM's *ARK International*, teaching and co-ordinating education programs such as *Live Life* and *Safe Child*. *Live Life* uses a holistic approach to ministry, teaching children to make the best choices for the future. Amy was on the ground when *Safe Child*, a child protection program, began after two children in one of the slums she works in were abducted and later returned.

Paul Cameron is the husband of Amanda, the father of three adult sons and the grandfather of one beautiful little boy. Paul grew up in a family steeped in the Churches of Christ story. After a short period working in a bank, he followed God's call to preparation for ministry, a call he still follows. He has had local church ministries in New South Wales and Victoria, and is currently the CEO of Churches of Christ in Victoria and Tasmania, as well as being a cheerleader and advocate for UNOH and the chair of its Reference Group.

Tony Campolo is professor emeritus of sociology at Eastern University, a former faculty member at the University of Pennsylvania, and the founder and president of the Evangelical Association for the Promotion of Education. He has written more than 35 books. He is one of the founders of the Red Letter Christian movement and blogs regularly at RedLetterChristians.org, offers resources on his website tonycampolo.org, and can be found on both Facebook and Twitter. Dr. Campolo and his wife Peggy live near Philadelphia and have two children and four grandchildren.

Shane Claiborne. With tears and laughter, Shane Claiborne unveils the tragic messes we've made of our world and the tangible hope that another world is possible. Shane graduated from Eastern University, and did graduate work at Princeton Seminary. His ministry experience is varied, from a 10-week stint working alongside Mother Teresa in Calcutta, to a year spent serving a wealthy mega-congregation at Willow Creek Community Church outside Chicago. During the war in Iraq, Shane spent three weeks in Baghdad with the Iraq Peace Team. Shane is also a founding partner of The Simple Way, a faith community in inner city Philadelphia that has helped to birth and connect radical faith communities around the world. Shane writes and travels extensively speaking about peacemaking, social justice, and Jesus. He is featured in the DVD series "Another World Is Possible" and is the author of the several books including *The Irresistible Revolution, Jesus for President,* and *Becoming the Answer to Our Prayers.*

Darren Cronshaw is passionate about training and resourcing leaders and missionaries. He serves locally as Pastor of AuburnLife, and is Mission Catalyst – Researcher with the Baptist Union of Victoria. He teaches as Associate Professor in Missiology with Australian Colleges of Ministries (Sydney College of Divinity), and is an Honorary Research Associate at Whitley College (University of Divinity). He is Editor-in-Chief of UNOH Publications. His own books include *Credible Witness: Companions, Prophets, Hosts and other Australian Mission Models* (UNOH 2006) and *Sentness: Six Postures of Missional Christians* (IVP 2014, co-authored with Kim Hammond). Other passions in Darren's life are being husband to Jenni, proud Dad to three children, lover of good books and movies, jogging or riding the paths of Melbourne, and enjoying the cultures and tastes of the world. He is contactable at editor@unoh.org.

Rosalee Velloso Ewell is a theologian from São Paulo, Brazil. She has a PhD from Duke University (USA) and taught biblical ethics and theology in Brazil for many years. Rosalee currently serves as the Executive Director for the Theological Commission of the World Evangelical Alliance and is the New Testament editor for the forthcoming Latin American Biblical Commentary. She is married to Samuel Ewell and they have three children. Together, they are trying urban farming in community and have 14 chickens, 2 rabbits, 6 fish and a goat.

Mary Kamau serves among the urban poor in the slums, particularly the Mathare Valley slum, of Nairobi with Missions of Hope International. She directs schools and Community Health Evangelism projects, as well as a microfinance loan program offered to parents for home-based businesses, cmfi.org/wherewework/missionary/wmkamau.

Lynette Leach is the Pastor for Urban Neighbours of Hope and has had a long association with UNOH as a mentor and guide since before UNOH officially began 20 years ago. In her pastoral oversight of UNOH as a missional order among the poor, she has many intentional conversations with workers and teams, offering support, advice and prayer to sustain them in their vocation. She and Athol enjoy family life with their eight grandchildren.

Geoff and Sherry Maddock make their home with their son, Isaac, in Lexington, Kentucky. They work as missionaries in an underserved neighborhood in their city. They finished their studies at Asbury Theological Seminary in 2001 with master's degrees in missiology and stayed in Kentucky. Geoff is from Melbourne, Australia and Sherry came to Kentucky from Marietta, Georgia. They are most passionate about neighborhood transformation through urban farming and creating awareness for urban dwellers about growing food. They have created a micro-farm (one tenth of an acre) on an urban lot next to their home where they have chickens, bees, fruit trees, berry brambles, and all manner of herbs, flowers, and vegetables. This experiment in urban homesteading (alongside other similar projects including community gardens and urban orchards) has proven to be the most effective and beautifying catalyst for building relationships and cultivating neighborhood transformation in their 15 years of missionary work in Lexington. They are contactable at: geoffandsherry@yahoo.com

Andrew Menzies is Principal of Stirling Theological College: MCD University of Divinity. He is also involved with supporting the executive as chairperson of Urban Neighbours of Hope as they seek to serve among slum communities.

Mari Muthu leads the work of Youth With A Mission in Trichy city, South India, and has been serving the Lord with YWAM for the last 16 years. He is married to Kavitha and they have three children.

Doug Priest was raised as a preacher's kid in Oregon U.S.A. He went with his missionary parents to Ethiopia in the 1960s. He lived in a remote part of the country during school vacations, while the rest of the year he was a boarding student in the capital, Addis Ababa. After Bible college and university in Eugene, Oregon, Doug attended the School of World Mission at Fuller Theological Seminary, with additional work in African studies at UCLA. This learning continues to inform his life's work, which includes living in Kenya and Tanzania for a decade, and being involved in holistic ministry—church work, community development, and anthropological studies. A regional role for CMF International was followed by a call to become its Executive Director a position he still holds. CMF International has its foundations in the Stone-Campbell Movement known also as Christian Church/Churches of Christ.

Natagamon Roongtim (Earth) works as an Interpreter and Translator in Bangkok, and is active in training and advocating for people with disabilities and their independent living, and for inclusivity development.

John H. Quinley, Jr. is CEO and Founder of Step Ahead Integrated Community Development www.stepaheadmed.org working in Bangkok's largest slum community of over 100,000 people since 2002, and across Thailand focusing on the poor, vulnerable, and at-risk. Step Ahead also runs mentoring and training programs that help youth gain growing confidence in English, computers, and sports. Following Kimberly Kae Paradee to Thailand twice in 1986—the second time with a diamond ring- cemented the Quinley's future in Thailand. They have worked together in missions, community economic development, family-based orphan care, microfinance, and even production of some of the finest woven leather purses never to come from Italy. Currently, new fashion leather and Thai silk ITSERA purses are in development with women's groups across the Northeast of Thailand. John, once father to four children under five; today seeks to keep up with four adult children on three continents. In 2013, John won the Alumni International Education Award from the University of Richmond. He's had six marathon finishes, and one heart attack. He looks to continue to add to the first total, and leave off on the second. You are welcome to contact John by email at: john.quinley@gmail.com

John H Quinley, III is a 2013 graduate of Eastern University in Economic Development. He has a keen desire to see justice and peacemaking initiatives go forward in South East Asia, and the Middle East. John has a goal to summit Denali before the age of thirty. His father hopes to spend a few miles on the Appalachian Trail with him in the early prep. You may contact John III by email at: jquinley@eastern.edu

Kimberly Quinley cofounded Step Ahead: Integrated Community Development Foundation with her husband, John. Currently she is the Director of Families at Risk programs for Step Ahead. She is passionate about partnering with local churches to keep widows and orphans together and loves helping communities understand safe and informed migration to decrease the risk of human trafficking among their youth. http://www.stepaheadmed.org

Matthew Wilson has been involved in Eden's work since its inception, being one of the first team members to get involved and move into an extremely disadvantaged social housing estate in south Manchester. He has been Director of the Eden Network for the last ten years. Matt also serves on the leadership team of Eden's parent charity – The Message Trust, a youth and community ministry based in Manchester, England. Over 20 years The Message has forged a reputation for being one of the most innovative youth ministries in Europe pioneering in areas of music, media, urban ministry, and large-scale mission mobilization. Matt came into vocational ministry from a career background in the advertizing industry and has since gone on to study master's degrees in management and in theology. He has written a book *"Concrete Faith"* which is available on Amazon. He lives in Salford with his wife Grace and two young sons, Izzy and JJ.

Cori Wittman lives alongside her Breakthrough Thailand team in a small, rural village in Thailand's Northeastern "Isaan" region – a region marred by socioeconomic challenges and high rates of rural-urban migration. The team engages in creative ways to facilitate individual and community breakthroughs in areas of families, education, and economics in an effort to stem the tides of migration to Thailand's sex industry. Cori worked as an agriculture policy advisor in Washington, DC before moving to Thailand in 2010. An original "Idaho farm kid," she continues to explore ways to use agriculture as a tool for individual and community restoration. Web: www.breakthroughthailand.org Blog: www.coriwittman.com Email: cori.wittman@gmail.com

Note: The authors acknowledge the assistance of participants who acted as scribes for the Working Group discussions at the Integral Urban Mission Summit, Bangkok, January 2013.

www.ingramcontent.com/pod-product-compliance
Lightning Source LLC
Chambersburg PA
CBHW051941290426
44110CB00015B/2068